"This is a deep, wide, wise contribution to a truly comprehensive Christian understanding of justice. I can't imagine a better biblical and theological introduction to the topic of justice, combined with pastoral wisdom and the urgency that comes from direct engagement with the brokenness of our world."

—**Andy Crouch**, executive editor, *Christianity Today*;
author of *Playing God: Redeeming the Gift of Power*

"I suspect that *The Justice Calling* will become one of those books I turn to again and again. Its message is grounded not only in a few key biblical texts but in the full story of God's people from Genesis to Revelation. Weaving biblical truth with personal experience, the authors lead us from God's glorious vision of human flourishing, through the fall and our need to lament, to Jesus's renewed call to his church, and finally to the restored vision of 'all things made new.' As one seeking to live justly in places of deep brokenness and violent conflict, I am grateful for the thread that stitches this whole book together: the possibility and promise of persevering hope."

—**Lynne Hybels**, advocate for global engagement,
Willow Creek Community Church

"Many books on justice have appeared in recent years. Three things make this one stand out from the crowd. First, instead of quoting only a few golden nuggets from Scripture, the authors trace the theme of justice throughout Scripture. Second, they give concreteness to their discussion with harrowing true-life stories of present-day sex trafficking and slavery. And third, they explicitly address the need of those who struggle for justice, patience, lament, and hope. An important contribution."

—**Nicholas Wolterstorff**, Yale University; Institute for Advanced Studies
in Culture, University of Virginia

"If we're not careful, the pursuit of justice can become more about us than about responding to the heart and character of God. In *The Justice Calling*, Hoang and Johnson have written a resource for the church that is theologically rich, biblically faithful, and practically engaging. I'm genuinely inspired by this book and pray that it will encourage, challenge, and inspire others not only to the work of justice but also to the God of justice."

—**Eugene Cho**, senior pastor, Quest Church; founder, One Day's Wages;
author of *Overrated: Are We More in Love with the Idea of Changing
the World Than Actually Changing the World?*

"This is a powerful and timely book that shows us why the God of justice must be at the center of the justice movement in this generation. The authors have combined their years of national and global experience with deep theological reflection to produce one of the best biblical theologies on justice that I've ever read. As an advocate for justice and racial reconciliation, I highly recommend it!"

—**Brenda Salter McNeil**, Seattle Pacific University; author of *Roadmap to Reconciliation* and *A Credible Witness*

"There is so much joy to be found as we follow God into his work of justice, so much strength to be gained in the Scriptures that he's given to us. *The Justice Calling* takes us deep into all of these gifts. As we face down the giants of injustice in the season ahead, this is a book I'd urge every follower of Jesus to dig into and carry close at hand."

—**Gary A. Haugen**, president and CEO, International Justice Mission; author of *The Locust Effect*

"We often think justice is merely standing against and stopping what is wrong. It is no less than that, but it is far more. With tender passion and immense wisdom, Hoang and Johnson invite us to see that the drama of the Bible is about growing goodness as a means to thwart what is unrighteous. Their development of justice as a primary passion of God's is brilliant and breathtaking. Their personal journeys will further open your heart to the wonder of how mercy and justice kiss in the person of Jesus Christ. This is a must-read, glorious book."

—**Dan B. Allender**, Seattle School of Theology and Psychology

"I've been waiting for a book that blends the depth of Scripture's call to justice with the breadth of how God is using the church today. We now have that book. While the stories of pain and injustice will haunt you, this fresh exploration of God's vision for our world will make you want to get up and do something—and invite others to join you."

—**Kara Powell**, executive director, Fuller Youth Institute

The Justice Calling

WHERE PASSION MEETS PERSEVERANCE

Bethany Hanke Hoang and
Kristen Deede Johnson

Foreword by Mark Labberton

BrazosPress
a division of Baker Publishing Group
Grand Rapids, Michigan

_David + Andrea,
So grateful for the amazing hospitality 👉 showered neighborhood you have ... on ... + ... ity!_

© 2016 by International Justice Mission

Published by Brazos Press
a division of Baker Publishing Group
P.O. Box 6287, Grand Rapids, MI 49516-6287
www.brazospress.com

Printed in the United States of America

Library of Congress Cataloging-in-Publication Data
Hoang, Bethany H., 1979–
    The justice calling : where passion meets perseverance / Bethany Hanke Hoang and Kristen Deede Johnson.
        pages cm
    Includes bibliographical references.
    ISBN 978-1-58743-363-4 (cloth)
    1. Christianity and justice. 2. Social justice—Religious aspects—Christianity. 3. Human trafficking—Religious aspects—Christianity. 4. Rescue work—Religious aspects—Christianity. 5. International Justice Mission. I. Title
BR115.J8H635 2016
261.8—dc23   2015030262

Unless otherwise noted, Scripture quotations are from the Holy Bible, New International Version®. NIV®. Copyright © 1973, 1978, 1984, 2011 by Biblica, Inc.™ Used by permission of Zondervan. All rights reserved worldwide. www.zondervan.com

Scripture quotations labeled ESV are from The Holy Bible, English Standard Version® (ESV®), copyright © 2001 by Crossway, a publishing ministry of Good News Publishers. Used by permission. All rights reserved. ESV Text Edition: 2011

Scripture quotations labeled NRSV are from the New Revised Standard Version of the Bible, copyright © 1989, by the Division of Christian Education of the National Council of the Churches of Christ in the United States of America. Used by permission. All rights reserved.

The proprietor, International Justice Mission, is represented by Creative Trust, Inc., Literary Division, 5141 Virginia Way, Suite 320, Brentwood, TN 37027, www.creativetrust.com.

16 17 18 19 20 21 22   7 6 5 4 3 2 1

For Anthony:
who walked with me into this work and
loved me into perseverance
—Bethany

For Tryg:
whose love draws me further
into the grace of God in Christ
—Kristen

Contents

Foreword

MARK LABBERTON

The God who is love calls the people of God to love. That same God who is just calls the same people to do justice. To extract or to separate love and justice from the character of God would be impossible, just as it should mean these qualities in action are inextricable from God's people. The body of Christ is meant to be the enactment of God's life in the world. Jesus says the evidence will be measured by whether we actually live our calling. It's not whether our lips say Amen, but whether our lives do.

This is the overarching argument of *The Justice Calling*. The central gift of this book is that its authors themselves say Amen to God's justice calling with their words and with their lives. Now, let it be said that Bethany Hoang and Kristen Johnson would be the first to admit they have a long way to go to live this calling as faithfully as they wish; yet, I want to witness to what I know about them. They obviously and deeply affirm the call to do justice even as they give themselves to live the calling they present to us here. They do so as fellow travelers who journey with God, and us all, in an unjust world of suffering and pain. Their privileged lives have been recast, reordered, and filled by God's love and by the world's need. The love and justice of God makes a claim on them, and they have responded with their hearts and minds, their abilities and time. What I have found in this book is that Bethany and Kristen's humble empathy, alongside their faithful biblical and practical teaching, strengthens my longing to live God's justice calling. I believe it will do so for you too.

Lives centered in the love and justice of God will make room for the poor, the widow, the orphan, and the slave. That changes everything, which is just what Jesus said we should anticipate. Individual and social cries for justice go out for transformation of people and of systems; justice in the real world means both, not either/or. "Justice is what love looks like in public," is the way Cornel West captures it. The body of Christ can and should move to enact the kind of incarnational justice that seeks, rescues, and restores individuals impaired by injustice. But likewise, God's people need to engage the abusive assumptions, habits, laws, and societal systems that leave billions without justice and without hope every day—sometimes for generations.

These personal and systemic crises exist in the United States and in nations all around the world. This book illustrates its message primarily against the backdrop of global violence and oppression where the scale of injustice is the most overwhelmingly extensive. The particularity of injustice against the vulnerable, placed in the context of massive global injustice, is mind-boggling. How can a mature follower of Jesus be less than engaged and responsive, not paralyzed, by these enormous, life-destroying realities for those who also bear the image of God?

Alongside these international illustrations, readers could add compelling stories of urgent personal and systemic injustice in the United States as well. Our nation contains so many plain, persistent, multigenerational stories of lives undermined—and even now being damaged—through economic, racial, educational, and sexual injustice. The stories we might add include the names of priceless individuals, even whole communities, tribes, and regions in our nation. It is always about the decisions and actions of individuals, but it is also about laws, institutions, and social practices as well.

The justice calling is at hand wherever we are, right where we are. May this book give powerful voice to a distinctive call of those who follow Jesus Christ. May we too be among those who say Amen with our tongues and with our lives.

Acknowledgments

We are so grateful to God for allowing our lives to intersect, making it possible for us to write this book together. It all began with a book proposal swap—realizing that we'd both been working on books that stemmed from a mutual concern about justice, we showed each other our respective proposals and realized they shared an uncanny, perhaps even Spirit-led synergy in what we were seeking to do. There was enough crossover between our ideas and yet enough distinction between our voices and contexts that we believed we could write a stronger book if we joined forces. We met for coffee in Michigan one afternoon in February 2011, hashed out our ideas, and then began. And began again . . . and again.

In the course of writing this book children were born and raised in our families, jobs and intense travel schedules were juggled, and—between the two of us—we moved more than half a dozen times. This book was a far longer journey than we anticipated, and its very existence is testimony to the Spirit of God working in our midst across the miles.

Throughout this project we've experienced God working personally in each of our lives, teaching us the very things about which we have been writing. As we wrote, God chiseled away at us, forming our understanding of who God is, who God is calling us to be as we follow Jesus, and what it takes to persevere. We are grateful—so utterly-beyond-words grateful—to God for his gracious love, presence, and power with us in this work.

We thank our editor at Baker, Bob Hosack, who was gracious to creatively reimagine with us what this book could be as we considered writing it together. We are grateful to Lisa Cockrel, Brian Bolger, and their editorial team for going deep into the weeds with us as we shaped and reshaped the manuscript. To International Justice Mission (IJM), we are grateful to have been given the opportunity to write together. And words cannot convey our depth of gratitude to IJM's Nikki Toyama-Szeto, who invested countless hours helping this book come to life.

From Kristen
In writing this book, I found myself reflecting with deep gratitude upon friends in Christ from my college days who first offered me a glimpse that God's heart for this world was bigger than I understood, even though talk of justice was not yet widely in the air in our Christian circles. I thank Christen Kay Schaefer Wiggins, whose faith has driven her to be passionate about urban housing, both then and now; Christy Borgman Yates, who has consistently cared about racial reconciliation and economic inequality; and that remarkable group of students who allowed first their friendships and then their callings to be deeply shaped by their commitment to live and actively love their neighbors together in urban Richmond for the long haul. All of these friends have persevered against the odds in their passionate love for God's justice; I am grateful for their witness and their deep roots.

Many of the ideas for this book were forged in the communities of Hope College and Third Reformed Church and came to life in the communities of Western Theological Seminary and Pillar Church. I thank God for prayerful and supportive colleagues, theologically inquisitive students, and grace-filled communities of faith that helped bring this book into being. I think especially of the faithful preaching of Rev. Jon Brown, which helped to shape the book's contents as it was being written; the fellowship of our dinner group through the years; the prayers and laughter of our Pillar women's Bible study; the "world's best prayer group"; the sweet summer fellowship of Fireside Sip; and the loving support of family and friends near and far such as Arlene and Dave Johnson, Jess and Erik Deede, Jill and Alex Pfeiffer, Susanna Leche, Deb Van Duinen, Beth Anderson, Amy Hagood, Jill Tanis, Kate Bolt, Abby Vanderbilt, Caron Gentry, Stephanie Mar Brettman, Gisela Kreglinger, J. C. Luckey Sadler, and Suzzette Rodriguez Hurley DeMers.

At pivotal points, a number of conversations helped to shape this book's contents. I think especially of conversations with Keith Starkenburg, Mark Husbands, Jeff Tyler, Charlotte Witvliet, John Witvliet, Jamie Smith, Todd Cioffi, Andy McCoy, Emily Gum, Chuck Mathewes, Bob Dodaro, Clay Cooke, Sean

Larsen, David Phillips, Chris Rice, Laura Goetsch, Tom Wright, Ellen Davis, Oliver O'Donovan, Kevin Slusher, John Brogan, Tom Boogart, Chris Dorsey, Chris Dorn, George Hunsberger, Ron Rienstra, David Stubbs, David Komline, Ben Conner, and Travis West. I am continuously grateful for the ways in which the thought of James Davison Hunter shapes and clarifies my own thinking.

I am grateful to my friends Todd Billings and Jason Byassee, who gave of their limited time to read the manuscript in an early stage, providing invaluable comments. Tee Gatewood generously read it at both early and middle stages and offered theological insights that sharpened the book tremendously. Han-luen Kantzer Komline, Dan Claus, Grace Claus, and Emilie Wierda offered exceptionally helpful feedback on the final draft.

My parents, Elka and Peter Deede, also invested innumerable hours behind the scenes. I cannot thank them enough for all they have done, especially for teaching me to give my best to the responsibilities entrusted to me. I will always remember the many books that Trygve Jr. "wrote" alongside me as well as Ella's love for books that emerged early and strong. I continue to pray that they both become deeply rooted in Christ and that, by the grace of God, they bear much justice fruit in their lives. And to my dearest Tryg, who more than any other has helped me to receive the grace of God in my life: our life together in Christ gives me my most hopeful glimpses of shalom.

From Bethany
To my dear family, colleagues, and friends who have walked with me through the years of bringing this book to life, I long for you to know a measure of my fierce love and overflowing gratitude for you, greater than any of my words could ever convey.

To my IJM colleagues who have poured conviction, beauty, courage, strength, and wisdom into my life and our work together: Gary Haugen, Larry Martin, Nikki Toyama-Szeto, Mark and Janet Labberton, Andy and Catherine Crouch, Amy Sherman, Tim Dearborn, Steve Hayner (who encouraged this work even into the last days of his life) and his wife Sharol, Laurel Henshaw, Sharon Cohn Wu, Shelley Thames, Constance Padmore, Sean Litton, Pranitha Timothy, Ruthie McGinn, Bill Clark, Kayrn Aguirre, Susan Conway, Greg Darley, and so many others from across the years.

To those who waded into the thick of this manuscript in its many stages, bringing clarity and vast improvement: Jim Martin, Chong-Ae Shah, John Richmond, Scott Kauffmann, Greg Tarrant, Saju Mathew, Philip Langford, Liz

West, Kristy Pyke, Abey George, Kelly Cotter Ingebritson, Lori Poer, Tierney Short, Amy Lucia, Stephanie Reinitz, Dan Raines, Matthew Robinson, Nhi Clement, and Caryn Dahlstrand Rivadeneira.

To those who have prayed and continue to pray so relentlessly and with such great love for my family, for me, and for this book: my parents Harriett and Jay Hanke and Trang Trinh, John and Linda Richmond, Christine Britton, my pastors John and Laura Crosby, Christine Caine, Amanda-Paige Whittington, Christiane Lang Hearlson, Becca Messman, the "listening prayer" group at IJM headquarters (Vera Leung, Bill Clark, Blair Burns, Amy Lucia, James Criss, Philip Langford), Barb Armacost, Holly Tilton, Joan Korenchuck, Alisha Bauer, Elizabeth Cullen, Jill Klaiber, Amanda Epting, Bonnie Yelverton, Andrea Fuderer and Lindsey Dennis.

To Christ Presbyterian Church in Edina, a haven where my family has grown together in worship and walking with Jesus since our move from the East Coast to Minnesota, and to the staff who so graciously gave office space, tea, and camaraderie as I worked on this manuscript.

To the very best coffee and public writing atmospheres of Minneapolis: FiveWatt Coffee, Studio 2, SpyHouse Coffee, and George and the Dragon. Countless hours of creating and composing were richly inspired within these walls.

To my community of friends in Virginia and Minnesota, who have been companions in wisdom, love, and life through each stage of this book: Susan and Nate Den Herder, Riley and Skip Powell, Stina and Steven Busman Jost, Sara and Troy Groves, Kate Harris, Carolyn and Cameron Doolittle, Heather and David Hammond, Matt and Kari Norman, Jaime Rau, Pam Block, and every one of my extraordinary neighbors "South of George." And to Sarah Gossman, now in Seattle, who gave herself in extravagant love and grace to Beckham, Zoe, Anthony, and me and paved the way for seasons of flourishing to come.

To Anthony's and my family, with whom our lives are filled to overflowing with grace and love: the Trinhs, the Hoangs, the Hankes, the Youngs. I could not do the work God calls me to do without all that our family gives to Anthony, Beckham, Zoe, and me.

To Esther Dim, whose faithfulness catapulted me into the work of justice before I even knew your name, and who continually spurs me on to this day. I will never cease to be astounded by the way God has given us the gift of doing life together!

And to sweet Beckham, so many of your beautiful questions about God, Jesus Christ, and the Holy Spirit have been wrestled with in these pages. I love that we are only at the beginning and have many years of learning together ahead. And to sweet Zoe, you summed up this book so well when you asserted, at the age of three, "Did you know that God is still making you?" Indeed. Indeed. Every moment of curiosity and joy and chaos with the two of you has spun beauty, and I cherish you more than you will ever know.

And to Anthony, on the eve of our tenth anniversary, with each new day I am caught by surprise at your never-capped capacity to dream and envision and build and make manifest what matters most for others. Thank you (so paltry these words!), thank you for connecting me to Kristen, for believing in both of us, for spurring this project along even in its hardest days, and for serving me and loving me over and over and over, and over and over again. I love you.

Solo Christo. Sola Deo Gloria.

Introduction

Justice and God

It seemed like any other day: wake up, grab breakfast, head to class, go to chapel, head to another class, then lunch. But it turned out to be a day that would change the course of my life.

It was the winter of 2002, and I (Bethany) was in my first of three years pursuing a master of divinity at Princeton Theological Seminary. I finished lunch in our cafeteria and headed toward the door, on my way to the next class. In the main foyer, I could see that someone had set up an information table. Typically I would have rushed past.

But something caught my eye.

A poster was featured prominently at the display table, and on the poster was the image of a young girl's face, a single tear streaming down her cheek. As I moved in for a closer look, I froze.

The poster had two sentences written next to the image of this young girl:

Slavery is alive.

Rape for profit must be stopped.

The poster—the girl, those sentences, that moment—is forever seared in my memory. I had no idea that slavery was still alive in our world. I knew nothing about it. I was a student and lover of history and knew a great deal about slavery from the past. But slavery, alive in our world *today*—this was a new reality for me.

1

The second sentence—"rape for profit"—pointed to a horror beyond anything I knew existed. For years I had carried a very personal burden for people who endure sexual abuse, but I had no idea that abuse was happening on a profit-driven, global scale or that an entire industry existed for the sake of exploitation. The existence of this reality, an industry that could be called "rape for profit," knocked the wind out of me.

As I unlocked my eyes from this poster, I turned toward the table and met the eyes of Lisa, a woman who, unbeknownst to me in that moment, I would grow to know and deeply respect over the months to come. Lisa had driven up from Washington, DC, and set up this display table on behalf of the Salvation Army. I remember looking at Lisa and quietly asking her what I could do, still stunned by the two sentences that forever reshaped my understanding of reality.

God is the one who reveals the justice calling upon our lives, because God is the source of justice.

Lisa pushed a piece of paper across the table toward me and handed me a pen. I wrote down my name and email address so that she could send me more information.

It seemed like a hopelessly small step. It was the kind of step that many of us almost disregard, simply because of how insignificant it feels. But looking back I realize that, regardless of its size, putting my name on Lisa's mailing list was a step *forward*. And because it was a step forward, it was a step that mattered. It mattered then, and it continues to matter to this day.

I began to get articles from Lisa in my email in-box and was shocked to learn that there are more slaves in the world today than during the four hundred years of the transatlantic slave trade *combined*. Today an estimated 35.8 million people are owned by slave masters who use violence and lies to trap those who are vulnerable.[1] I also learned that this industry of selling human beings nets tens of billions of dollars annually. The estimates today exceed $150 billion, with about $99 billion coming from the sex trafficking industry alone.[2]

These statistics were completely new to me. The massive number of people in slavery, combined with news stories of actual children, women, and men all over the world being trapped in this scourge, was enough to leave me utterly overwhelmed. The more I learned, the more I felt like I was drowning in information I had no tools to navigate.

Seeing that poster and beginning to learn about human trafficking in all its forms ignited in me a passion that was immediate and strong. But in tandem with this new passion I was also fighting an even stronger instinct to recoil. I remember wishing there was a way that I could put what I was learning back on a shelf and forget about it for a while.

But I couldn't turn back. Unimaginable violence committed against the poorest and most vulnerable people in our world; suffering beyond anything I had ever imagined—I couldn't put it out of my mind. So what did I do? I hung my head. Quite literally. After opening yet another email full of nightmares I could not fathom, I buried my face in my hands and hung my head. I was sitting in the computer lab at the seminary library, and I was *done*. I couldn't move another step forward.

When I eventually lifted my head and stared at the computer screen again, I found myself composing an email to Lisa. "How do you do this?" I asked. "How do you wake up every day and face these terrible stories and somehow keep going, much less find a way to make a difference?"

Lisa wrote me a reply that I will never forget. She shared at length from her own story of engaging the needs of justice in our world and gave me a simple yet profound admonition: "Remember, this battle belongs to the Lord. It is not our battle. It is his. And he has invited us to join him. And he holds the victory. This battle belongs to the Lord."

The Source of Justice

Knowing the reality of injustice in our world was never going to be enough to get me out of my computer lab chair. Far from spurring me to action, my newfound knowledge felt instead like a weight pulling me to the bottom of a fathomless sea of suffering. But Lisa's email reminded me that justice has a source, and that source is not dependent on what we have or don't have in our hands, or on our good but faulty intentions. The source of justice in the midst of even the most heinous injustice in our world is Jesus Christ. God's very character is one of justice, and he has given us Jesus as the manifestation of his justice both now and for eternity. God is the one who reveals the justice calling upon our lives, because God is the source of justice.

Ever since that moment in the computer lab I have been on a journey to discover justice rooted in Jesus, to know this call that comes first from God, and to navigate the brokenness of this world with biblical hope as my sure-footed guide. Justice rooted in Jesus broke open for me the possibility and promise of persevering hope—the possibility that I could shed my paralysis and actually move forward one small step at a time because there is a God who is and will be victorious over injustice. And while God certainly could and does act on his own, God beckons us to join him, calling us into his family to be part of his work of redemption and healing through Jesus Christ and the Holy Spirit.

The Whole Story

As God makes his call upon our lives, he connects us with companions for the journey. It turns out that we (Kristen and Bethany) were both wrestling with the reality of injustice in our world, and we were coming to similar realizations about the necessity of knowing Jesus as the source of all justice pursuit. Kristen comes to this book primarily from her context as a professor of theology and Christian formation interacting with questions and struggles that arise from her students, colleagues, studies, and life. Bethany's perspective comes primarily from her biblical and theological training in the context of Cru, Princeton Theological Seminary, and more than a decade of engaging pastors and local churches through leading a think tank for International Justice Mission (IJM)—an organization of attorneys, criminal investigators, and social workers providing direct service to victims of violent injustice.

Over the years we have both increasingly grown to understand that our passion for the needs of this world must be grounded in the reality of who *God* is and what God's vision for justice is and has always been. We've written this book as a Genesis-through-Revelation exploration of God's justice calling upon his people, God's invitation to us to participate in his work of healing what is broken and setting things right in this world. As we've wrestled with the enormity of the needs of the world, we've become convinced that Scripture is as essential guide that each of us needs; through Scripture God offers us an ever-unfolding invitation to know God's love for justice and strength to respond to his calling.

Our hope for ourselves and for all who follow Jesus is that we would not only grow to know the needs of the world and find ways to respond to these needs, but also that we would come to know more deeply the God who is able, above all we could ever ask or imagine, to bring beauty and glory out of the ashes of suffering.[3]

Because of this conviction about who God is, we've written this book not as a guide to how you can muster more inspiration and find ways to "try harder" in response to the needs of the world. We are not going to tell you that the lives of the vulnerable and the advance of the kingdom of God rest on your actions. We are not going to tell you that you are the only hands and feet of Jesus and that Jesus can't act in this world unless you do. We are not going to try, whether overtly or subtly, to guilt you into caring about justice.

> *What we hope to do through this book is draw you more deeply into knowing who God is, what God loves, and who God calls us to be.*

What we hope to do through this book is draw you more deeply into knowing who God is, what God loves, and who God calls us to be. We hope to offer a vision of what our lives and our communities can look like as, by the grace of God, we respond to his call for us to live the way of life revealed in Scripture. This way of life is the way of justice and righteousness.

We want this book to guide you and aid you in guiding others into pursuing justice rooted in Jesus—not because justice has become a buzzword in our era but because from the beginning of Scripture until the end we see a God who longs for justice and righteousness in this world and who calls his people to join him in seeking it. God is alive and active in this world; his light blazes in the darkness. And God calls us to join what he is doing through his strength, his presence, and his grace.

Watchwords

We've broken the story of Scripture into six movements, each of which is connected to a major segment of the Bible: creation, the fall, Israel, Jesus, the church, and all things being made new.[4] Throughout the entire story we've found that five key words—watchwords, as we call them—emerge as essential and interconnected for understanding who God is and who God calls his people to be: holiness, *hesed* (faithful and active loving-kindness), justice, righteousness, and shalom (flourishing wholeness).

From the beginning of Scripture through to the end, the Bible reveals a God whose holiness and active loving-kindness (*hesed*) lead him to care deeply about justice, righteousness, and the flourishing of all that he has created. We see these passions of God most clearly in the person of Jesus Christ as our holy and loving God enters this world in human flesh. God in Jesus Christ personally and powerfully takes the fullness of the world's injustice, unrighteousness, and brokenness upon himself in order to overcome the sin that prevents humanity and creation from flourishing. Jesus Christ will come again to complete this victory and fully usher in his kingdom of justice, righteousness, and shalom. In the meantime, God calls us to live as his holy people. Empowered by the grace of God in Christ, as we wait for the fullness of his kingdom, we live his justice and righteousness, actively loving and seeking the flourishing of all. And while we passionately respond to the justice calling as the people of God, we remember that the battle and the victory ultimately belong to the Lord.

Mapping the Story

Each movement of the biblical story opens the door to a deeper understanding and invitation to respond to who God is; who God calls his people to be; and the justice, righteousness, and shalom that God longs to see in this world. At each turn in the story we find God beckoning us further into the justice calling he has placed upon our lives.

In chapter 1 we invite the reader to consider the whole of the Bible as one story and the implications of this interconnected story for understanding and living justice and righteousness. What *is* justice? What does righteousness *mean*? As we grow to know the whole story of God's love for justice and righteousness, in what ways will we respond as the body of Christ?

In chapter 2 we delve into *creation*, the first of six movements of the biblical story. Understanding justice in the context of God's original vision for creation leads to a counterintuitive invitation to rest. God is continually inviting us, even commanding us, to receive and extend Sabbath rest as a gift.

In chapter 3 we explore justice by juxtaposing it with *the fall*, and we seek to understand God's invitation to move *toward* the darkness of this world, in the light of Christ. We then consider what we can learn about God's commitment to justice from his covenant relationship with Israel (chap. 4). In this context, God invites us to lament rather than despair as we face suffering and injustice in our own lives and communities and throughout the world.

In chapter 5 we look deeply into who Jesus is as he enters and redeems this fallen, broken world of suffering and injustice. As we look to Jesus, we are invited to consider how we are being formed as we follow him. We need to be honest with ourselves; as we pursue justice, are we enticed by the possibility of being heroic? Or are we seeking justice by the power of Jesus Christ, whose victory over sin and evil enables us to receive and seek God's justice and righteousness as God's beloved saints?

Turning to chapter 6, we explore what it means for the church today to respond to God's invitation to be sanctified and sent in kingdom mission. As we look to the end of the biblical story (which is only the *beginning* of all things being made new), we remember that Jesus Christ will fully usher in his kingdom of justice and righteousness in the age to come and how this invites us to be a people of persevering hope as we pursue our callings in the midst of injustice (chap. 7). In the conclusion to the book we consider what it means to live this story in our daily lives, embracing Scripture and the practices we have learned from Scripture as gifts that draw us deeper into communion with God, knowing that only as we abide in Jesus Christ will God bring lasting fruit from our lives.

A word of caution: many of the concepts in this book, such as *injustice* and *oppression* and *slavery*, are all too easily relegated to the (safer) realm of abstract ideas. Remember that this calling is about real people. People suffering from injustice are our neighbors, both nearby and throughout the world, right at this moment. Each person has a name, a face, a family, and dreams.

To help us remember this, we have woven specific cases of people suffering injustice throughout this book. In most stories pseudonyms were used to protect their identities. We also include stories of churches and other communities and organizations responding to injustice in this world. In sharing stories of suffering, rescue, healing, and following Jesus our hope is that ideas will spark as to how God is inviting you and others in your community to respond to the justice calling. Many of these stories focus on victims of violent injustice in countries *outside* the United States because this is where God has drawn Bethany to focus her response. But we believe that God calls us to engage people, places, and structures both near and far with a persevering passion for justice, and we encourage readers to consider how God is opening your eyes and hearts and lives to injustice and where specifically to focus your actions.

A Word about Stories

Our intent is that this book will provide a Genesis to Revelation biblical theology of justice. Above all, we hope that this book will serve you, our readers, by drawing you nearer to our God who loves justice and is himself the embodiment of justice. But it must be said, with complete candor, that even as we seek to offer a biblical theology that is timeless and thorough, we are by no means able to exhaustively cover the riches of the Scriptures. And even as we seek to draw you, our readers, into an experience of the reality of injustice in the lives of individuals and communities today, the stories of injustice that we tell are far from a thorough representation of the fullness of the wrong that justice seeks to right in our world.

As the authors of this book, created in partnership with International Justice Mission (IJM), our own expertise centers upon violent injustice being committed against those who live in the most poverty-stricken regions of the world, and the stories we tell lean heavily in this direction. However, it is incumbent upon every one of us who follow Jesus to be constantly mindful of and committed to engaging the myriad faces of justice and injustice beyond what any one book might present. In the United States alone today there is a groundswell of racially-charged violence and murder, there are waves of unaccompanied children and entire families seeking refuge from unstable nations, there is urgent need to reform our prisons and the systems that lead to mass incarceration, just to scratch the surface. None of the stories in this book, however, center on these or other deep injustices in the United States, nor do our stories touch upon Syria or Iraq or Israel/Palestine or so many other regions that could and should be named and engaged. But we want you to know that all throughout the writing of this book, we've sought to hold out in front of ourselves all that we could not address, and we've sought, even with the smallest of steps, to learn deeply and engage with injustice far beyond the areas we explore in the book itself.

As each of us moves ever more steadily toward the darkness of injustice by the light of Jesus Christ, we will discover there is far more that is broken than any of us could ever piece back together, and that there is far more beauty in the healing that God will bring than we could ever ask or imagine. We put forward this book as an offering, and we're counting on each reader to move deeply into the stories we've experienced while also allowing your hearts to be broken and your lives disrupted by the injustices in your own immediate context. As we enter into the stories of injustice in our world and as we enter into the biblical story with its persistent call for us to seek justice and righteousness in this world, God himself will lead us by the sun of righteousness that comes with healing in its wings (Mal. 4:2).

1

Engage the Whole Story

Justice and Righteousness

Boola was out of options.[1] He knew he was risking his life, but he secretly found a way to make a phone call to his brother. When his brother answered, Boola whispered into the receiver what was happening: he had incurred a small debt and in the midst of this transaction he was taken a thousand miles from home and locked into a brick-making facility. He was enduring vicious beatings, grueling eighteen-hour workdays under a blazing sun, and given very little food or rest. He was trapped and desperate to get out.

Boola had been trafficked into labor slavery. The terms *human trafficking* and *slavery* both refer to the use of coercion (whether through force or deception) to exploit a person for labor, sex, or other means of profit or gain.[2] The good news today is that, unlike in generations past, slavery is now illegal in nearly every country on the planet. Boola's own country has good laws against slavery. The problem is that, on the whole, these laws are rarely enforced.

When government authorities choose to turn a blind eye (and often even profit through bribery from their willingness to overlook the crimes) rather than protect those who are most vulnerable, slave owners and others who choose to abuse their power are able to wreak havoc on the lives of whomever

9

they can pull into their traps with no fear of consequences. In this culture of impunity the ones who pay the highest price are the victims like Boola.

Slave owners often lure the vulnerable into their control through lending money and holding over them the ruse of debt that needs to be worked off in order to be repaid. The loans in question are not large, typically borrowed to cover an urgent need such as a medical emergency. And yet, it turns out that the amount of the loan doesn't actually matter. The truth is that slave owners are not interested in being repaid for the money loaned. International Justice Mission (IJM) has documented scores of cases demonstrating that the financial debt owed is not the currency the slave master is most interested in; a physical human body, turned into chattel, is far more valuable to the slave owner than the original money lent.

Taken by force and fraud, Boola was trapped in this highly lucrative trade in human beings. The estimated annual profits for the human trafficking industry today exceed those of Microsoft ($22.1B), BP ($23.5B), Samsung ($27.2B), Exxon ($32.6B), and Apple ($37.0B) *combined*.[3]

Vividly corroborating the evidence of what slave owners really want, one of the most harrowing forty seconds of video footage I (Bethany) have ever seen comes from an undercover surveillance camera brought inside the walls of a rice mill in South Asia. The video captures a slave master throwing his head back in laughter about the idea of a debt needing to be repaid. With an enormous smile and cackle he says, "The debt? We're not so much interested in the debt."

In his laughter, the slave owner reveals that he knows the incredible profitability of owning human beings. A living, breathing human being is exponentially profitable once secured as a commodity. A drug owner can sell a drug only one time because it is then consumed. A human being can be sold and worked over and over again. Slave masters—whether brothel keepers, or labor compound owners, or the traffickers who broker a transfer of sale—profit many times over from a single human being, working them for months and years until their bodies are simply discarded.[4]

What Is Justice?

Whatever you might be thinking or feeling about what you've read above, you likely have a sense, at root, that *this is not right*. When we intentionally put these realities on our radar, when we choose to know the stories of slaveowners who gleefully profit from the suffering of millions of slaves like Boola, when we encounter stories and situations of brutal injustice, we might have a deep, intuitive sense that *this is not the way things are supposed to be.*[5] But what is the basis for our sense that things can and ought to be different? And what can we do to be part of that difference?

In its most direct biblical formulation, justice can best be described as *setting things right.*[6] But how do we even know what "right" is? How do we make sure that we are pursuing God's vision of "right" rather than our own distorted or culturally constricted vision as we seek justice? The short but crucial answer is that we learn what is right when we look to Jesus Christ and the whole story of Scripture.

> *What is the basis for our sense that things can and ought to be different? And what can we do?*

When I (Bethany) was in high school, I learned how to reshingle a roof. After several years of mission trips around the United States, I grew to love being up on a roof with a crew of friends. I loved ripping through layers of tar-laden shingles with a sharp shovel, using a crow bar to pull up the old nails, and heaving it all to the ground in a massive heap, creating a clean slate. Once we rolled out rows of tar paper to cover the cleared-off plywood roof structure, we needed to complete a critical step. Before the first shingle could be laid, we needed to stretch a horizontal line across the length of the roof. Covered in chalk, this thin line of twine was held by one person on one side of the roof and then stretched taut by another person on the other side of the roof. "Snap!" One of us pulled the line high, let go, and watched it ricochet off the tar paper, leaving a perfectly straight, level marking of chalk. We repeated this process at intervals up to the ridge of the roof. Only then, when we knew the precise standard against which we would mark out all of our work, could we begin to lay the first row of shingles that would guide the following rows.

Like a chalk line's offering of a horizontal reference point, plumb lines offer a vertical reference point. Both leveling tools have been used in construction since the civilization of ancient Egypt. As we grapple with the idea of *righteousness*, it is illuminating to note that the Scriptures describe righteousness using the imagery and metaphor of a plumb line (Isa. 28:17). God's righteousness helps us to see the path of right living we are called to follow and to gauge whether we are living "rightly" and treating one another and the created world in accordance with how God created and redeemed us to live.

Every leveling tool needs a point of reference. In our pursuit of what it means to be "right," Jesus Christ is that standard. Jesus embodies what is perfectly right, and his life serves as a measure against which we can determine what is right and what is not right. As God in the flesh, Jesus had all the power and the authority in the world, and he consistently used his power and authority not for his own gain but for the flourishing of others. He "did not come to be served, but to serve, and to give his life as a ransom for many" (Matt. 20:28). Living in perfect communion with God, Jesus not only dedicated his life to love and service but he also gave his life to conquer sin, death, and injustice of every kind. Exemplifying how God intended humanity to live from the very beginning, he showed us right relationships, right living, and the right use of power, undertaken out of love for God and love for others.

> *As God in the flesh, Jesus had all the power and the authority in the world, and he consistently used his power and authority not for his own gain but for the flourishing of others.*

We need the righteousness of God in Jesus Christ—"the Righteous One" (1 John 2:1)—to know what is right, but Christ doesn't just leave us with a measure of what is right. He is more than a plumb line or a chalk line against which we measure ourselves, leaving us to do the work of fixing what is not right in ourselves and in this world. Through his life, death, resurrection, and ascension he *shares* his righteousness with us. He sets us right with God so that we can live in right relationship with God and offer every part of our lives as instruments of justice and righteousness in this world (Rom. 3:21–26; 6:13). Ultimately, "setting things right" is God's work. We don't fully see Christ's justice reflected in this world, but we live in hope of Christ's return, when he will finally and fully set all things right.

Meanwhile, the Holy Spirit invites followers of Jesus to join him in his work of setting all things right; God gives us the ministry of reconciliation in this world (2 Cor. 5:14–21). God calls us to join him in the pursuit of justice as we use our power to seek what is right and just in this world. When people use their power to enable others to flourish and live as they were created to live, justice is the result. Injustice occurs when power is used to exploit, abuse, and even destroy.

The biblical sense of justice as setting things right comes into play after the fall, when humans begin to use the power God has given them to seek their own selfish ambitions rather than seeking God's vision. *Shalom*, the Hebrew word used to refer to the flourishing of all of God's creation, involves God, humans, and the rest of creation living together in harmony, wholeness, justice, and delight. The English translation of *shalom* is "peace," but that word fails to capture the rich and vibrant life that the Hebrew concept entails. In keeping with God's intentions, a world that truly embodies shalom is a world of justice and righteousness, with everyone and everything flourishing as a result of living "rightly"—that is, living in accordance with the ways God created them to live and to flourish.

When God created humans, he charged them with stewardship of the created world. He shared his very own power and authority with them so that they had the power and authority to faithfully care for God's world and for each other, using their God-given power to seek the wholeness of everyone and everything. But we know that the story takes a tragic turn. Instead of gratefully receiving the calling God had given them and faithfully using the power God had entrusted to them, the first humans chose their own way. Instead of trusting God's vision for them and for the flourishing of the world, they used their power to seek what they thought would be best for themselves. When they made that choice, they were essentially rejecting not only God but also the justice calling God had given them.

> *Jesus is more than a plumb line. . . . Through his life, death, resurrection, and ascension . . . he sets us right with God so that we can live in right relationship with God and offer every part of our lives as instruments of justice and righteousness in this world.*

As a result, the door to injustice opened. Separated from right relationship with God, generation upon generation of people have used power not for love of God and others but rather to seek their own distorted notions of what is right, thereby seeking their own glory, security, or authority. Along the way, the people and the world that God created for flourishing have instead been exploited, abused, and even destroyed.

I (Kristen) was reflecting on this idea of "setting right" when my son broke his arm. The brokenness was immediately evident, as the bone jutted sideways

in a clear distortion of God's intended design. The top priority of the or-
thopedic doctor was to set the bone right (*ortho* comes from the Greek for
"right" or "straight"). With the bone painstakingly set straight by the doctor,
the healing process could begin.

My son's broken arm, this departure from the way arms are supposed to
be, reminded me of the way God's original picture of justice, wholeness, and
delight gave way to an unjust and tragic world. In the midst of this fallen world,
God called Israel to be his holy people and reaffirmed his justice calling. By
drawing them into relationship with him and
giving them his law as a guide, God called
them to use the power and authority he'd
given them to create a nation that reflected
and pursued God's vision of justice, righteousness, and shalom. Justice as "setting
things right" is what God is referring to when
he tells Israel to "follow justice and justice
alone" (Deut. 16:19–20). He is calling them
to be a people set apart by their consistent
commitment to seek what is right in a world
full of wrongs, to return to the plumb line he has set, to seek justice in a world
marked by injustice, to bring light to the darkness around them. Eventually, in
his loving faithfulness, God sent Jesus Christ to set right all that was wrong,
broken, and distorted. In and through Christ and the Spirit we are invited
into God's family and called to participate with God in seeking and living
God's vision of what is right.

God's righteousness provides the backdrop against which we can understand God's vision for justice and the justice calling that God has for us today.
As we explore the biblical story, the five concepts of holiness, *hesed*, justice,
righteousness, and shalom—which are all embodied in Jesus Christ and evident
throughout the biblical witness—will be important guides.

> *Separated from right relationship with God, people use their power to abuse and exploit rather than to love and serve.*

One Interconnected Story

Writing in the second century AD, Irenaeus, bishop of Lyons, is the earliest
surviving example of a Christian who sought to combine the different parts
of the biblical narrative into one story.[7] Irenaeus also believed that each of us
is a character in the story of the Bible.[8] As you engage the story of Scripture

throughout this book, know that you are part of a long tradition dedicated to immersion in the whole of Scripture—a story in which you are also a character with a calling.

My (Bethany's) friend and mentor Ruth Padilla DeBorst has committed her life to creating space for others to live more fully into this full story of Scripture. She and her husband Jim founded Casa Adobe in Costa Rica (www.casaadobe.org), and it has become a place to both learn and embody what it means to live in mission not only among neighbors in your own community but also globally amid the needs of the world as a whole. People are invited to come to Casa Adobe as visitors for a brief retreat or as community members for a year of immersion and service.

> *We are part of a long tradition that is dedicated to considering the whole of Scripture.*

Ruth has been witness both to shattering suffering and unspeakable beauty, and every conversation with her imbues my life with wisdom. She's written and taught widely on the critical importance of engaging the whole of Scripture and living into the fullness of God's intentions for justice in our world. In particular, I find the following excerpt from an interview she did with Andy Crouch to be a helpful snapshot regarding what is at stake in our approach to reading Scripture:

> I've been struck by how fragmented our reading of the Bible is. It's a kind of Sunday school version of the Bible: all these isolated little Bible stories, taught out of their context. What we need to reclaim is the big story, the big picture. "In the beginning God . . ."—that's where we need to begin. In the end, we find the new Jerusalem and all people bowing before the Lord of all nations. The story between that beginning and that end is not divorced from human history. Rather, it is a picture of God's involvement in history.[9]

One of the most pervasive themes throughout the Bible is freedom. Stories, illustrations, and allusions to freedom and slavery (both physical and spiritual, as well as the intersection of the two) abound, from Genesis through Revelation. Understanding Scripture as one connected story helps us to see how our pursuit of justice fits within God's long-standing desire for the freedom, the flourishing, and the wholeness of this world and everything in it. The larger story of Scripture gives us a picture of what God intended when God created and redeemed the world and what full redemption will look like when Christ comes again. It provides a picture of how things are meant to be so that when we witness how deeply things have gone wrong, we can name them as wrong and join in with the work of God—who is *always* moving and inviting us to join him in making things right.

As Ruth explains, "I often think about the disciples on the way to Emmaus. When they were blind to Jesus, he explained 'all the Scriptures.' Too often we don't look at all the Scripture, all of life, and God's comprehensive intentions of not leaving any corner of the earth untouched by his love."[10] Jesus is with us on this road, just as he was with the disciples, and by his Spirit he will provide everything we need to know to understand the interconnected story of Scripture more deeply, to love the world and those in it, and to join him in all he is doing in this world.

> *As we wade into the murky waters of injustice, corruption, and violence, we need to know God's Word in such a way that we are buttressed by its truth in the face of darkness and lies.*

As we wade into the murky waters of injustice, corruption, and violence, we need to know God's Word in such a way that we are buttressed by its truth in the face of darkness and lies. We need to be immersed in the story of Scripture to see more and more of the God who is leading us and calling us as we follow him beyond the borders of what we know. If we ask God to help us better know the entire story of Scripture, God will show us not only his consistent concern for justice but also his consistent calling to his people to seek justice in this world.

When we move from the story of Scripture to stories of injustice in this world, we realize that real lives are at stake, every day. But the reality of what is at stake is not meant to be a burden of guilt; it is a gracious invitation from God to join him in seeking justice through the saving work of Jesus Christ, who has given us all we need to respond to this justice calling.

Jesus at the Crux

Jesus Christ is the hinge on which the whole story turns. The life, death, resurrection, and ascension of Jesus Christ are collectively the climax of it all. In the form of redemption, salvation, and reconciliation, Jesus Christ is the resolution within the whole that changes everything. It takes the rest of the story, which is ongoing, to work out this resolution. Clearly, then, Christ and the outworking of his saving love and sacrifice are central to the parts of the story that follow him.

We also need to keep in mind that Jesus Christ was present and active in the story from the very beginning, long before he was named. The Gospel of John tells us that all things came into being through Christ, who was with God in the beginning and who, in fact, *was* God from the beginning. Through the person of Jesus Christ, God made himself known to humans. Even though we didn't see him in the flesh until he was born as a baby in Bethlehem, Jesus Christ has always been God. The same is true of the Holy Spirit. These three persons of God make up one God, the Trinity, who has always cared about justice and called his people to seek it.

Jesus did not intend the justice calling to be a solo journey. Throughout the story of the Bible, God has called and equipped *a people* to live in relationship with him and to seek his justice in this world. As we immerse ourselves in the biblical story in order to learn more about God and his calling upon us, we need to do so as a part of God's family. We need to grapple with Scripture together and discern together; we need to draw on the wisdom, knowledge, and example of those in the body of Christ who have gone before us or who live in other parts of God's world. We need to spur one another on to rely on the gift of the Holy Spirit who guides us, forms us, strengthens us, and draws us further into life in Christ as we read God's Word together.

The Justice *and* Righteousness Calling

The two greatest commandments identified by Jesus—to love God and to love your neighbor as yourself—are the flip side of the two most prevalent sins throughout Scripture: idolatry and injustice.[11] Failing to love God leads to idolatry, while failing to love others leads to injustice. Another way of putting this is to say that the call to love God and love our neighbors is a call to righteousness and justice.

Righteousness is a term used throughout the Bible, and it is critical for us to understand what it means as we seek to know the whole story of Scripture and God's love for justice. Unfortunately, *righteousness* is a word laden with negative connotations in many cultures today, and it can be difficult to discern its original meaning. While it is easily relegated to the theoretical, the biblical call to righteousness is meant to have tangible implications for daily life and love. However, instead of bringing to mind love for others, the idea of righteousness and being "righteous" more likely brings to mind notions of *self*-righteous people who are full of pride and arrogance. Depending on your perspective, *justice* might also have some troubling connotations.

Seeking the Lord and pursuing justice and righteousness belong together and were never meant to be separated. Justice and righteousness flow from the same source: God's steadfast love.

But when we look to Jesus in particular and the Bible as a whole, we see that justice and righteousness get to the heart of what it means to love God and love others. God's justice and righteousness are manifestations of God's character of love, and God, in turn, calls his people to be set apart by their justice and righteousness. And as God shares his own justice and righteousness with us through Christ, he enables us to love, justify, and be righteous. The entirety of Scripture shows that seeking the Lord and pursuing justice and righteousness belong together and were never meant to be separated. Justice and righteousness flow from the same source: God's steadfast love.

In Scripture, the justice calling cannot be separated from the righteousness calling. Although the connection is harder for us to see than it was for those familiar with Scripture in its original languages, when we look at the call to justice and righteousness throughout the whole story of Scripture, the significance of their interconnection and the implications for our lives today are staggering.

The New Testament words *justice* and *righteousness* are English translations of the same Greek word, *dikaiosyne*. These two words are part of a larger family of words that are prominent in Scripture and connect to the very heart of our life in Christ; the words *justice, righteousness, justification,* and *justify* all come from this same Greek root. Our English renderings fail to capture these significant family ties. As a result, our English understandings of justice, righteousness, and justification often don't reflect the fullness of what these words meant to the first followers of Jesus.

Take the words that Paul writes in Romans 3. A common English translation of the chapter includes the following phrases: "righteousness is given through faith in Jesus Christ to all who believe" (3:22); "all are justified freely by his grace through the redemption that came by Christ Jesus" (3:24); God's offering of Christ is a sacrifice of atonement that demonstrates God's "righteousness"; and God is both "just and the one who justifies" those who have faith in Jesus (3:26).

In its original language, this passage involves a fair amount of creative wordplay around the Greek root *dikaio-*. Through that wordplay, the readers (or more accurately, the listeners) of Paul's letter would have seen obvious links between Christ's work of justification and their own righteousness and call to justice. They would have seen that Christ's atoning sacrifice justified them, making them right with God. They would have understood this act of reconciliation as a demonstration of God's own righteousness and justice, a gift that enabled them to love God *and* others rightly and justly. As Tim Keller describes this connection, "Justice and justification are joined at the hip."[12]

The Hebrew language of the Old Testament uses two different words for justice and righteousness, but the two concepts are closely connected to each other. They appear together repeatedly[13] and form a distinctive phrase called a *hendiadys*. An example of a common hendiadys in English is the phrase "sick and tired." The words *sick* and *tired* provide a stronger and slightly different effect when placed together than each does on its own. Think of the phrase, "I'm sick and tired of waking up early." (As parents with young children who don't always sleep well, we are well acquainted with this particular hendiadys!) We would use such a phrase for added emphasis, to convey something more than just "I'm sick of waking up early" or "I'm tired of waking up early."

Within the Bible itself, the most common word-pair used to convey our understanding of justice in relationship is "justice and righteousness."[14] In Psalm 33:5 we read,

> The LORD loves righteousness and justice;
>   the earth is full of his unfailing love.

This is but one example of an intentional pairing found throughout the Old Testament. The parallelism of this verse also tells us that God's love for righteousness and justice is the way in which God fills all things; therefore we cannot understand God's faithful love apart from righteousness and justice.

This inextricable connection between justice, righteousness, and love is at the core of God's vision for the flourishing of all he has created.

The Hebrew word usually translated as "justice" in the Old Testament is *mishpat*. This word comes into play only when things have gone wrong with God's original vision of shalom and restoration is needed. When a situation is not going according to the way of life God intends for his people or creation—when injustice of any kind is present—judicial intervention may be needed to help make things right (in this way, the word *mishpat* also has legal connotations and is sometimes translated "judgment"). Once the situation has been set right, then justice is in place. Without this restoration, injustice remains. *Mishpat* can also be defined as *the restoration of a situation or environment so that equity and harmony are promoted in the community.*[15] Simply put, *mishpat* means *setting things right.*

In contrast to many legal systems today, both justice and righteousness in ancient Israel were based on *relationships.* Justice was understood to be both inherently personal and communal. As scholar Elizabeth Achtemeier writes of the Old Testament sense of justice, "That which is right in a legal sense is that which fulfills the demands of the community relationship, and the sole function of the judge is to maintain the community, to restore right to those from whom it has been taken."[16] This was also one of the main responsibilities given to the king, to protect and restore right relationships in the community entrusted to him.

> *God's love for righteousness and justice is the way in which God fills all things.*

Even though righteousness can have negative connotations in our culture today—conjuring up images of people who care more about following rules and laws of the faith than loving others—this could not be further from the biblical intention of righteousness. Biblically speaking, the word *righteousness* (rather than *mishpat* alone) probably better captures the big vision toward which we who are passionate about justice today are aiming. We want to see a world in which all people and all of creation are treated rightly and are given what they need to be able to flourish. This is a vision of abundant life, rather than the scarcity and disorder that come with injustice. *Righteousness* (*tsedaqah*) is the biblical word that connects us to this bigger picture of human flourishing, while *justice* (*mishpat*) focuses more specifically on the action that needs to be taken in order to restore a situation to its intended righteousness.[17] As an integrated, holistic understanding of what it means to live rightly, loving others and following God's rules are both essential to living in a deeply connected way with one another as God intended.

The root of the Hebrew word for righteousness, *tsedaqah*, refers to behavior that is called for based on the relationships between people or between people and God. Righteousness is not about an abstract moral standard to which we need to adhere perfectly but rather about living faithfully in each of our relationships. As one biblical scholar writes, "There is no norm of righteousness outside of that of personal involvement. When people fulfill the conditions imposed on them by relationships, they are righteous."[18] Just like justice, righteousness is concerned for the community. At its core, righteousness is about loving others more than it is about ourselves.

> *Righteousness is not about an abstract moral standard to which we need to perfectly adhere but rather about living faithfully in each of our relationships.*

Scholar and ministry practitioner Amy Sherman notes that biblical righteousness expresses itself in three directions—up, in, and out.[19] Righteousness expresses itself in an upward direction as we live our lives in ways that glorify God and demonstrate our love of God, in humble dependence on God's grace and Spirit. It expresses itself inwardly as we live with internal holiness and purity, with transformed and purified hearts, and through the grace and transforming work of God in Christ and the Spirit. Righteousness also needs to manifest itself outwardly in righteousness toward others, as we love our neighbors near and far through Jesus Christ and the Spirit.

The "righteous man" described by the prophet Ezekiel gives us a picture of what this upward, inward, and outward love can look like.

> Suppose there is a righteous man
>   who does what is just and right.
> He does not eat at the mountain shrines
>   or look to the idols of Israel.
> He does not defile his neighbor's wife
>   or have sexual relations with a woman during her period.
> He does not oppress anyone,
>   but returns what he took in pledge for a loan.

> He does not commit robbery
>> but gives his food to the hungry
>> and provides clothing for the naked.
> He does not lend to them at interest
>> or take a profit from them.
> He withholds his hand from doing wrong
>> and judges fairly between two parties.
> He follows my decrees
>> and faithfully keeps my laws.
> That man is righteous;
>> he will surely live,
> declares the Sovereign LORD. (Ezek. 18:5–9)

Notice the different layers involved in being righteous and just within this passage. It begins with faithfulness to God, as the righteous person does not worship idols. It extends to loving treatment of others by addressing personal sexual ethics, the importance of just judgments, and the faithful use of finances. It marks the righteous person as one who follows God's laws and avoids wrongdoing not for personal gain but to become one who treats others well, shares with those in need, uses personal finances for the greater good of others, and judges fairly when called on to enter into situations of injustice. It assumes the righteous person is one who can and will do what is just and right.

Justice as Judgment

Within Scripture the justice and righteousness of God are also linked to judgment. In today's world, we don't often think of God's judgment against unrighteousness as good news. When we need comfort in the face of our shortcomings or encouragement in the face of the injustices of the world, we don't tend to turn to the idea of God as our Great Judge. In the Old Testament, however, the people of God did just that. Look at the prayer contained in this psalm, calling God to judge on behalf of the afflicted:

> O LORD, you God of vengeance,
>> you God of vengeance, shine forth!
> Rise up, O judge of the earth;
>> give to the proud what they deserve!
> O LORD, how long shall the wicked,

how long shall the wicked exult?
They pour out their arrogant words;
    all the evildoers boast.
They crush your people, O Lord,
    and afflict your heritage.
They kill the widow and the stranger,
    they murder the orphan,
and they say, "The Lord does not see;
    the God of Jacob does not perceive." (Ps. 94:1–7 NRSV)

The people of God understood that appealing to God's righteous inter-vention involves the condemnation of evil, which means the condemnation of all that goes against God's good intentions for the shalom of the world. While the justice (*mishpat*) God and his people aimed for may have included punishment of the evildoer, this punishment was not mere payback. It was for the greater good—a restoration of that which had gone wrong. It was set-ting things to right. As Elizabeth Achtemeier writes, "Only because Yahweh saves does he condemn. His righteousness is first and foremost saving. He is a 'righteous God and a Savior' (Isa. 45:21)."[20]

So God's justice and righteousness are displayed through God's saving action on behalf of his people. As we read in Isaiah:

My righteousness draws near speedily,
    my salvation is on the way,
    and my arm will bring justice to the nations. (Isa. 51:5)

God's righteousness—that is, God's relational faithfulness—involves righting the wrongs that impact the people whom God creates and loves. It involves saving his people from sin and evil. God's righteous action leads to judgment (*mishpat*), which results in the restoration of harmony and flourishing in the community. In this way, God's righteousness leads to *justice*.

Furthermore, God's righteousness cannot be separated from "God's mercy," which is one way of translating the Hebrew word *hesed*. Like justice and righteousness, *hesed* is another foundational biblical concept. It appears through-out the Old Testament in reference to God's faithful, active loving-kindness. "The Lord, the Lord, the compassionate and gracious God, slow to anger, abounding in love and faithfulness" (Exod. 34:6). This description of God emphasizing his *hesed* runs like a refrain through the Old Testament.[21] God's *hesed* helps us to understand why God created humans in the first place and why God remained faithful to his people in the face of human sinfulness generation after generation. "The steadfast love of the LORD never ceases," we read in Lamentations 3:22 (NRSV).

> *God's righteousness—that is, God's relational faithfulness—involves righting the wrongs that impact the people whom God creates and loves.*

No one English word captures all the connotations of covenant faithfulness and active devotion that the word *hesed* conveys, which is why it is alternately translated as "steadfast love," "mercy," and "loving-kindness." Old Testament scholar Ellen Davis has beautifully translated *hesed* as "God's love in action."[22] Because of God's *hesed*, God commits to faithfully and actively loving his people. According to Scripture God's righteousness, justice, and active love all work together on behalf of God's people and the world God created. We read an example of this in Jeremiah:

> "I am the LORD, who exercises kindness [*hesed*],
>   justice [*mishpat*] and righteousness [*tsedaqah*] on earth,
>   for in these I delight,"
> declares the LORD. (Jer. 9:24)

Hesed is not only a mark of God's character. Like the justice and righteousness calling, it is also a call God places upon his people. We see this perhaps most clearly in Micah 6:8:

> He has shown you, O mortal, what is good.
>   And what does the LORD require of you?
> To act justly and to love mercy
>   and to walk humbly with your God.

The word translated here as "mercy" is *hesed*. We are called to love and act in ways that reflect God's own mercy, steadfast love, faithful loving-kindness—love in action.

The same is true for holiness. Holiness is another biblical term that refers both to God's own character and to the call God places upon his people. God is sometimes called the "Holy One of Israel" (Ps. 71:22), and God calls his people to be holy as he is holy (Lev. 19:2). The Hebrew word *qadosh*, which is translated "holy," means something set apart for a special purpose. The Sabbath day was the first thing in Scripture to be called holy, as it was set apart from the other six days of the week to be a special time during which God dwelled in rest and enjoyment with his creation. The place where God's presence dwelled—first within the tabernacle and then within the temple—was called the most holy place or the holy of holies.

> *To be holy as God is holy, the holy people of God must be set apart by drawing near to others with justice, righteousness, and merciful love in action.*

The people of God were called to be holy, set apart as the people with whom God dwelled. They were set apart for a special purpose—to be the people of God who lived with justice, righteousness, and *hesed* in this world. Because holiness carries with it the idea of being set apart, it can be easy to forget that the holy God of Israel makes himself known as a God who draws near. As theologian John Webster points out, God is the Holy One *in the midst* of his people (Hosea 11:9). He is the Holy One who in his majesty, freedom, and power *turns toward* his people in righteousness and mercy.[23] As we read in Isaiah,

> The LORD Almighty will be exalted by his justice,
> and the holy God will be proved holy by his righteous acts.
> (Isa. 5:16)

Paradoxically, to be holy as God is holy, the holy people of God must be *set apart by drawing near* to others with justice, righteousness, and merciful love in action.

Love Is Justice and Righteousness

God's holiness and righteousness are made visible within the Bible as God draws near to his people with justice and merciful love. This becomes especially clear within the biblical story when God helps the poor and powerless. As Swiss theologian Karl Barth points out:

> It is important to notice that the people to whom God in His righteousness turns as helper and Savior is everywhere in the Old Testament the harassed

and oppressed people of Israel, which, powerless in itself, has no rights, and is delivered over to the superior force of its enemies; and in Israel it is especially the poor, the widows and orphans, the weak and defenseless.[24]

The mighty and all-powerful God chooses to make a covenant with an unknown and powerless people (Israel). Within that powerless and frequently oppressed people, God gives special attention to those who are especially beleaguered: the poor, the widows, the orphans, the weak, and the defenseless. God's consistent choice to use his power to love and rescue those who do not have power and strength of their own is the expression of God's justice and righteousness.

> *God's consistent choice to use his power to love and rescue those who do not have power and strength of their own is the expression of God's justice and righteousness.*

This brings us to one more important understanding of the word *righteous* in the Old Testament. Those being mistreated within a relationship and those not receiving "right" treatment—the poor, needy, and oppressed—are all considered righteous in the Bible. In the words of the prophet Amos as he condemns the actions of the Israelites:

> They sell the righteous for silver,
>   and the needy for a pair of sandals—
> they who trample the head of the poor into the dust of the earth
>   and push the afflicted out of the way. (Amos 2:6b–7a NRSV)

This does not mean that the righteous spoken of here are without sin themselves but that they are looking to God to make right what has gone wrong. God keeps a special eye out for these righteous ones because they are in need of restoration. As Psalm 146:7–8 puts it:

> He upholds the cause of the oppressed
>   and gives food to the hungry.
> The LORD sets prisoners free,
>   the LORD gives sight to the blind,
> the LORD lifts up those who are bowed down,
>   the LORD loves the righteous.

God's commitment to the righteous poor, needy, and oppressed is a reflection of God's faithful love in action and his desire for justice and righteousness in this world, not a "reward" for the reliance or faithfulness of those who are suffering. Because God created the world and the people within the world to live in harmonious unity that all might flourish, it makes biblical sense that God would want to look after those who are living especially far from shalom.

God's justice and righteousness lean toward the poor, widows, orphans, and resident aliens, and in our calling to justice and righteousness we are to steward, as Barth has said, "against the lofty and on behalf of the lowly; against those who already enjoy right and privilege and on behalf of those who are denied it and deprived of it."[25]

Because God created the world and the people within the world to live in harmonious unity that all might flourish, it makes biblical sense that God would want to look after those who are living especially far from shalom.

Contemporary philosopher Nicholas Wolterstorff refers to the poor, widows, orphans, and resident aliens as the "quartet of the vulnerable" because of how often they are named by God as needing particular attention when it comes to doing justice. Neither Barth nor Wolterstorff is suggesting that God loves those who are part of this quartet more than he loves others or that only people who fall within one of these groups can be victims of injustice. Rather, they are acknowledging how often the Old Testament links God's call to act with justice and righteousness with these groups of people. As Wolterstorff puts it, those most likely to live in or be vulnerable to ongoing conditions of injustice are Scripture's priority.[26] God calls his holy people to seek justice on behalf of those living farthest from his vision of shalom so that all in the community might flourish.

The sinfulness of humanity prevents us from responding faithfully to God's justice calling. We are not able to love God and love others on our own. We do not even know what it means to love God and love others, at least not in the full and rich and whole ways that God intends us to love in keeping with his character of and vision for holiness, *hesed*, justice, righteousness, and shalom.

This is why we need Jesus Christ, as God in the flesh, to show us what love is. Jesus shows us what it means to love God and be loved by God. He shows us what it looks like to live as a beloved child of God, to love our neighbors as ourselves, even to the point of death. Not only did Jesus show us these things but he also did these things on our behalf so that we might be transformed into people who can rightly love God and others. As we love God and others in Christ through the Spirit, we are not merely imitating the example of Christ; through our love we are expressing an analogy of God's mercy toward those in great need, a mercy that we ourselves have received in Christ.[27]

In the light of Christ, we come to see that we are *all* poor, wretched, helpless, and utterly dependent on God's saving grace to rescue us. Outside the grace of God, we are incapable of getting right with God, others, ourselves, and the rest of the created world. As slaves to sin, we find it impossible to be holy, to act justly, and to love mercy, but thanks be to God that Jesus Christ came to this earth to find the lost and free the enslaved. Through Christ's righteousness we can become righteous and be restored to right relationships. Because of this grace, we can live the way of life God intended for his holy people, the way of justice and righteousness, the way of shalom.

As one of my (Kristen's) students wrote: "When we marvel at the saving power of God's extravagant love and mercy, whatever imperative we are called to is only in response to the grace, righteousness, and life already given to us by him. Our response is to move in the direction of justice that God is already moving in. Grace calls for justice."[28]

Invitation for Today: Engage the Whole Story

Abraham Heschel is a Jewish rabbi whose study of the Hebrew Scriptures (what Christians call the Old Testament) offers incredible wisdom as we seek to understand the fullness and depth of justice represented in the Bible. Heschel eloquently points out that justice is a call that comes from the very character of God himself, and it is a call that God gives to *all* of his people. From his study of God's Word, Heschel became convinced that "to do justice is what God demands of every man: it is the supreme commandment, and one that cannot be fulfilled vicariously." Scripture reveals further that to do justice is "not only to respect justice in the sense of abstaining from doing injustice, but also to *strive* for it, to *pursue* it. . . . The term 'pursue' carries strong connotations of effort, eagerness, persistence, inflexibility of purpose."[29] When we look to Scripture, we see that God's call to do justice not only comes to every single one of us as God's people, but it also requires each of us to actively pursue it.

I (Bethany) have been spurred toward more deeply immersing myself in the Scriptures and intently pursuing God's call by dear friends who lead an organization called the A21 (Abolishing Injustice in the 21st Century) Campaign.[30] This organization is dedicated to rescuing victims of human trafficking, providing restoration through aftercare, and prosecuting traffickers in some of the most corrupt cities in our world. A21 was founded by Christine Caine, a woman who lives and breathes Scripture daily and deeply. Most mornings she rises before dawn and fills her mind, heart, and whole being with the Word of God—immersing herself in Scripture, writing in her journal as the Holy Spirit leads, and then teaching the Word of God to others throughout the day ahead. Even though she frequently preaches before thousands, she also sits in hidden corners with those who have suffered unspeakable abuse. Daily she lives to know and give the Word of Truth and the healing love of their Creator. She allows the Holy Spirit to pour the Word of God into her life and pours her life out to others, wherever God leads her to serve.

The A21 Campaign has been a beautiful example of partnership in the pursuit of justice, repeatedly sending their United States director, Amanda-Paige Whittington, and other staff members to join IJM for the Global Prayer Gathering in Washington, DC, each April. Amanda-Paige powerfully expresses this commitment to kingdom partnership in prayer, telling us, "We are armor-bearers with you." Ever committed to partnership in the gospel, Amanda-Paige has become a constant companion in my own journey to continually renew my mind with the words of Scripture—the "sword of the Spirit" (Eph. 6:17)—in the face of the intensity of the casework we are exposed to each day. She frequently sends me text messages from her own book-by-book study of the Bible, worship songs that fuel her for the day, or sermons that feed her with truth. Through her friendship I am reminded and also discover anew the many ways that followers of Jesus can bring life to one anther simply through a daily, diligent commitment to sharing truth, wisdom, and strength from the Bible, no matter how many thousands of miles away we may live from one anther. This too is righteousness; this too leads to justice.

The Bigger Story Always at Hand

God is constantly beckoning each of us to draw near to him, and one of the best gifts he gives us is the opportunity to know and engage the bigger story of his kingdom. Every one of us needs to be reminded, every day (and by each other), that our call to justice is part of a larger vision that God has had for this world and for his people since the very beginning. When we are faced with the reality of suffering and violence beyond what we can bear to hear, much less actually confront, the Bible reminds us that it is God who leads this work, and it is God who will empower us to respond to his justice calling. Most important, it is God who will enable us to keep responding day in and day out, year after year, over the long haul.

For every image, story, and statistic that overwhelms us, for every victim and perpetrator whose name we learn or even meet in person, for each and every glimpse of injustice that we see as we open our eyes wider, God sees infinitely more, and Scripture invites us into this seeing *with* God. God hears every cry of every single person who suffers, every victim who is abused, and every perpetrator who banks on the lie that God does not see or hear or act. God invites us to hear the cries and to respond *with* him—fueled by his words, empowered by his Spirit.

God saw Boola. God saw the darkness and hopelessness engulfing Boola. God saw him in his suffering. God saw as Boola called his brother, risking his life to reach out with this phone call from a thousand miles away.

Boola's brother reached out to local law enforcement authorities and told them what was happening to Boola, asking for help. It was likely, however, that his call for help would go nowhere. Or worse, calling the police could have resulted in the authorities sending a tip to Boola's slave owner, ensuring that Boola and his fellow slaves would be punished. My colleagues at IJM have seen this over and over again: government authorities in many countries will receive hard evidence of mass atrocities happening to people like Boola, and they will either turn a blind eye because there is no political will to intervene, or they'll turn a blind eye because they are actually profiting from that slave industry themselves by accepting bribes from the slave owners in exchange for protection.

But in this case there was a backstory at work, a *kingdom* backstory of the body of Christ, steeped in the whole story of Scripture, knowing deeply God's passion for justice. God saw Boola, and God was moving through people who didn't even know yet that Boola existed but who *did* know the God of justice revealed in Scripture. God was preparing his people to intervene.

Two weeks before Boola made his phone call, there were about a thousand people gathered to pray near Washington, DC. IJM holds this gathering for prayer and worship every April (the Global Prayer Gathering) out of the conviction that throughout Scripture we see a God who loves justice and beckons his people to pray in the face of injustice. This Global Prayer Gathering is a time to engage the whole story of Scripture and the story of those who are suffering in our world and respond by talking with God, together. It's a time to ask God to move and act as his Word promises and to prepare our own hearts to be ready to move as God leads.

And so, two weeks before Boola made his phone call, two weeks before any of us even knew that a man named Boola existed, that's what we were doing—a thousand members of the body of Christ, responding to God's love for justice throughout Scripture, responding by showing up in prayer. None of us knew Boola as we prayed for his country that night. But when Boola called his brother, and then his brother called the government authorities, this time something completely unexpected happened. Instead of ignoring Boola's brother's pleas or tipping off the slave owner, this time the government authorities *asked IJM for help.*

There was a kingdom backstory at work—the body of Christ responding to Scripture, knowing God's passion for justice, and coming to God in prayer.

The tide was beginning to turn. In all my years of work with IJM it would be impossible to count how many times we have prayed together and pleaded with God about cases that had come to a complete halt because government officials were refusing to move. My colleagues would bring evidence and plan the rescue operations and would be left waiting. IJM refuses to conduct rescue operations without government officials because each country's own government needs to lead the way to enforce their laws. The governments themselves need to do the linchpin work of arresting slave owners and freeing victims. And so year after year it has been a game of waiting, showing up over and over again, and digging in with dogged perseverance.

But in this case, after Boola called his brother and his brother called the government, the government actually *called IJM.* They *initiated* the rescue operation themselves. It was astounding. And that's why we need to remember the kingdom backstory and be prepared through prayer to move with the God who sees.

If my colleagues had just rescued Boola that day, that would have been in itself a great miracle because Boola, on his own, matters to our loving, faithful, just, and righteous God. Every single one of us matters to this God. And even if just one person is rescued, just one slave owner arrested, a strong message starts to make its way through an entire corrupt system.

> *God hears every cry of every single person who suffers, every victim who is abused, and every perpetrator who banks on the lie that God does not see or hear or act.*

If they had been able to rescue even a *dozen* others along with Boola, that would have been a massive feat in itself, because rescue is not just about taking someone out of a slave facility. There are a host of steps that must be taken at the point of rescue: protection for each victim, release certificates issued and reparation money paid by the government to each victim, return of the former slaves to their homes, and the beginning of a multiyear aftercare program to ensure each former slave has the opportunity to flourish in his or her new life of freedom. Sometimes it can take weeks for these steps to unfold, if at all. But in this case, the government authorities not only led the operation to rescue Boola and others but they also worked throughout the night and into the next morning to secure every need for each slavery victim *immediately*.

At the end of the rescue operation Boola was among not just a handful or even a dozen people released from slavery, but he was one of *514 people* rescued. Release certificates were issued for all 514: 514 victims paid reparation by the government, 514 people transported a thousand miles back to their homes. The government completed every single step and without a moment of delay. All these former slaves were taken into a robust aftercare program to help them learn how to live lives of freedom. Their slave owner was arrested.

By far the largest rescue operation in IJM's history to this day, it was unlike anything we had ever seen before. Prompted by the Spirit of God, this was what we had been asking God to do—to move through his people and begin breaking open a deeply ingrained system.

The massive sea change continues today. There have been rescues of unprecedented size, with local government authorities in Boola's country continuing to lead the way.

For the rest of my life, as I carry Boola's story in front of me, and as all of us continue to work together as the body of Christ to see freedom come and slavery end, I will remember the thousand followers of Jesus gathered together in prayer on one side of the world, and the followers of Jesus on the other side of the world who were ready to bring rescue as God flung wide the gates. I will remember that the Holy Spirit formed all of these followers of Jesus to respond to God's call throughout the whole story of Scripture to seek justice and righteousness. And I will remember that this beauty is yet only a glimpse of all God has, is, and will continue to do.

How Will You Engage the Story?

How might the Holy Spirit be leading you and others in your community to consistently receive the gift of God's Word as you seek to be formed into God's holy people, set apart to receive and pursue God's faithful love, justice, righteousness, and shalom?

What steps might you take with your church, a friend, a colleague, a family member, or a neighbor to draw each other to open the Bible, enter into the whole story of Scripture, and receive truth that God will use to renew and equip you to respond to the justice calling in your lives?

How might you grapple together with the ways in which the sermons you are listening to and the passages from the Bible that you are reading connect to the richness of God's vision for this world and for his people?

How can you and your community begin to see justice through the whole story of Scripture?

As Ruth Padilla DeBorst reminded us earlier in this chapter, we are used to reading the Bible in fragments. It takes intentionality to receive the pieces of Scripture we encounter through sermons, Bible studies, or daily devotions and hold them up to the light of the larger story of Scripture. But when we do, beautiful connections and refractions emerge that we might otherwise miss.

I (Kristen) fell in love with studying Scripture when I was in high school. I can still remember the day I received an exhaustive concordance, which (back before the internet) was the best way to find all the places in the Bible where a particular word or topic was mentioned. I remember looking up the word *joy* and then looking up every single verse that mentioned *joy*; I then compared those verses to the verses that included the words *happy* and *happiness*. I repeated that process word after word after word. The only problem was that I looked up each verse in isolation from the verses surrounding them, which provided the immediate context to make sense of them; I looked them up in isolation from the larger story of Scripture in which they found their fuller meaning.

I have no doubt that God used my study of his Word through that concordance to form me, but I was amazed at what I discovered when I learned to place these verses within the larger story of the Bible, moving from God's creation of the world to Christ's return. Connections that I had never seen before emerged, and confusing parts began to make sense, bringing to life the extent and scope of God's gracious commitment to our salvation. Now whenever I hear a passage in a sermon, read a passage during devotions, or study a passage with my church Bible study group, I try to ask: How does this passage fit into the verses around it and the larger narrative of the book in which it is placed? How does it fit into the larger story of the Bible?

> *It takes intentionality to receive the pieces of Scripture we encounter through sermons, Bible studies, or daily devotions and hold them up to the light of the larger story of Scripture.*

As you study Scripture through sermons, Bible studies, and devotions, we encourage you to ask how your reading connects to the larger story of Scripture. When you ponder a favorite verse, take the time to consider how it relates to the grand, gracious sweep of God's commitment to the salvation of the world. Bethany and I have each experienced the ways in which verses and passages that we love and that call us to justice—such as Micah 6:8; Amos 5:24; and Isaiah 58—become more meaningful when we are immersed in the *entire* story of Scripture. As you encounter the movements of the story of God in each chapter of this book, and in the short rendering of the story that we offer for your reflection on the following two pages, we hope that you can see God's commitment to justice and God's calling upon his people to seek justice more fully. We hope that through deep engagement with the whole story of Scripture, the Holy Spirit will open your eyes to see opportunities to seek God's justice and righteousness all around you.

The Whole Story—A Rendering for Reflection

God created the world and everything in it with the intention that humans, animals, and the rest of the created world would flourish as they lived together in mutual harmony, justice, and delight. God's vision for the flourishing of all that he has made is a reflection of God's own character of justice, righteousness, and steadfast love.

The original biblical word for this flourishing is *shalom*. Shalom is often translated "peace," but it describes a reality much larger and deeper than the absence of conflict or a pleasant state of mind. The word *shalom* and its biblical counterparts express a holistic vision of the vitality of all of creation—from seed-bearing plants and trees on the land to the fish of the sea, the birds of the air, the beasts of the field, and human beings. God created humans to live in loving union and harmony with him and to care for one another and the rest of creation in keeping with this shalom vision. God called humans to undertake this stewardship in ways that reflected God's own way of justice, righteousness, and love.

Instead of trusting God and remaining in loving union with him, the first humans questioned whether God's commands were intended for their flourishing and made the choice to disobey him. This rupture in the trust and union between God and humans resulted in what we have come to call "the fall" of humanity, a reality with far-reaching ramifications. The fall resulted in disunity between God and the humans he had made, between humans themselves, within each human, and between humans and the rest of the created world. This was the case not only for those first humans but also for all their subsequent kin. God's creation was no longer a place that expressed the fullness of the justice, righteousness, and shalom for which it was intended.

Despite the significance of the fall, God in his loving faithfulness did not abandon his original desire for union with his people and for the flourishing of humans and creation within a harmonious order. God made a covenant relationship with the people of Israel, graciously calling them to live in union with him. In calling Israel to be his holy people, God set Israel apart by their relationship with him and by the way he called them to live, exhibiting justice and righteousness in this world. God provided guidelines and laws for the Israelites to create a society in which they could live in union with God, one another, and the (still fallen) created world in ways that continued to reflect God's own heart for and character of justice, righteousness, and love.

The law given by God made provisions for the ramifications of human sin so that the Israelites could worship God and care for all in their midst, so that everyone could flourish, and so that their kingdom could be a place of refuge and shalom. As the people of Israel lived with justice and righteousness, as they looked after each person in their midst and tended the creation and institutions entrusted to them, God intended that they would be a witness to other nations of God's own love, righteousness, and justice. However, in their fallen state, the people of God continually failed to worship God with their whole hearts and love others in the kingdom of Israel. And yet, through the ups and downs of Israel's efforts to live with and reflect justice, righteousness, and shalom, God remained faithful to his people.

In God's steadfast love he eventually provided his own son, Jesus Christ, who embodied God's justice, righteousness, and shalom in ways that went beyond what anyone could have predicted or imagined. In Christ we can see the fullness of what God intended for his creation and his holy people. Because of what Christ did to set things right through his life, death, resurrection, and ascension, we—the people of God—can finally live the way God calls us to as we are invited into and receive God's own justice, righteousness, shalom, and love through the Holy Spirit.

As both God and man, Jesus was able to live in perfect relationship with God, others, and the created world throughout his life on earth. Through his death, resurrection, and ascension he overcame the consequences of sin on every level. This means that God's kingdom of justice, righteousness, and shalom can and will be made known through Christ. Jesus promised to return to this earth to fully usher in his kingdom, which has already begun but is not yet fully realized in this world.

With Christ as our savior and king, we are invited into a new covenant of restored union with God, one another, and creation. This new covenant ushers in both the kingdom of God and the church—the people of God united to God as his children through his Son Jesus Christ and the Holy Spirit. The people of God are still called to live as God's holy people in this world in ways that reflect God's own character of justice, righteousness, and love; now that we are united to God through Christ and the Spirit, we receive God's very own justice, righteousness, and love. As we are both justified and sanctified by the saving grace of God in Christ, we are reconciled to God and given the ministry of reconciliation in this world. This is our place in the story now, as we live by the grace of God and in anticipation of Christ's return: through the Spirit, we join in Jesus's ongoing kingdom mission in this world, bearing witness to the justice, righteousness, and reconciling love of God in Christ and anticipating the fullness of God's kingdom when all will be made new.

2

Receive God's
Vision of Flourishing

Justice and Creation

August 5, 2009

If I think about the future, my future life, I imagine nothing but tears, bruises on my body, being beaten for no reason, just because he is in a bad mood.

This is not life; if it is, it's only the life of a slave. Am I really such a bad person that I deserve this kind of life and treatment?

I can no longer live being scared all the time, I am tired of being manipulated all the time, and being physically and mentally hurt.

My God I need your justice!!!

Why is all this happening to me?

Am I so bad that I deserve it?

I tolerate it as much as I can but I am exhausted already.

Help me God! I need you.

John is a dear friend and colleague of mine (Bethany) serving as a federal prosecutor for human trafficking crimes in the United States. He spends long days and nights visiting traffickers in jail, prosecuting them in courts across the

nation, and listening to their victims' stories of terror. John recently shared
the journal excerpt above with me, which was written by a woman enduring
horrific abuse at the hands of her traffickers. John explained her situation:
"When she wrote this prayer in captivity, I was away from my family working
on her case. But she had no idea there was anyone working for her rescue. And
none of us knew who she was yet, since we were targeting her traffickers. After
her rescue, when the case went to trial her personal journal was admitted as
evidence of what she had endured at the hands of her traffickers."

As the woman sat on the witness stand and read her journal entry aloud in
court, John suddenly realized that he was living in the midst of a miracle—that
he was getting to be part of the answer to her prayers.

"God used all sorts of local cops, federal agents, prosecutors, and many
others who never met her and who never saw that prayer," said John. "But
ultimately it was God who answered her prayer."

God knew this woman. God created her, knew her name, knew her need.
And God knew whom he would send to her rescue.

John's work abounds with stories of people suffering horrific nightmares
of abuse and crying out for help. His wife, Linda, and their children walk
alongside him in this work; they uphold him, his clients, his colleagues, and
the traffickers in prayer. John's whole family is shaped by their pursuit of Jesus,
and in their daily sacrifices they are strengthened by God's call to be part of the
flourishing, righteousness, and justice God longs to bring to all of his creation.

"People often wonder how I can travel so much. People ask my wife why
she sacrifices, and how does she possibly handle it all." John said. "The simple
answer is that—in some incredibly small way—together we get to be answered
prayers for victims crying out to God."

"The jury convicted this woman's trafficker on all counts," he continued.
"Life in prison for her trafficker. Life in freedom for her. Neither have an easy
road ahead. But she got justice. She got a Sabbath."

After crying out to God for justice from her deep exhaustion and pain, this
trafficking survivor was finally able to rest after years of enslavement. John's
use of the familiar word *Sabbath* to describe this extraordinary rescue opened
me to a new level of understanding of the fullness God intends Sabbath to be
as he commands it throughout the Scriptures.

The word *Sabbath* comes from the Hebrew word for rest, and the command
given to God's people to keep the Sabbath day holy by resting from work is
linked in Scripture both to God's original creation of the world (see the Ten

Commandments in Exod. 20:8–11) and to slavery (see the Ten Commandments in Deut. 5:6–21). The Sabbath commandment is, in fact, the *only* one of the Ten Commandments that refers back to creation and the *only* one that refers back to slavery. God made the heavens, the earth, the sea, and all that is in them, and then he rested on the seventh day. Generations later, God delivered his people from ceaseless toil in slavery under the Egyptians. God calls his people to remember this great creation and great rescue by instructing them to rest on the seventh day.

The giving of the law in Exodus and Deuteronomy connects creation and slavery with the Sabbath commandment because Sabbath-keeping not only impacts the individuals or families who observe it, but Sabbath-keeping also impacts their neighbors and the surrounding community. As God's people remember that they were slaves rescued by the hand of God, they are to extend Sabbath rest to *everyone* around them, especially those who might not be able to choose the day of rest for themselves (Deut. 5:12–15). God makes it clear in this commandment that Sabbath rest is not a minivacation for God's people, given as a reward for enduring years of slavery while others continue to do hard work. According to the commandment, every son and daughter, every servant, every foreigner, every animal, and the land itself is to join in this Sabbath rest, and God's people are called to actively protect and extend Sabbath on behalf of others. No one is permitted to prevent anyone else from resting, and everyone is invited to keep the day holy by resting. Through the act of keeping and extending the Sabbath, God's people receive a glimpse of the world as God created it to be—a world in which God reigns, where beauty can be seen and tasted and experienced, and where God's own delight in his creation can be savored by those he has created. It is a world intended to flourish, marked by justice, righteousness, and love. The Sabbath is central to what it means to love God and love our neighbors as ourselves: God rested, God commands us to honor him through rest, and God commands us to extend and provide rest to our neighbor.

> *The command given to God's people to keep the Sabbath day holy by resting from work is linked in Scripture both to God's original creation of the world and to slavery.*

The more we probe Scripture for a deeper understanding of justice, the more we will find a surprising connection between two commands that seem to compete with each other, at least on the surface: seek God by obeying his command to do justice for others; seek God by obeying his command to rest. When God inextricably connects justice and Sabbath, he is making it clear that justice never begins with our own reactions to the needs in the world but rather with knowing him, the God of justice.[1] In this way, the active work of justice often begins when we stop rather than move forward on our own.

As we stop our "doing" to enter into Sabbath rest, we acknowledge that we are joining God in the work he is already doing in this world and are not ultimately responsible for its success. It is work centered in Jesus Christ, who saves us by grace and yet has created us as his own workmanship to accomplish good things (Eph. 2:8–10). The Sabbath helps us to recognize that our Creator and Redeemer is Lord, and we are not. He is Lord. We can rest in this truth and know that any and all good that comes from our labor is ultimately from the hand of God beckoning us to know him and serve from his strength. The practice of Sabbath today invites us further into God's vision of flourishing for all of creation, even as it roots our actions for justice in the ongoing creative and redemptive work of God in Christ.

Flourishing in Creation

A deeper look at God's act of creation (of which the Sabbath was the crowning moment) opens for us the truth that our Creator God has, from the beginning, always cared about justice. Even before it became clear that justice would be needed to right the wrongs ushered in by the fall, even before injustice entered the world, God loved justice—the flourishing that results from the right ordering of power.

From the very beginning of the story, God brings order to creation. The Bible opens with God calling into being light from darkness, separating water from land, and ordering the roles of humans and animals. God creates the sun, moon, sky, land, seas, plants, trees, stars, birds that fly, creatures that swim, animals that move along the ground, man, and woman. At the end of this creative extravaganza, "God saw all that he had made, and it was very good" (Gen. 1:31).

God intended that all of these different parts of creation would live together in wholeness, harmony, and mutual flourishing. As we learned in chapter 1, *shalom* is the Hebrew word from Genesis that captures this vision, which we translate as "peace" in English. The problem, as we've noted, is that peace does not fully capture all that is meant by the biblical idea of shalom. Just as the idea of justice involves far more than simply the absence of injustice, shalom implies more than the absence of conflict or a general feeling associated with calmness and trust. Shalom also incorporates what it means to be whole, complete, safe, and sound, and it refers to all of humanity and creation in relation to each other and to God.[2] Shalom offers a vision of the vitality of all of creation, a reality in which all things are just and right. Shalom describes a reality in which nothing needs to be set right because everyone and everything is flourishing. With shalom flourishing, God's justice and righteousness are everywhere because the good and just and beautiful order God created from the beginning is in place for all of creation.

The Sabbath is central to what it means to love God and love our neighbors as ourselves: God rested, God commands us to honor him through rest, and God commands us to extend and provide rest to everyone around us—especially those who cannot choose rest for themselves.

Sometimes when we think back to creation within the Bible, we focus so much on the relationship that God wanted with humans that we miss the extent of God's vision for the entirety of his creation. When God paid attention to every detail of creation as he brought it into being, it was because he had a vision for how all of those pieces of creation would work and flourish *together*. Imagine plants, trees, birds, fish, livestock, wild animals, men, women, the land, and the sea living together, interacting with one another in harmony, so that each part flourishes, each part has its place without being in competition with any other part.

From the human perspective, we see four interrelated layers of shalom in the biblical story of creation that we are called to care about: relationship with God, relationship with others, relationship with self, and relationship with creation. God's concern for every aspect of this shalom vision can be seen throughout Scripture. Every layer of the shalom vision is distorted by the fall and addressed within God's covenant relationship with Israel; every layer is restored in and through Christ's redemptive work, incorporated into the church's calling, and will be fully reestablished when Christ returns.

God's original vision for creation involved an abundance rather than a scarcity of resources. Within this abundance, humans were called to stewardship and care (justice and righteousness) rather than domination and misuse (injustice). Humans were to live in union with God, get along with each other without friction or mistrust, be whole and integrated within themselves, and faithfully care for each aspect of creation.[3] According to God's provision of abundance, if we had remained dependent on God and trusted his counsel and provision, we would have been given all that we needed to thrive as all of creation lived together in harmony and wholeness.

> *Every layer of the shalom vision is distorted by the fall and addressed within God's covenant relationship with Israel; every layer is restored in and through Christ's redemptive work, incorporated into the church's calling today, and will be fully reestablished when Christ returns.*

Continuing to explore God's vision of creation, we find in Genesis that God's purpose in creating humanity to dwell with him and one another was inextricably linked to the calling he gave humans to care for the rest of the created world. This call to care for creation comes in both Genesis 1 and 2. In Genesis 1 God blesses Adam and Eve and tells them to "be fruitful and increase in number; fill the earth and subdue it. Rule over the fish in the sea and the birds in the sky and over every living creature that moves on the ground" (1:28). This verse has been misused and misunderstood in some very serious ways through the centuries, contributing to the mistaken belief that the created world exists solely for the sake of humanity.[4] But this call to "rule" is about promoting the welfare of the created world, not about domination.

In its original context and in keeping with the larger shalom vision of these creation accounts, Genesis 1:28 is actually a commission to be responsible stewards of the created world. We can see this reflected in Genesis 2:15, "The Lord God took the man and put him in the Garden of Eden to work it and take care of it."[5] As the sovereign king, God has the power and authority to create and rule over all he has made. When God delegates his authority to humans, giving them the charge to care for the world he created, he expects humankind to wield power in a way that is consistent with his own character and rule.[6] God uses his power to create and bring forth life that is designed to thrive and flourish in relationship. This same vision of shalom is to guide human stewardship of creation as well.

God's call to "be fruitful and to have dominion" can even be understood as a creative calling intended to include the creation and stewardship of culture. That is to say, the cultivation of culture can be understood as a part of our God-given calling rather than culture being a sinful by-product of the fall that we should avoid.[7] Regardless of the fall, as more and more humans were created they would have engaged together in things that we tend to call "culture." They would have received the gifts of creation and eaten together (creating various foods), lived together (creating housing), talked together (creating languages), learned and thought together (creating education), traveled to see one another and tend creation (creating means of transportation), sang, made instruments together, danced, painted, made drawings, and told stories together (creating different kinds of music and art). This would also have necessitated the creation of institutions, as humans imagined ways to organize their cultural activities and their relationships with one another.

> *This call to "rule" is about promoting the welfare of the created world, not about domination.*

If all of this creative cultural work would have been shaped by the reality of life with God, in keeping with the vision of shalom, *hesed*, justice, and righteousness that guides the call to steward creation, it would have fostered the flourishing of humans and the created world while glorifying God. In spite of the fall, this vision of shalom flourishing for our cultures and their practices and institutions is the vision that God holds before us still. God has always desired his created world to be a place of justice and righteousness, and he has always called his people to seek justice and righteousness in it. This is as true today as it was at the very beginning of the biblical story.

Flourishing in Relationships

This vision of an abundant, thriving, interconnected creation outshines the default images that come to mind for many of us when we think about God's intentions for humans and our relationships with one another. We often think that God cares about our souls, not our bodies. More than that, we often assume that God cares the most about our souls living in eternity with him in some future age rather than how we live here and now in the world that he created. As a child, whenever I (Kristen) saw rays of sunlight streaming through clouds I pictured myself following those rays up to where God lived in heaven. I thought that Jesus would guide us up those rays when we were called home to eternal life with God in the clouds. This kind of vision of the Christian life—which focuses primarily on living with God in the clouds after we die, possibly strumming harps and singing songs to God, disconnected from the earthly realities of life and from one another—does not match what we see in the beginning of the biblical story. Yes, God does long and invite us to live with him for all eternity; yes, God is preparing a place for us, as Jesus describes (John 14:2–3). But God also created us to live in deep and rich communion with him and with one another and the rest of the created world *right now*, in the world that God created. The kingdom of heaven is at hand—it is within us and it is here, even as it is yet coming.[8] Through Christ and the Spirit, we can enter into this vision and respond to this calling as we live here and now in relationship with God, as we love others, and as we care for the world that God has made.

When God delegates his authority to humans, he expects humankind to wield power in a way that is consistent with his own character and rule.

Looking closely at Genesis, it's clear that God's vision of abundant flourishing for creation includes human relationships with one another. After creating Adam, God decides that "it is not good for the man to be alone" (Gen. 2:18a). God then creates Eve out of Adam, making their bond so close that upon Eve's creation Adam says,

> This is now bone of my bone,
>   and flesh of my flesh. (Gen. 2:23a)

One of Christianity's early significant thinkers, Augustine of Hippo, believed that God chose to begin all humanity from the single person of Adam so that the human race would "be bound together by a kind of tie of kinship to form a harmonious unity, linked together by the 'bond of peace.'"[9] God created us to live in unity with one another, rooted in the fellowship we have with him. Living harmoniously with one another is just as much a part of God's original creation vision of shalom as living harmoniously with God.

Augustine wrote a great deal both about this "bond of peace" intended for all human relationships and about justice, while simultaneously engaging in significant work on behalf of victims of injustice.[10] He believed that God "created all things in supreme wisdom and ordered them in perfect justice."[11] Perfect justice marked the original creation order and will mark the kingdom of God in the age to come; it leads to the realization of shalom, which Augustine describes as "everlasting and perfect peace." He calls this peace the "Supreme Good," which is another way of saying that it is the most important thing that God gives to his creation.[12] This peace has everything to do with the restoration of relationships between God and humans and between humans themselves; as a result, injustice plays no part. Augustine describes this peace as "completely harmonious fellowship in the enjoyment of God, and of each other in God."[13] In part, we can experience this enjoyment in Christ while we await the full and everlasting peace that Christ will bring when he returns.

> *Augustine points us toward an important truth about biblical justice: relationships are at the heart of God's vision for justice in this world.*

Augustine points us toward the important truth about biblical justice that we've been unfolding: relationships are at the heart of God's vision for justice in this world. God's vision of shalom is a vision of relationships that are so rightly and lovingly ordered that they are just in every way. It is a vision of justice rooted in rightly ordered relationships that begins with humanity's relationship with God.

Flourishing and the Image of God

The creation story in Genesis is also the place where we learn that humans are made in the image of God. The image of God is an important biblical truth about each created person (Gen. 1:26–27), and it endures in every human on the planet despite the fall (Gen. 9:6). This image can be fully and properly understood only in light of Jesus Christ who, as the true image of the invisible God (Col. 1:15), reveals and restores that image in us (2 Cor. 3:18; Col. 3:10).[14]

While all of this is true, God's call upon us to seek justice is not grounded in the appeal to the image of God alone. When God encourages his people to care about justice and righteousness through the law and the prophets or when he encourages his people to seek first the kingdom of God and his justice and righteousness through Jesus, he does not base his appeal on his own image in humankind. When we think about the biblical basis for seeking the flourishing of others, it is important that we hold together what we learn from the entire biblical story—from creation to redemption—all of which is grounded in God's love and manifest in Christ, the image of the invisible God.

Every human being is loved by God and precious in his sight because God created each person in the image of God and because God sent his Son on behalf of every person so that redemption might be made available to all people. We are called to love others because God's desire for the flourishing of all people and of all creation is built into the very story of creation and carried throughout the rest of Scripture. We are called to pursue justice on behalf of all people because the very character of God—his everlasting loving-kindness (*hesed*)—is displayed in his ongoing commitment to justice and righteousness in this world. Taken together, all these aspects of the biblical story can teach us to more deeply live our call to love and care for others.

Flourishing and Delight

It's fascinating to note that the climax of God's creation lies neither in the creation of Adam and Eve nor in the charge given to them to steward creation. As the very first element (and the only day) of creation to be made holy, the Sabbath is the culmination of God's work, as seen in the first account of creation given in Genesis; it is the embodiment of what God intends for us as he stops to enjoy creation and reigns over its flourishing.

This part of the creation story invites us to see that God's vision of shalom includes the intentional experience of joy: enjoyment. On the seventh day of creation, God saw that what he had made was very good, and then he rested. God sits down on his throne to admire and delight in his good creation. God reigns, and because God is the one who reigns, he can rest. Because he reigns, we can rest. God's rest was marked by delight in what he had made, and God invites us to share in his Sabbath rest; therefore, we too are invited to freely enjoy all that God has created.

Philosopher Nicholas Wolterstorff emphasizes that God's shalom vision in creation is not simply the absence of conflict or hostility, and it is not limited to humans, animals, nature, and God being in right relationship. Rather, shalom is *expansive* and *overflowing* with enjoyment and delight in these relationships. Wolterstorff writes, "To dwell in shalom is to enjoy living before God, to enjoy living in one's physical surroundings, to enjoy living with one's fellows, to enjoy life with oneself."[15] Wolterstorff asserts that while there can be no shalom without justice, shalom goes *beyond* justice. Justice is essential for shalom to be realized, but the full biblical picture of just order and right relationships also includes joy and delight.[16] Building on Wolterstorff's assertion, we would go so far as to argue that justice enables true joy.

> *God reigns, and because God is the one who reigns, he can rest. Because he reigns, we can rest.*

By delighting in God's love for us and lovingly responding with grateful service, we can delight in loving relationships with other humans and care for everyone in our midst. By delighting in our relationship to the created world, we can nurture what God has made and responsibly use what God has entrusted to us in our own acts of creation, thereby living the way of life God intended. To live the call to justice is to live as God has planned from the very beginning. Fittingly, the word *Eden* means delight.

Invitation for Today: Receive and Extend Sabbath

Joy and rest may not be the first ideas that come to mind as we undertake the pursuit of justice today, but joy, rest, and justice are inextricably connected in a world replete with overwhelming needs. We will discover the connection only as we commit to Sabbath rhythms in our daily and weekly lives.

We need the grace of God to enable us to intentionally step back (and help one another step back) from the relentless demands and needs that stretch far beyond our capacity to meet them. By doing so, we will better see and receive (over and again) God's vision for and commitment to the flourishing of this world. God created this world, and God is the one who redeems it. Clearly, God is committed to its flourishing. His passion never wanes. Our decision to stop and rest—day by day and week by week—is a decision empowered by the Holy Spirit to keep the Sabbath holy and set apart; it declares our trust that God will provide all that we and others need and that God is at work in this world even when we are not. When we persistently trust God, we can rest and enjoy the works of God's hands.

Millions of people today cannot choose rest the way those of us reading this book can likely choose rest. Sabbath is the crowning moment of creation, a lavish invitation from God to rest and joy, but millions of people in our world cannot receive this invitation because of injustice.

> *Sabbath is the crowning moment of creation, a lavish invitation from God to rest and joy, but millions of people in our world cannot receive this invitation because of injustice.*

Think back to the Sabbath command as Moses brings the Ten Commandments to God's people following his time on Mount Sinai. The Israelites had been held in captivity for generations and disheartened by what seemed to be God's detachment from their plight. But then God brought them out of this slavery and moved them toward the promised land, commanding them to rest on a regular basis, every week. While readers in our context today may consider the Sabbath commandment to be a burden on top of other commands that are difficult to keep, in its original context the Sabbath was intended by God to be a gift extended to his people, and it is meant to be received by us as a gift today. Furthermore, throughout the books of the law and the writings of the prophets God makes it exceptionally clear that the gift of Sabbath is not for God's people alone; it is to be extended to others. The giving of Sabbath was (and is) for everyone: servants, slaves, strangers, animals, and the land all participated in Sabbath rest in Israel. One person's rest was not to come at the expense of another's, and neither was God's rest reserved for the privileged few.[17]

As we practice Sabbath today, we need to remember that we are called to extend this gift to those who do not have the power or privilege to experience rest themselves. What steps can you take to more fully receive the Sabbath as a gift from God intended for delight? What steps can you and your community take to intentionally extend the Sabbath to others in this world who are in need of rest?

Receiving

The closer we get to the real needs of others, the more we face an enormous temptation to respond and react out of our own resources and strength. The best way to live faithfully within the limits of our God-given abilities while relying on the limitlessness of God's power to heal, restore, and love is to proactively limit ourselves before we inevitably "hit" the limit by other means. When we proactively set apart an entire day *not* to be "productive," or set aside specific parts of each day for quiet listening, prayer, and the study of Scripture, the Spirit opens our lives to receive the gift God is always offering: the capacity to delight in God's presence in our lives and in this world.

Sometimes when we reach "the end of our rope," we find ourselves seeking an ultimately unsatisfying rest in a glass of wine, a television show, or sleep brought on by exhaustion. But if we stop and intentionally switch off our efforts to "get things done" (even when we haven't finished everything), we can experience the grace of God as he reminds us that he is the one who reigns and we are not. As a result, we can take joy in the fact that it doesn't all come down to what we can get done or what we have the ability to accomplish.

Sabbath rest might mean turning off technology for a day every week (or longer if you're like us and it takes a while to settle in and fully embrace being unplugged). It might mean committing to getting all of your schoolwork or business projects and meetings completed before your day of Sabbath and intentionally trusting God with whatever you have not been able to finish. However Sabbath rest manifests itself in each of our weekly rhythms, we will always need the Holy Spirit to help us to make an intentional choice to *receive* the Sabbath that God offers as a gift to us. We intentionally receive Sabbath when we join with others for worship and rest through fellowship. Likewise, we intentionally receive Sabbath when we make small decisions every day that prepare and enable us to live in light of the Sabbath throughout the week. Cultivating daily practices and taking moments to rest amidst our work "move[s] us into the heart of Sabbath," as Norman Wirzba explains. Even in the midst of the sometimes overwhelming work of justice, the Spirit uses such practices to enable us "to

> *One person's rest was not to come at the expense of another's, and neither was God's rest reserved for the privileged few.*

participate regularly in the delight that marked God's own response to a creation wonderfully made."[18]

As we receive the gift of Sabbath rest, by God's grace we are nourished in at least two significant ways. First, we are drawn back into God's vision for the world; we remember that God is the Creator of the world, and we are not. In all areas of life, it is far too easy to let our ideas, ambitions, and visions take over. In our pursuit of justice, we can be overly shaped by our own short-sighted notions of what justice entails. We need the grace of God to allow us to remain rooted in God's vision. As we pause to enter into a day of rest, the Holy Spirit reminds us of God's rich and beautiful vision for justice, righteousness, and shalom, going all the way back to creation. The Holy Spirit reminds us that our relationship with God lies at the heart of this vision.

> *We need to make an intentional choice to receive the Sabbath that God commands us to take.*

As we enter into the rhythms of a Sabbath day, we remember that *who we are* as God's holy and beloved people is more important than anything we do for God and others in this world. As God's holy and beloved people, we are called to love the things that God loves and seek the things that God seeks. Through the nurturing rhythms of our Sabbath rest we are shaped by God's vision and formed into people who seek God's justice, righteousness, and shalom in this world.

Second, as we receive God's gift of Sabbath rest we are reminded that we are utterly dependent on God's grace and provision. Sabbath is not an easy gift to receive because it is designed to show us our dependence on God. The Exodus version of the command to keep the Sabbath links God's people to the significance of God's work in creation, while the Deuteronomy version tells God's people that the Sabbath is to remind them of their deliverance from slavery by God's hand. In both cases, the people are reminded that who they are and what they have received are a direct result of the generous hand of God in creating them, calling them to be his people, setting them free, and sustaining them. The same is true for us as we live by the rescuing and saving grace of God in Christ.

The gift of Sabbath rest forces us to acknowledge that God's work in this world is more important than our own. God calls us as his people to seek justice and righteousness in this world, but God does not depend on our work. On the contrary, we need constant reminders that our work depends on God's ongoing work. As Eugene Peterson writes, "Sabbath is a deliberate act of interference, an interruption of our work each week, a decree of no-work so that we are able to notice, to attend, to listen, to assimilate this comprehensive and majestic work of God, to orient our work in the work of God."[19] God has cared about the flourishing of the world he created from the very beginning, and God never ceases to be at work in this world. The brokenness and injustice that we experience are real, but this world is a part of God's kingdom and falls under God's reign. Failure to rest reveals that we are relying on our own work and reflects a lack of trust in God's provision and grace.

Living in an agrarian society, the Israelites were dependent on the land for their daily sustenance. It can be hard for people who are not directly dependent on the land to realize that God's call to the Israelites *not* to work the land one day a week involved deep trust that God would provide the food they needed. But that was part of the Sabbath's purpose—to remind the Israelites that though they depended on the land and their ability to cultivate it for their nourishment, on a deeper level they depended on God, who created the land, entrusted it to them, and continued to be involved in its productivity. Norman Wirzba reminds us that "Sabbath rest is thus a call to Sabbath trust, a call to visibly demonstrate in our daily living that we know ourselves to be upheld and maintained by the grace of God rather than the strength and craftiness of our own hands."[20] As we pursue justice, we do so as the people of God, called to be faithful in our pursuit of God's

> *The gift of Sabbath rest forces us to acknowledge that God's work in this world is more important than our own.*

vision in the same way as the Israelites, who faithfully tended their land; we must acknowledge that the realization of justice depends on God's work, not our own.

Sabbath rest is not simply about a break from the normal workweek; it is about intentionally entering into and enjoying God's presence in community. This is why we consider weekly worship with others to be so central to the meaning of Sabbath: gathering in church for worship is an opportunity to be reminded together of who God is and who we are and to be shaped into people who seek God's vision in this world. As I've (Bethany) written previously, days of Sabbath and daily set-apart moments of Sabbath can feel more like a wrestling match with ourselves than joyful rest.[21] It's hard to stop. It's hard to get our minds and bodies to settle, to slow, to stop producing or stop worrying or stop checking our phones or stop "doing" for the sake of doing alone. It can be especially difficult to get ourselves out the door to join in worship with others, especially if we don't feel like it (which, if I'm honest, is how I feel more Sunday mornings than not, especially with small kids in tow). A Sabbath day may not always "feel" dramatically nourishing as it's happening. But over time, we can find grace-filled rhythms of worship in our churches and in our homes sharing meals, music, prayer, and Scripture. We might also go for walks or enjoy God's creation in other ways, participating in recreational activities that provide enjoyment and refreshment, both with our families and with the larger family of Christ. In doing so, we are better able to see the Holy Spirit at work,[22] moving through these rhythms and spurring us to enter more fully into God's vision for this world and our lives—into trust and dependence on the grace of God.

For some people it may seem hard to carve out an entire day once a week. Those in church-based ministry may need to find another day of full rest to supplement the day of worship. Whatever you can do to establish a weekly rhythm that involves different practices from the rest of the week, we encourage you to try. We encourage you to find others with whom you can make this commitment, people who can provide encouragement, accountability, and mutual enrichment. Allow these practices to spill over into the rest of the week, perhaps by sleeping more (as an act of trust in the sufficiency of God's work), carving out consistent mealtimes and regular prayer and Scripture times, or turning off technology for a certain amount of time each evening. Practice not "doing"; entrust your activities and your worries into God's hands as you receive the gifts of God to strengthen you and draw you further into God's vision of justice, righteousness, and shalom for this world.

> "Sabbath-keeping is a way to love your neighbor, a simple act of justice. . . . It erects a weekly bastion against the lethargic procrastination that breeds oppression."

Jesus says, "Come to me, all you who are weary and carrying heavy burdens, and I will give you rest. Take my yoke upon you . . . for my yoke is easy and my burden is light" (Matt. 11:28–30). In our discussion on the importance of the Sabbath, we need to remember that by the grace of God Jesus has already given rest to us; he offers us his yoke and takes away our heavy burdens. Because of Jesus Christ's life, death, resurrection, and ascension, we are set free and drawn into intimate communion with God. Through Jesus and the Spirit, we live each moment in the presence of God, and being in the presence of God is the heart of biblical rest. As we undertake the Sabbath, we do so remembering that we can rest because we have received all the rest we need in Christ. As Tim Keller writes, "Avoiding overwork requires deep rest in Christ's finished work for your salvation (Heb. 4:1–10). Only then will you be able to 'walk away' regularly from your vocational work and rest."[23] Through Sabbath rhythms, the Holy Spirit is simply drawing us further into the rest we have already received in and through Jesus Christ.

Extending

We'll say it again—the closer we get to the real needs of others, the more we will face the enormous temptation to respond and react out of the poverty of our own resources and strength. The rest and nourishment we receive by God's grace through the practice of the Sabbath rhythms is not just for our own sake but so that we might be formed and strengthened into people who love God and love others with God's vision for this world as they depend on God's grace and strength. Remarking on this, Peterson writes, "Sabbath-keeping is a way to love your neighbor, a simple act of justice. . . . It erects a weekly bastion against the lethargic procrastination that breeds oppression, that lets injustice flourish because we are not attending in holy obedience and adoring love to the people and animals and things God has placed around us."[24] As God invites us to take Sabbath rest, he is also calling us to find ways to offer Sabbath rest to those who cannot yet receive this gift for themselves because they suffer under the oppression of others. If our own rest comes at the expense of others that God has placed in this world and in our lives, it does not honor God.

The commandment to keep the Sabbath was revolutionary. At the time when it was issued to the Israelites, the concept of "the weekend" did not exist. The only people in that society who ever had time off from labor were the elite and the wealthy. Everyone else worked relentlessly. When God gave the commandment to his people to keep the Sabbath one day each week, he offered an unprecedented day off work for all Israelites, regardless of status. Furthermore, it gave an unprecedented day off to all *foreigners* living in their midst. No matter what a person's background or origin, regardless of their employment or their status, they could receive this gift of rest. However, the Sabbath required those with more power to use their power to extend this gift to others.

In our culture today, we may not feel like we have the direct power to give others a day of rest. But as we are nurtured and formed by our own Sabbath-keeping as the people of God, we can ask God to show us how to use whatever power we have and whatever gifts we've been given to pursue his justice, righteousness, and shalom in his world. For some like my friend John, the federal prosecutor who prosecutes traffickers and secures freedom for human trafficking victims in the United States, this may entail dedicating paid working hours (and beyond) to pursuing the justice calling. For others it may involve volunteering at a local domestic violence shelter, trafficking aftercare home, or another nonprofit dedicated to helping those who are suffering to flourish in our midst. It may look like intentional church partnerships with ministries that pursue the work of justice in our own contexts as well as in other countries.[25] For all of us, it can involve being engaged in our neighborhoods and schools, being open to entering into friendships and to engaging structural issues that keep those near us from flourishing. It may look like conscientious decisions about what we buy and what we eat, being attentive to the conditions under which the goods we consume were produced.[26] It may involve consistent prayer and financial support of organizations and ministries with the background and expertise to pursue freedom for others that extends beyond our own. It may be taking time to hear a stranger's story of oppression and connecting them with resources and gospel hope as we listen and respond. It may mean bringing foster children into your own home and working with churches throughout your city to provide foster care for as many children as possible, giving protection from traffickers who prey on the vulnerability of kids in the foster-care system.

As we steward our time, money, gifts, and callings on a daily basis, we need to be attentive to the ways in which our practices can help us offer the gift of rest to others. As the Holy Spirit uses our own Sabbath-keeping to form us into a holy people who enjoy God and the works of his hand, may the Spirit empower us to seek justice for others that they may enjoy rest from oppression and find the ultimate rest that comes from living in the presence of God through Jesus Christ.

3

Move toward Darkness

Justice and the Fall

Rosa was sixteen years old. [1] She had been pregnant, clearly full-term, and the time had come and gone for the baby to be born. But, as a neighbor noticed, the baby was nowhere to be seen. Rumors began to circulate around the neighborhood as days passed and no one saw the baby. When International Justice Mission staff in Bolivia heard about Rosa from a doorman in their building, they began to investigate.

They learned that Rosa's stepbrother began raping her when she was twelve years old. Compounding his assaults, he threatened to hurt her in even more ways if she ever told anyone. He was twenty-five, unemployed, and at home with Rosa every day. He raped her two or three times a week, and Rosa ultimately became pregnant.

Rosa lived in constant fear that others would find out about her pregnancy. She tried to hide it for as long as possible, but her stepmother found out when Rosa's situation inevitably became obvious. Terrified but desperate for help, Rosa courageously shared with her stepmother the nightmare of abuse she had endured. But help is not what she received.

Rape is a crime of pandemic proportions throughout Latin America—a plague endured by hundreds of thousands of girls every year. The police make

virtually no attempt to stop rapists, much less hold them accountable by prosecuting their crimes. When the rare rape trial does make it to court, defense
lawyers and judges regularly fail to appear at the hearings. My (Bethany's)
colleagues recently obtained a conviction in a case that needed only fifteen
hours in court; it took eight months to get those trial hours.[2] Such obstacles
and delays discourage prosecutors and parents who lose precious daily wages
to attend a hearing only to have it rescheduled.

> *When the world
> is brimming with
> pain and decay,
> why does it matter
> that we know that
> God created the
> world with a vision
> of flourishing,
> wholeness, and
> delight?*

Children who have been raped become weary of
the emotionally tumultuous process of preparing
to testify, reliving their abuse with each retelling,
only to have their hearing canceled again and
again. Many families give up and abandon a case
before it ever comes to completion, and without
witnesses, the prosecutor dismisses it. Even more
cases are never brought to authorities and the
culture of impunity for rape is reinforced. The
cost for a victim to speak up is simply too great.

Living in the caustic air of a culture where
unprosecuted rape is rampant, Rosa's stepmother
chose not to report the crime to the police. Furthermore, she hid the truth from Rosa's father.
As Rosa's pregnancy grew closer to term, she
took Rosa out of school and moved her to a distant city where questions
would not be asked.

Rosa returned to La Paz to give birth to her daughter. When her baby was
born, Rosa succumbed to threats from her stepmother and told her father
that a friend had gotten her pregnant, but Rosa's ordeal was far from over.

Once back home in La Paz, Rosa's father and stepmother refused to let
her care for her baby. She was not allowed to nurse the baby, and when the
baby cried—sometimes for three or four hours at a time—Rosa was not even
allowed to pick her up. Rosa was forced to watch her daughter deteriorate.
Rosa at last held her weak baby and pleaded with her father and stepmother
to let her go to the doctor. They refused. The baby girl died in Rosa's arms.
Rosa's father and stepmother took Rosa two hours from home into the remote
countryside to bury her daughter's body.

The very next month Rosa's stepbrother attempted another assault, and
Rosa fell and hit her head as she ran away. Bleeding, she fled to her aunt's

nearby home and told her everything that had happened. Rosa's aunt took her in and together they told Rosa's father the truth—that the dead baby was fathered by his stepson and that his stepson had serially raped Rosa. But her father remained unmoved and did nothing. He never visited or asked about Rosa.

Meanwhile, Rosa's stepmother continued to cover up the crime and threatened all involved to stay quiet. Rosa's aunt bravely went to the child welfare agency, but in fear she made only vague allegations about Rosa's physical mistreatment. The agency is overwhelmed with hundreds of cases like Rosa's each month (though these hundreds are only a drop in the bucket compared to the number of rapes not even being reported) and took no action.

Our Calling in the Darkness

When I (Bethany) hear of a story like Rosa's, layered with the reality that her story echoes that of millions of other girls throughout the most poverty-stricken areas of our world, I'm tempted to dismiss the idea of looking to Scripture for guidance. I'm tempted to see the Bible as trite and irrelevant, unable to bear the weight of suffering in our world. When I allow myself to look closely at Rosa's life, much less all the lives that her story represents, I find that my conviction that God cares about justice and calls his people to seek it becomes deeply challenged.

If God is all-powerful and has always cared about and commanded justice, then how could this have happened to Rosa? When the world is brimming with pain and decay, why does it matter that we know that God created the world with a vision of flourishing, wholeness, and delight? When there's such a magnitude of suffering to contend with, what's the point of pursuing what seems to amount to mere pockets of shalom? We might experience glimpses of healing and flourishing, but delight is certainly not the pervading reality in our world.

And yet, if I were to resign and dismiss Scripture as irrelevant or as having nothing of enduring substance to offer, I would be acting with deep hubris. For all the weight I feel in knowing a story like Rosa's, the God who *made* Rosa and who *made* the man who became Rosa's assailant knows that weight infinitely more. And the God who created the world and governs it toward redemption is the God who is beckoning us, through Scripture and through the living Word of Jesus Christ, to join him in knowing the only hope that will never disappoint—the hope that God will be glorified, that his justice, his healing, his vision of flourishing will be made known.

Moving through the story of Scripture from God's creation vision in Genesis 1 and 2 to the fall in Genesis 3, we can see that the darkness of injustice pervading our world plays no part in God's intent for the flourishing of this world; it is an utter distortion. This does not mean that God is impotent or that his power has been thwarted. But in order to understand that injustice does nothing to thwart God's power, we need to better understand the ways in which shalom has been marred, enabling the proliferation of suffering. At the same time, we need to carry with us the truth—even when it is hard to hold—that God has always been passionate for justice and has always called us to join him in this passion. We need to carry with us the truth that justice precedes the advent of injustice.

> *Invoking the reality of sin gives us language to describe and protest all that is wrong in this world and in our lives.*

Justice is more than the work of setting what has gone wrong back to right, and yet the work of setting things to right is a massive undertaking—more than any of us can accomplish. Sin has ruptured every layer of the righteousness and shalom that God intended for this world. If we are going to pursue the flourishing of shalom and the fullness of justice and delight, it is important to thoroughly understand why the world we live in festers in such pain. We need to face the darkness of our world head-on and move toward it, even into it. As we do so, we go with the gift of the light of Christ. Isaiah tells us that as we seek to right the wrongs of injustice, our light will be as bright as the noonday, and the glory of the Lord will be our rearguard (Isa. 58). We do not go as our own broken selves. We bear the light of Christ, who dwells within us and cannot be overcome (John 1).

Regardless of how humanity has rebelled against God and proliferated injustice and enmity, God in his loving-kindness (*hesed*) actively works in our midst through all generations, continually moving and calling us to join him in righting all that has gone wrong, in re-creating this world as a place of justice, righteousness, and shalom. This is a calling that we, the body of Christ, need and can respond to by the grace of God as we move toward the darkness and injustice of this world in the light of Christ.

As we move forward it is critical to name the source of all that has gone wrong. The name of the source is *sin*—a term and concept that is one of the most avoided and yet compelling aspects of the Christian faith. Sin is routinely denied in many societies today, and yet it can be life-giving to understand and acknowledge it. Invoking the reality of sin gives us language to describe and protest all that is wrong in this world and in our lives. As Emmanuel Katongole and Chris Rice have expressed in the context of their work on violence and reconciliation, "The way things are is not the way things have to be."[3]

When sin entered the world, as the apostle Paul describes it in the New Testament, "creation was subjected to frustration," and it remains in "bondage to decay" (Rom. 8:20–21). All of the brokenness, evil, and injustice that we witness in creation and experience as a result of fallen creation goes against God's original intentions for the flourishing of the created world.

Tracing the biblical concept of sin—beginning in Genesis with Adam and Eve—enables us to name what we are witnessing when we encounter injustice in our world. When we think about sin, it is common to picture our individual shortcomings. The sin within each of us is important to acknowledge, but this individual understanding does not capture all of the ramifications of sin that unfold according to the biblical story. Knowing the many layers of brokenness that entered into this world after the fall opens up the opportunity for us to protest against the darkness we see with ever more frequency, knowing that it does not reflect God's intentions for this world. It opens the possibility for us to mourn this brokenness and its ramifications. It helps us to believe that things can be different. And by the grace of God it enables us to live as the people of God who move toward the darkness of this world in pursuit of justice, surrounded and strengthened by the light of Christ and the power of the Holy Spirit.

The Fall: Creation Distorted

The opening of Genesis makes it clear that God created man and woman to be in fellowship with him and each other and to care for the created world. Adam and Eve live and work in harmony until the serpent enters the picture.

In issuing the call to take care of the garden of Eden, God says, "You are free to eat from any tree in the garden; but you must not eat from the tree of the knowledge of good and evil, for when you eat from it you will certainly die" (Gen. 2:16–17). The serpent latches on to this piece of God's instructions and says to Eve, "Did God really say, 'You must not eat from any tree in the garden'?" (Gen. 3:1). The woman responds by saying that they may eat fruit from all but one tree; if they eat of that one tree or touch it, they will die. The serpent questions this pronouncement and tells Eve that if she eats the fruit she will be like God, knowing good and evil. The woman looks at the beauty of the fruit and the prospect of God-like wisdom and makes the decision to eat it. She then offers this fruit to Adam, who also decides to eat it.

> *The scope of the fall was . . . cosmic, disrupting the relationships between God and humanity and the entire created order.*

The consequences of this choice are swift and significant. If shalom can be understood as the flourishing of all creation, then sin can be understood as the fundamental disruption and distortion of what God envisioned for his creation. The original shalom vision was a cosmic vision of wholeness, harmony, unity, justice, and love between God and humans, between man and woman, within each human person, and between humans and the rest of the created world. The scope of the fall was also cosmic, disrupting the relationships between God and humanity and the entire created order. After sin entered, the layers of shalom intended for the flourishing of all relationships were corrupted. As Cornelius Plantinga puts it, nothing is any longer "the way it's supposed to be."[4]

Sin and the Layers of Shalom

As the account of the fall unfolds in Genesis 3, we see how injustice enters the world through the distortion of each of these layers of shalom. While reading through the following summary of the biblical story of the fall, notice how the introduction of sin impacts not only the fundamental relationship between God and humans but also the created world itself and human relationships with one another.

The first thing we read after Adam and Eve eat the fruit is that they realize they are naked. In poignant contrast to the time when "Adam and his wife were both naked, and they felt no shame" (Gen. 2:25), the couple is mortified and make the first clothing to cover themselves. Here we see the first indication that the relationship between Adam and Eve has been impacted by their sin. Through the entrance of shame we also see a disruption in the harmonious relationship that had existed between God and humans. Instead of delighting in God's presence, Adam and Eve hide from God, full of shame.

A bit later, when the man explains to God what he has done, he blames the woman for giving him the fruit, a further sign of the ruptured relationship between man and woman. The woman, in turn, blames the serpent. In stark contrast to the blessings that God bestowed as he created the world, God issues his first curse to the serpent and then curses the ground as well. As a result, the created world itself is distorted by the fall.

In God's *hesed* (his merciful loving-kindness), he does not curse Adam and Eve themselves, and neither does he abandon his commitment to be their God. But he does outline severe consequences for their behavior that underscore the multiple layers of suffering that enter creation as a result of their sin. God's original charge to Adam and Eve is to be fruitful and multiply and to take care of the created world; the consequences of the fall impact both aspects of this charge. The woman is told by God that she will experience pain in childbirth and that her desire will be for her husband, who will rule over her, which is a clear distortion of the mutuality envisioned for them. The man is told that his caretaking work will involve toil and pain and that the cursed ground will produce thorns and thistles, an obvious disruption to the harmonious relationship he was intended to have with creation.

Ultimately, God banishes Adam and Eve from the garden that he had earlier entrusted to them, the garden in which they had once shared intimate union and fellowship with God. However, the depiction of the fall in these early chapters of Genesis is not entirely without grace and mercy. Before sending them out, God initiates an act of generous provision, making garments for the man and the woman from animal skins. Having said that, these animal skins are the first indication of death of any kind in the Bible and another sign of the disruption of flourishing relationships.[5] In another act of grace and mercy, God ensures that Adam and Eve do not eat from the tree of life again, lest they live forever in their broken condition (Gen. 3:21–24).

> *In God's* **hesed** *. . . he does not curse Adam and Eve themselves, and neither does he abandon his commitment to be their God. But he does outline severe consequences for their behavior that underscore the multiple layers of suffering that entered creation as a result of their sin.*

Although the man and the woman do not immediately die as a result of their decision to eat the fruit, "the curse, the disruption, the toil, the banishment, are all outworkings of the divine word from 2:17: 'in the day that you eat of it you shall die.'"[6] Biblical scholars note that this reference to death alludes to the stark changes that have resulted from Adam and Eve's disobedience: "from the blessing, freedom, vitality, and fellowship of the Garden, to curse, bondage, toil, and alienation outside the gate on the East of the Garden."[7] This picture of life after the fall could hardly be more different from the shalom vision that characterized life before the fall. Things are no longer the way they were created to be on any level.

The next several chapters in the biblical story (Gen. 4–11) provide evidence of the layers of brokenness and evil that now mark the created order—sibling envy, murder, toil, wickedness so great that God regrets creating humans, and a community of people that tries to reach the heavens as a way to make a name for themselves and find unity without God. The snowball effect of the fall is highlighted throughout the biblical story as broken people interact with one another and create cities, cultures, institutions, and structures that reflect and amplify brokenness rather than reflecting and amplifying the justice and righteousness of God.[8]

More Than Individual Wrongdoing

On multiple levels, the understanding of sin as "not the way it's supposed to be" is certainly rooted in Scripture. And yet it's important to acknowledge that the current ways in which we talk about sin do not always match this more wide-ranging understanding of sin. We often assume that sin refers primarily to individual wrongdoing. As I (Kristen) enter into times of prayer and confession, I notice that I usually pray about sin only in terms of the ways I have individually fallen short of living God's will. Not too long ago, my son reminded me that we can and need to expand what we bring before God as we pray about sin.

Every night in our times of prayer I ask my four-year-old son what he is grateful for and what he is sorry about as a way to introduce him to the long-standing practices of thanksgiving and confession. For months, he refused to name anything he was sorry for. It may be that he was not developmentally ready to understand and answer the question, but since I usually need to confess my impatience as a parent to my son and to God at the end of the day, I kept with the practice, hoping he would grow into it. Then one night we read a story about Jackie Robinson, the African American baseball player who courageously paved the way for other African Americans to play professional baseball. We read that when Jackie was a baby, white people set fire to black churches in his community. That night, for the very first time, my son answered my question: "I am sorry that they burned those black churches," he said, quietly but with deep conviction. As I began to pray, he reminded me again, "Please say sorry to God that they burned those churches." In that moment, I realized that my son grasped the truth that sin is larger than our personal shortcomings. When we acknowledge sin before God and others, we need to include all the ways that the world is not the way it's supposed to be.

The Emergence of Injustice

That God allowed these ramifications of the fall to play out on so many levels does not mean that God no longer cared about the flourishing of his creation after the fall. As we continue to explore the story of Scripture, we see that God consistently cares about justice and righteousness in this world and consistently calls his people to care about justice and righteousness in this world.

As we discussed earlier, *righteousness* refers to people being rightly and lovingly connected in relationship with God, others, themselves, and the created world. According to God's design, people are meant to love in ways that promote the flourishing of everyone and everything as they faithfully live into God's intentions for all of their relationships. As a result, a world marked by shalom would be a world of rightly ordered love, a world of justice.

Sin broke open the way for unrighteousness and injustice to enter the world. The intimate relationship humans had with God was broken, and the way of life he intended for his people—a way marked by righteousness and justice flowing from their right relationship with God—was no longer possible. Injustice entered and prevailed.

Once their relationship with God was distorted, humans were no longer able to respond faithfully to their call to steward creation. Rather than acting in ways that honored God's call upon them to love him and love others, they became self-seeking. They began to use power and domination to serve themselves rather than using their power to seek the welfare of others and the larger created world. Justice is manifest as people use their power to enable others to flourish, injustice is what happens when power is used to exploit, abuse, or destroy.

Augustine wrote this about the fall: "The essential flaw of the devil's perversion made him a lover of power and a deserter and assailant of justice."[9] It's not that power is bad in and of itself. If we believe that everything that God created is good, that goodness includes the power God gave us to steward this world on his behalf.[10] However, anything that God created good can be manipulated for bad purposes. As Augustine puts it, fallen humans tend to mirror the fallen angel Satan in their pursuit of power over justice; people "imitate him all the more thoroughly the more they neglect or even detest justice and studiously devote themselves to power, rejoicing at the possession of it or inflamed with the desire for it."[11]

Living as God's people today involves receiving the gifts that God has given us and using them to seek God's justice and righteousness in this world.

Take the gift of sex. In the creation story we read that God created humans to "be fruitful and multiply," implying that the capacity for sexual intimacy is a God-given gift that humans receive as part of their call to be faithful stewards of this world. Because it involves the power to procreate and the power that comes with shared intimacy and vulnerability, sexual intimacy needs to be engaged in ways that are in keeping with God's intentions for shalom in this world. Just as with justice and righteousness, sexual intimacy is intended both to flow from and encourage a "right" love of God, self, and others.

The power that comes with the gift of sex is intended to be used to love others and seek their flourishing in ways that correspond to God's vision of human flourishing. However, this good gift—perhaps more often than not—is deeply distorted and perverted for selfish gain. The abuse of power in sex happens in relationships all over the world, both outside and inside of marriage and at all ages. We see this in the suffering Rosa endured, and we see it every time sex is used for someone's gain rather than as a gift that is given and shared. Injustice occurs when one person takes and demands intimate use of another's body instead of reciprocally receiving and sharing the gift that God meant physical intimacy to be.

Sex is but one example that points to a deeper truth: justice happens when people use the gifts and power God has given to them in ways that promote the flourishing of humans and creation.

Receiving and Depending

The story of Scripture consistently shows God's commitment to justice and righteousness and reveals God's desire for his people to be set apart by their pursuit of justice and righteousness with him. Called to live in dependent trust, God's people are to gratefully receive what God has given to them and offer their gifts back to God for God's sake and for the sake of God's vision for the world. God gave Adam and Eve every good gift—life, union with him, food, one another, and the opportunity to participate in his rule and power as stewards of creation. But instead of gratefully receiving these good gifts and using them to promote the flourishing of God's world, they took the one thing that had not been given to them. The act of eating the fruit that God had forbidden them to eat is the first instance of humans *taking* for themselves rather than *receiving* that which was given as a gift from God. They used the power that had been entrusted to them—the power to rule over the earth with justice and righteousness, the power to seek shalom—to choose their own way.

> *Justice happens when people use the gifts God has given to them in ways that promote the flourishing of humans and creation.*

Thinking in terms of taking versus receiving helps us to see how important gratitude is to living lives of justice and righteousness. Karl Barth writes, "Radically and basically all sin is simply ingratitude—man's refusal of the one but necessary thing which is proper to and is required of him with whom God has graciously entered into covenant."[12] Creation itself is a gracious act; God generously created the world and then created humans to live in relationship with him. Along with the gift of being in relationship with the loving and faithful Creator of the world came the gifts of being in relationship with others and caring for the world that God made. Gratitude is the only fitting response to these gracious gifts. Understood in an active, all-encompassing way, Spirit-empowered gratitude entails receiving the gifts God has given with thanksgiving and offering our entire lives back to God in response, in pursuit of the things God cares the most about.

As Barth writes, "Grace and gratitude belong together like heaven and earth. Grace evokes gratitude like the voice an echo. Gratitude follows grace like thunder lightning."[13] If the amazing grace of God is at the center of this world and our lives, enabling us to be God's beloved people, then as God's people we ought to gratefully offer our entire lives back to God. This conviction about the centrality of grace and gratitude led my husband and I (Kristen) to give our daughter the name "Karis" as one of her middle names. *Charis* is the Greek word for grace, and it forms the center of the Greek word for gratitude, *eucharistia* (from which we derive the word *Eucharist*, the term used within many Christian traditions to refer to the Lord's Supper). The close connection between grace and gratitude in the biblical Greek reflects how closely they work together in our lives. Our hope and prayer is that just as "Karis" is at the center of our daughter's name, she will always have the grace of God at the center of her life and, empowered by that same grace, will offer her whole life in grateful service to God.

> *How would the story have changed if Adam and Eve had gratefully received from God rather than ungratefully taken what they wanted for themselves?*

How would the story have changed if Adam and Eve had gratefully received from God rather than ungratefully taken what they wanted for themselves? In response to the serpent's loaded questions, they could have said, "God has given us so many good and gracious gifts—these gifts are more than enough, and we will use them to lovingly care for this world." Even more simply, they could have said, "We trust God," and walked away.

Had they trusted that God's plans for them and for the rest of creation would truly lead to their flourishing, they would not have been tempted to think the tree offered something better. Had they fully trusted God, they would have gratefully received the innumerable gifts that God in his mercy had given them and faithfully used those gifts to pursue the vision of justice, righteousness, and peace that God has for this world.

Rooted in loving union with God, Adam and Eve could have lived in a relationship marked by gratitude and dependent trust. From this right relationship with God, right relationships with other people and the created world would have followed, ushering in a world stewarded by God's people that reflected God's commitment to righteousness, justice, *hesed*, and shalom.

In Paul's letters Jesus is called the last Adam (Rom. 5:12–18; 1 Cor. 15:42–49). As God took on human flesh in the person of Jesus Christ and lived his life on our behalf, he "redid" the life that Adam was called to live, with perfect faithfulness. Among other things, this means that he embodies the gratitude, trust, and righteousness that Adam and all subsequent humanity was intended to embody. We will take a more comprehensive look at the person of Jesus in a later chapter, but for now we want to point out that in Jesus we see the righteousness of God manifest in a living person. Jesus lived in full and perfect union with God the Father, and from this faithful relationship with the Father, empowered by the Holy Spirit, Jesus lived in right and loving relationships with others and creation. Jesus Christ both sought and embodied God's righteousness, justice, *hesed*, holiness, and shalom.

What did righteousness, justice, *hesed*, holiness, and shalom look like in Jesus's life? Total, constant trust in his Father. Jesus manifested this dependent trust over the course of his time on earth, culminating in the persecution, suffering, and death he underwent as he offered everything he had been given back to God. This included giving his very life, so that through his death, resurrection, and ascension Jesus would reconcile all things, and God's vision for humanity and the world would be victorious over the distortions that arose after the fall. Jesus used his power not to dominate others but to enter the world in humility in order to serve others—even to the point of death on a cross (Phil. 2). This same power enabled him to conquer sin, death, and every evil injustice in this world when he was raised from the dead and ascended to the Father, where he continues to serve as Lord and King.

Whether or not we perceive ourselves to have power, through the gift of the Holy Spirit we have received the very power of God. After his resurrection, Jesus promised his disciples that they would receive power when the Holy Spirit came upon them so that they could become his witnesses in this world (Acts 1). This promise was fulfilled on the day of Pentecost, when the gift of the Holy Spirit was given to the disciples (Acts 2)—the same Spirit we who are called to follow Jesus Christ receive today. This Spirit draws us into the grace of Jesus Christ, which means that through the reconciling love of Christ we are set right with God. Rooted in this righteousness we receive God's love and are freed to love God, others, and this world as God intended. With gratitude for this overflowing grace, we can offer our entire lives and all of our gifts back to God for God's sake and for the sake of God's vision for the world. We do this through the power of the Holy Spirit, using all that God has given us to seek justice, righteousness, and shalom right where we are.

Overcoming sin through Christ involves moving toward the darkness of this world, which is itself the result of sin. Living this power that God has given us involves sitting with and listening deeply to the stories of those who are suffering from injustice so that we can understand the real consequences of the world's brokenness, lament the evil we encounter, and rely on the Spirit to use our lives to join God in the work of setting things right.

Whether or not we perceive ourselves to have power, through the gift of the Holy Spirit we have received the very power of God.

As we move toward darkness, we need to prepare for what we will encounter and know that we do not go on our own but bearing the light of Christ. We need constant guidance for this counterintuitive act of trust. But before we move into specifics as to what it looks like to take these steps forward, it's important to note some pressing questions that arise in the face of evil and injustice in this world. By looking at these questions we till and prepare the soil so that we can plant courage rather than fear.

The Origins of Evil and Injustice

Where did the temptation to turn away from God come from? Where did evil and injustice originate, and what was the role of Satan? These and many other important questions are not addressed in the story of sin that is recounted in the early chapters of Genesis. For example, why did the "crafty" serpent (Gen. 3:1) ask questions that seem intended to lead Eve to question God's trustworthiness? And where did the serpent's craftiness come from? Although no direct connection is made in Genesis between this serpent and the power of evil or the fallen angel who has come to be known as Satan, within Christian tradition and elsewhere in Scripture (see Matt. 4:10; Rev. 20:2) a snake is associated with Satan. The connection of the serpent with Satan has helped to make sense of why the story of Adam and Eve is not just about the interactions between a woman, a man, and a serpent but rather a cosmic story with ramifications for all of humanity and the whole created world.[14]

Genesis shows how sin and evil enter into God's good creation without addressing their exact origins. And yet there are some things we learn about the nature of evil from Scripture that are important to address as we face evil and injustice in this world. According to the biblical account of good and evil, evil is *not* an independent entity in competition with good. Evil is not a created force locked in an eternal battle with the forces of good. Most of the Christian tradition has held with Augustine that evil is a turning away from God's goodness; it is a diminishment or privation of that goodness. The word *deprived* may come to mind here: those who are deprived lack something they need or want. Similarly, in Augustine's view, evil doesn't enjoy its own independent being but is a lack of the good. Privation is linked to the idea that by turning from God we turn from the good: from what we need, from God's good gifts and intentions, and from his provision for flourishing.

The illustration of a parasite can be helpful here as we think about the nature of evil, because a parasite—by definition—lives off other living creatures, getting its food at the expense of the creature that is unknowingly hosting it. Parasites cannot live on their own, just as evil depends on goodness for its existence. Rather than being a part of the living creature or essential to the creature's flourishing, parasites take life from the creature that hosts them and use it for their own ends. They have life and the power to do real harm and inflict substantial hurt, but they cannot and do not exist on their own.

Evil is a turning away from God's goodness; it is a diminishment or privation of that goodness.

Sometimes Christians offer the explanation that evil and sin needed to enter the world so that we could recognize the nature of goodness, but we would counter that such an explanation gives evil far too prominent a role in God's creation. One would not say that a host creature needs a parasite to function as it is supposed to; neither do we need evil to exist so that we can flourish. Evil is a distortion of what God intended, and it is not essential to this world. Furthermore, we believe that the day will come when evil will no longer be a part of this world, when it will be fully and finally overcome in Christ. While God's aims are not thwarted by evil, evil's existence is something we must always protest.

When we witness the brokenness of this world, we are witnessing a *turning away* from what God intended, as well as a misuse of God's good gifts. Our ability to turn away does nothing to mar God's power and goodness. Rather, it demonstrates that God has given us the ability to choose either to obey, love, and trust or to turn away. Even angels turn away from God's goodness and gifts, for reasons beyond our understanding. We need to recognize that these fallen powers exert tragic influence in this world.

At the same time we must remember that, ultimately, the forces of evil and injustice are not greater than God and his victory over them, which is secured in and through Jesus Christ. Evil is not an independent force. The injustices of this world are real, but they fall under the greater power and authority of God in Christ (Eph. 1:18–23).

One would not say that a host creature needs a parasite to function as it is supposed to; neither do we need evil to exist so that we can flourish.

Significantly, God's response to evil was not to remain distant from evil and suffering but to enter into this world's darkness as God in the flesh. God in Christ came near, endured and experienced the reality of sin, wept in the face of the brokenness of this world, and then suffered death on the cross in order to bear the consequences of sin and evil for us. In Christ's resurrection and ascension, the final victory of God over all the evil and injustices of this world was secured.

We can say with confidence that the light of Christ shines in the darkness, and the darkness cannot overcome it (John 1:5). We know that Christ experienced the suffering that results from the brokenness of this world (Heb. 2). More than that, Jesus himself was the victim of injustice—he was unfairly arrested, beaten, imprisoned, and crucified—so we trust that he understands the tragic plight of victims of injustice. All of this helps us to live with faith and hope even as we move toward the darkness and become more aware of evil and injustice in this world. We look forward to the day when all the darkness of the world will be fully and finally overcome by the light of Christ, and in the meantime Christ's light is present, even in the darkest places of brokenness and injustice.

Invitation for Today: Move toward Darkness

After my (Bethany's) colleagues listened to Rosa's story, Rosa led International Justice Mission's (IJM) investigators to the hidden, unmarked grave of her baby on a hill in the countryside, two hours outside La Paz, Bolivia. Rosa ran to the grave plot on the far side of the hill, tears streaming down her face. DNA evidence was needed to prove that Rosa's stepbrother was the father, which meant that the baby's body needed to be exhumed.

I find myself achingly devoid of words when I attempt to express how excruciating this would be for any mother—to be taken to the grave of your child and to watch as your baby's tiny body is exhumed for evidence of the crimes that led to her being lifeless in a grave rather than alive in your arms. And yet it was critical that the evidence be properly gathered so that it could be submitted in court. My colleagues took the DNA sample from the baby's body and reported the full details of Rosa's nightmare to the local authorities as our social workers prepared Rosa to share her story with the prosecutor. Rosa gathered her strength and spoke with great courage. The forensic examiner noted that the investigative work was exceptional, and so the team continued to push the case forward, using the full strength of their collective expertise and energy.

Without the effort of my colleagues, neither the investigation nor the exhumation would have taken place. The rape of a teenager and the subsequent murder of her baby would have gone unnoticed, and Rosa would still be suffering alone. But this story does not yet have an end.

In early 2012, the prosecutor ordered the arrest of the father, stepmother, and stepbrother on charges of rape and murder. The father and mother were placed on house arrest (permitted to leave only for their daily work). Rosa's stepbrother disappeared. According to informants, he is believed to have fled to Brazil. Overall, despite the very best work the IJM team could offer, no further progress has been made to bring justice to bear against the crimes Rosa has endured.

And yet, God's call to justice remains. God's call to us to join him in his work of bringing justice to the oppressed remains. Sometimes justice seems to come swiftly on the heels of rescue, and sometimes the years slip by as we wonder if justice will ever come at all. We know there is a day when all will be made right, when all will be made new. But in the waiting, we ache with Rosa.

Rosa has a long road ahead of her. She needs to be reminded day after day that she is not alone. God loves her and loves the baby she lost, and even though justice has not yet come against her perpetrators, there is a body of believers around the world who want her to flourish rather than wither in the wake of this tragedy.

Rosa's case is a critical reminder of broken justice systems everywhere that desperately need to be repaired so that they can function on behalf of the most vulnerable people in our world. Rosa's story reminds us of the depth of suffering at hand, sometimes in our own neighborhoods and most prevalently throughout the most poverty-stricken regions of the world. When injustice prevails and things need to be set right, the body of Christ must continue to draw near to those who suffer, as we draw near to our God of justice to intervene, heal, and redeem.

> We must remember that, ultimately, the forces of evil and injustice are not greater than God and his victory over them. . . . Evil is not an independent force.

By the power of the Holy Spirit, we *must* move toward darkness, spurring one another on, especially when the light of Christ seems dim.

> For now we see in a mirror, dimly, but then we will see face to face. Now I know only in part; then I will know fully, even as I have been fully known. (1 Cor. 13:12 NRSV)

The world is broken.

Across the globe today, girls are routinely assaulted in their own communities with no recourse; men are beheaded one by one and by the dozen; widows are left destitute by their own family members; and citizens are beaten, tortured, detained, and even murdered by the police who were meant to protect them. Millions of women and children are trapped and sold into the sex-trafficking industry. Untold numbers of families are bound in slavery. Death, disease, broken relationships, and abuse are within everyone's reach and far too close at hand.

For most people, despair seems to be an inevitable destination, at least at some point in their lives. But we hold fast to the hope that despair is *not* our inevitable end, and that God has called people to himself so that his healing and power will reign and new life will flourish. Even so, the way toward this hope is through the valley of the shadow of death; we will certainly face enemies, but we need not fear evil (Ps. 23). To find life for ourselves and for the world God is calling us to love, we must run toward the darkness with the light of Christ. Thankfully, we do not run alone. We need to seek out and surround ourselves with friends and colleagues and brothers and sisters in Christ who, when they hear and see darkness, do not cower but spur us forward with them.

My (Bethany) instinct is to shrink back. I remember a vivid image that came to mind as I was praying a few years ago: I was hiding behind a rock as a battle raged on a field that stretched out in front of me. I wanted to stay hunkered-down behind that rock, but God was inviting me to stand up, covered in his armor (Eph. 6), and walk straight down the middle of the field—no matter how many flaming arrows came my way, no matter how many hits I took. Moving *through* the very thing I feared and trusting God for protection was the only way forward if I wanted anything more than a life hidden behind an immovable barricade. Moving toward darkness in the armor of Christ does not mean that we won't get hit. Weapons will be forged against us. But those weapons will not prevail (Isa. 54:17). This is our sure hope. This is our promise.

> *To find life for ourselves and for the world God is calling us to love, we must run toward the darkness with the light of Christ.*

This image—of myself hiding behind a rock versus standing up and walking onto the battle-field in the armor of God—has stayed with me for years, simply because I so often find myself *longing* to take shelter rather than receive God's invitation to go into places of suffering where the light of Christ can and will heal. I need to be spurred on by the courage of others in order to even peek out from behind my rock, much less put on the armor of God and step onto the field.

God knows this about me. God knows my preference for the safe and sound, and so God has surrounded me with followers of Jesus all over the world who are relentless in their pursuit of justice for the most vulnerable. When my colleagues at IJM hear about girls like Rosa and her baby, they surge into the darkness with everything God has given them. As they work, they hold fast to the assurance of final victory in God's kingdom, but in the meantime, they understand there are no guarantees. More often than not, they are met with heartbreak on the way to healing and hope.

Moving toward darkness is counterintuitive, but the more we understand that we "are the light of the world" (Matt. 5:14) because of Jesus Christ living within us, the more we will know the power we possess even when faced with darkness that seems impenetrable (Eph. 1:19–21). As the Holy Spirit empowers us to know Scripture, connect with God moment by moment in prayer, and intentionally reach out to be in community with others in the body of Christ, the Spirit draws us toward the blazing light of Christ that forms our identity. It is not simply a light that we carry; it is a light that we *are*. And we are not meant to keep it to ourselves. Knowing the light of Christ within us, empowered by the Spirit, we can move with confidence toward darkness with sustained attention. Rather than simply glancing at people who are suffering, we can look deeply and intently, taking the time to explore why they are suffering and to ask God what step he might invite us to take.

The more we understand that we "are the light of the world" because of Jesus Christ living within us, the more we will know the power we possess even when faced with darkness that seems impenetrable.

Moving toward the darkness involves hearing and seeing stories of injustice that we'd rather not witness. Moving toward the darkness means moving toward actual people and listening intently to those who are hurting, whose situations are messy, chaotic, painful, and not easily fixed. Truth uncovered in Christ and Scripture must be our companion—the pain and confusion and struggle we meet in the darkness of suffering and injustice cannot overcome God's fierce love or his desire for this world to be a place of justice, righteousness, and shalom. Darkness does not nullify God's call upon us, but rather Christ's love propels us to move toward darkness as his people, set apart by the same love, justice, righteousness, and shalom that comes from God's own character.

Jesus Christ has already claimed victory over evil and injustice; darkness will never have the last word. The light of Jesus Christ really does penetrate and change the darkness, so that even the darkest places can be transformed and set right. By the mysteries of God's grace the light of Christ shines in and through us, enabling us as the body of Christ to bring light to the darkness as we offer our lives and gifts to God.

Moving toward darkness requires an intentional choice. Personally, I have to ask God to give me the strength and courage to step out from behind the illusion of my safe rock; I have to ask him to put his armor on me and draw me close with other believers in vulnerability and prayer. Then I start moving my feet one step at a time onto the field, asking God to open my eyes to see what he wants me to see—to really see it—not just offer a passing glance. At times the suffering of others catches our attention, especially if it seems particularly tragic, but there are too many ways to flip the channel and move on to another topic rather than continue to move intentionally toward actual people who are suffering and in need. But with God opening the way before us, we only need to take one step at a time.

Start by talking to God and taking inventory. What gifts has God lavished on you, of any shape or size? Thank God for these gifts and ask him to show you ways to use these gifts as he spurs you toward dark places. Don't know where to start? Confess that to God. Even those of us who think we know the step we need to take are better off confessing to God our need for him to guide our steps.

Prayer is critical preparation for moving toward darkness. It cannot be skipped or skimmed over.

Prayer is critical preparation and our constant companion as we move toward darkness. It is both a source of strength and connection with the God of justice, as well as the power by which God so often chooses to act. Our connection with God in prayer is meant for all times. It cannot be skipped or skimmed over. Prayer transforms us as prayer transforms the world.[15] And yet the work of justice daily puts our belief in the importance of prayer to the test. Whether or not we understand prayer or experience answers, God gives us prayer as a means by which to draw us further into relationship with God our Father, Jesus Christ, and the Holy Spirit. Prayer is the grace-filled fuel that drives the work of justice in our world.

When it comes to responding to injustice in our world, I (Bethany) have been asked more times than I can count, "What can I do besides pray?" My answer is always that there is quite a lot you can do. But then again, there's absolutely nothing you can do without prayer. It's important to remember that God can do his work whether we join him or not. God hears the cries of those who are suffering whether we talk to him about it or not. God is with us whether we ask him to be or not. But here is the mystery we may never fully comprehend: God wants to do the work of justice in *communion* with us. God has given us the gift of prayer so that we can be drawn further into life with him, receiving power and knowing God's love, grace, justice, and power at work in this world.

Ask God in prayer, "Who is suffering? Who is sitting in a place of darkness and having a hard time believing that you, God, are good because they are in so much pain?" God will direct your gaze. Even more important, God will also enable you to take a step forward. Ask God to point you to others in your local church with whom you can join in prayer. Don't go it alone.

Another step you can take is to focus on one specific book of the Bible. Even as this book means to immerse the reader in the entire biblical story, we encourage you to choose one book of the Bible and study it beginning to end. Find (circle, highlight, etc.) every mention of the word *justice* and/or *righteousness* and/or *peace* and/or *freedom* and/or *slavery*. Write down what these words mean in each instance and use study tools such as online or published commentaries (or ask a trusted pastor who has preached on the book) to find out the wider context of the book as you specifically seek to understand God's call to justice. The following books are a good place to start: Micah, Luke, Galatians, Psalms, Isaiah, and Job.

> *Here is the mystery we may never fully comprehend: God wants to do the work of justice in* communion *with us.*

As you step intentionally toward darkness, it can be helpful to identify two justice-oriented organizations you can learn from. Choose one that is focused on injustice issues "close to home" (wherever that may be for you) and one that is focused on injustice issues on a different continent or in a different hemisphere. The website globalmodernslavery.org can assist you in finding organizations that specifically target human trafficking, but there are certainly many other forms of injustice to be engaged with as well, such as racial inequality; child abuse; domestic violence; refugee resettlement; environmental degradation; and health, educational, and housing disparities. Once you've identified a couple of organizations, go to their websites, contact a representative, and ask questions. Invite a speaker to your church, and consider an on-site visit.[16] Just don't go it alone—invite a friend or neighbor to learn about these organizations with you.

As you take stock of the justice needs in your own community, you might find tools like The Community Justice Assessment (ijm.org/resources)—which is free, downloadable, and comprehensive. As you discover how to see injustice around you, talk with, learn from, and encourage law enforcement officers, social workers, and other justice professionals in your town.

As you learn, share stories with your friends, coworkers, neighbors, and kids about people suffering injustice. Share stats, but go beyond stats—share names, show pictures and videos, and share stories of hope and rescue. Powerful stories can be found through the websites of many organizations. When you hear stories of suffering and hope, share them regularly and engage in conversation with others, especially those who might not know what slavery and violent injustice look like in our world today.

Keep the conversation going by hosting an event in your home, or join up with someone else who loves to host events in their home. Show a feature-length documentary on modern-day slavery[17] or a sampling of shorter YouTube clips that educate about slavery and other forms of violence against the poor. Use the evening to creatively focus on one issue or one country or one city and raise funds to give to an organization doing exceptional work.[18] Gathering with others spreads awareness and also brings energy and focus to your steps.

As you get to know the needs in your own community and what other organizations are doing, consider joining an advocacy group in your city or start one of your own with leaders at your local church. Opportunities to join up with others can be found through IJM Advocacy teams in each state (check www.ijm.org or Facebook to join) and "A Teams" with A21 (Abolishing Injustice in the 21st Century, at www.A21.org). Get to know others who are already in this fight.

With each step forward that you take, read all you can and digest what others have to teach. Here's a sampling of books written in the past decade that are filled with biblical teaching on justice, as well as some that include practical action ideas:

- *The Just Church* (Jim Martin)
- *The Dangerous Act of Worship* and *The Dangerous Act of Loving Your Neighbor* (Mark Labberton)
- *Kingdom Calling* (Amy Sherman)
- *Good News about Injustice* and *Just Courage* (Gary Haugen)
- *Generous Justice* (Tim Keller)
- *Reconciling All Things* (Emmanuel Katongole and Chris Rice)
- *Undaunted* (Christine Caine)
- *With Justice for All* (John M. Perkins)
- *Evil and the Justice of God* (N. T. Wright)

- *Justice* and *Justice in Love* (Nicholas Wolterstorff)
- *Overrated* (Eugene Cho)
- *Refuse to Do Nothing* (Kim Yim and Shayne Moore)
- *The Spiritual Danger of Doing Good* (Peter Greer)
- *The World Is Not Ours to Save* (Tyler Wigg-Stevenson)

Pick a book and pull together a few people to read it as a group. Invite your pastor to read it too. Convene at a favorite restaurant or over dessert at someone's home for discussion.

As we move toward darkness Christ is with us, forming us into people who actively seek God's kingdom and righteousness in the places most overlooked and abandoned in our world, even in our own communities. Surrounded by other believers, buttressed by Scripture, and filled with the Holy Spirit, we remember that "the light shines in the darkness, and the darkness has not overcome it" (John 1:5).

Because we believe that all things have been conquered by Jesus Christ and that he has the final victory over the dominion of darkness, we can go in hope that Christ's light has overcome and will continue to overcome the darkness until the darkness is finally vanquished.

4

Lament

Justice and Israel

The grainy black-and-white footage showed little girls smiling and giggling, gathered tightly in a small space. One of them was only five years old, perched on the hip of a girl just a few years older. Their smiles belied the words they spoke in their native Vietnamese, offering a menu of what sexual acts they would perform and the going rate for each. The footage also showed young boys serving as tour guides, apprentice pimps who were trained to lead customers into the recesses of the brothels, where the youngest girls were being held.

These young girls were forced to smile; after vicious beatings they knew the consequences of noncompliance. And if the beatings weren't convincing, the brothel owners reminded the girls that they knew their families and had full access to bring them harm. The footage of these girls, taken in 2003, contained the first images I (Bethany) had ever seen of trafficking victims.

The girls had been trafficked to a town in Cambodia where the entire village—fourteen square blocks—was dedicated to the lucrative industry of selling children for sex. If ever there was a place in the world that I could point to as evidence of how deeply this world is "not the way it's supposed to be," this little village in Cambodia was it.

In my mind's eye the footage of these girls morphs into images of children from East Africa—children who belong to a woman named Grace. Grace's husband died of AIDS, and in the wake of this tragedy she was threatened by her own in-laws, who attempted to take the only possession she and her children had left—their one-room home and the land surrounding it. Land is critical to life for Grace and so many widowed women in countries throughout East Africa. Land enables them to grow and harvest food to eat and to sell in order to pay school fees and get access to basic medicines. Even the smallest plot of land and even the most ramshackle of homes are precious commodities for women like Grace who have no other means for survival. Grace's tiny home contains the entirety of her possessions, her land the only inheritance she has to offer her children. She is vulnerable not only in her poverty but also because she has no one to protect her from violent exploitation now that her husband has died. Even though Grace's land legally belongs to her, there are many in her own community (including those in her husband's family) who could easily profit from threatening to harm Grace and her children and claiming her land as their own without paying for it. For thousands of years, people have exploited widows and children, knowing they can get away with it.[1]

One night when Grace was not home, her in-laws began breaking through the walls of her house, working to tear it down brick by brick as her children huddled in a corner. As I recall the images of Grace's home and the gaping destruction of the front wall the words of Jesus come to mind: "They devour widows' houses. . . . Such men will be severely punished" (Mark 12:38, 40).

The home belongs to Grace. By *law* in her country no one has the right to violate her property and destroy her future. But if no one protects Grace, if no one stands up for her by enforcing the law against those who want to take advantage of her, Grace and her children are utterly vulnerable to the lies and force of anyone with more power than she has. Grace and her children share this plight with millions of other women and children who have been widowed and orphaned by the AIDS epidemic and left open to attack by opportunistic neighbors and family members.[2] Without property of their own, families like Grace's are left destitute. My colleagues in East Africa know children who have become crippled from malnourishment and carry with them the names of children who weren't able to survive at all. But poverty is not the primary assailant—it is violence.

From East Africa my thoughts next move to West Africa. Near the coastal ports where for four hundred years Africans were hauled into the bellies of slave ships and chained for transport in the transatlantic slave trade, another form of slavery is thriving today. Young boys are taken from their families and forced to work in the fishing industry on Lake Volta. Tens of thousands of children labor on massive Lake Volta, across more than three thousand square miles of surface water.[3] International Justice Mission (IJM) began investigations on the lake in 2013, and what we know so far is that traffickers or recruiters go to very poor towns and villages looking for young boys because, according to the fishing masters, younger boys are easier to control. Many of the children IJM investigators have met and rescued have lost contact with their families because of the many years of captivity and the long distance from home. Some were brought into the industry at such a young age that they don't remember where they were born.

> *How do we hold in tension the truth of God's goodness and love for justice with the reality of pandemic suffering?*

Fish avoid the heat of the day and so the boys must begin their work before dawn each morning, reeling in nets that were set the previous day. My investigator colleagues at IJM have met children as young as four years old, and the conditions are harrowing. They've seen children with "distended stomachs, scars from beatings and physical abuse, skin diseases, hair falling out, and open sores and wounds." The children who are enslaved (versus being part of a family fishing business) typically have little or no clothing, are visibly malnourished, have vacant expressions on their faces, and are banned from interactions with strangers. Drowning is common as traffickers force the boys into the water to do the treacherous work of disentangling nets from tree stumps and limbs. As a photographer documenting slavery on Lake Volta wrote in *The Atlantic*, "I didn't meet one child who didn't know another who had drowned."[4]

A million girls and boys trafficked for sex each year.

Millions of widows like Grace facing violence and destitution at the hands of their own family and neighbors.

Tens of millions of slaves, such as Boola and the boys on Lake Volta, locked in crushing labor.

Hundreds of millions of girls like Rosa raped.

How do we hold in tension the truth of God's goodness and love for justice with the reality of pandemic suffering? There are countless stories of people all over our world—people created by God for a life of wholeness and flourishing but who instead undergo a living nightmare of injustice. How do we open our eyes and see the dire needs of our neighbors while holding fast to hope in a God who rescues, heals, and restores?

Lament enables us to keep moving forward with perseverance in the justice calling; it is a way to remain deeply connected to the God who loves us and loves justice even when injustice makes us ask the hardest questions of God.

Derailment in the face of suffering is far too often the norm rather than the exception. Even those of us launching forth with the deepest passion for justice and conviction of God's goodness can lose heart and fail to persevere over the long haul. Everyone is vulnerable to derailment; injustice can breed disillusionment and doubt. Suffering can drive cynicism or, even worse, despair.

But God invites us to come to him—not in spite of doubt and derailment but in the midst of it. Woven throughout Scripture is an unguarded type of prayer known as *lament*. To lament is to ask "Why?" and "Why not?" as well as "What are you doing God?" and "Where are you?" To lament is to pour out our hearts, holding nothing back. It is to pray without trying to be more full of faith than we actually are. Lament is prayer that honors the honesty of pain and anger while also honoring the truth that God is the one who reigns and whose *hesed* love never fails. Lament holds in tension all the suffering that seems to make no sense with a determination to believe that God is just. Lament draws us near to God when we are tempted to turn away. Lament enables us to keep moving forward with perseverance in the justice calling; it is a way to remain deeply connected to the God who loves us and loves justice even when injustice makes us ask the hardest questions of God.

To understand and enter biblical lament it is helpful to know Scripture's story of God's people Israel, with whom the practice began. When we wrestle with questions of injustice and suffering and search for footholds to keep moving forward, the story of Israel reminds us that God consistently cares about justice and righteousness, calls us to join him in his passion, invites our honest questions, and brings his judgment so that justice and righteousness can prevail. Israel's story is vast; it fills about three-quarters of the entire Bible, which is certainly more than can be adequately addressed in a single chapter. To get at the heart of the story, we'll take a close look at some key parts: *God's covenant with Israel*, including Israel's fall into slavery and God's great rescue in the exodus; *God's gift of the law*, given to Israel after their rescue and in the midst of their wandering in the desert; and *God's prophets*, with a specific emphasis on Habakkuk and seeking God in the midst of suffering. Knowing Israel's story will provide critical context as we continue our pursuit to understand how the wrong in this world has been and will be set right through the coming of Jesus Christ.

God's Covenant with Israel

Despite the far-reaching ramifications of the fall, God's formation of a covenant with Israel underscores that God's desire for his people has never waned. God's consistent desire is that his people live in union with him and in loving, life-giving relationship with one another, seeking justice and righteousness. God's own righteousness and justice join together with God's *hesed* (lovingkindness) to propel his saving action as he makes a covenant with Abram. God's saving action is what the rest of the biblical story is about, as God begins the work of setting right what had gone so tragically wrong in the fall. God's covenant relationship with Israel shows us that rather than abandoning his vision of flourishing for the created world, God remains committed to seeing his justice and righteousness on this earth.

> *God's covenant relationship with Israel shows us that rather than abandoning his vision of flourishing for the created world, God remains committed to seeing his justice and righteousness on this earth.*

In the events of the biblical story we've explored up to this point, the ramifications for humanity and the world have been universal in scope—the creation of the world, the call to flourish, the fall of humanity, and the spreading stain of sin, which affects all that God made and every layer of shalom. As we turn to God's covenant with Israel in the arc of the biblical story, we shift to a particular person—Abram—and his descendants, the eventual nation of Israel.[5] And yet even in this particularity, the ramifications are cosmic. Through the covenant that God makes with Abram, God promises to bless all people and all generations to come:

> I will make you into a great nation,
>   and I will bless you;
> I will make your name great,
>   and you will be a blessing.
> I will bless those who bless you,
>   and whoever curses you I will curse;
> and all peoples on earth
>   will be blessed through you. (Gen. 12:2–3)

God changed Abram's name to Abraham to reflect that he would be "the father of many" and that those descendants would be God's special covenant people, set apart from all others. An invitation to live in communion with God lies at the heart of the promise God made to Abraham. God's intent was for his holy people of Israel to be set apart, unique in the world, as they lived in right relationship with God and, rooted in that relationship, reflected God's justice and righteousness in their way of life. As God's love and justice were made known through the way Israel loved with justice and righteousness, many nations would be drawn to want to know this God.

The blessing God gives to his people is never solely for the benefit of one community but always connects to God's desire for others to be blessed as well. This is one of the core reasons why the prophets get so upset when the people of Israel fail to live righteously. When Israel fails to love and care for those in their midst as God intended, they fail to reveal the truth of who God is to the wider world.[6] When the people of God mistreat others, God himself is misrepresented.

Ultimately, God will fulfill his promise to bless all people through Abraham and his descendants in and through Jesus Christ. God's people, broken by sin, would never be able to show the fullness of God's love and justice through their witness. By sending a Messiah descended from the genealogical line of Abraham—God's own self through God the Son, Jesus Christ—God fulfills his covenant promise to the one person of Abraham, opening the way for the blessing of *all* people through the one person of Jesus.[7] The coming of Jesus Christ and the Holy Spirit makes the revelation of God's holiness and justice visible in a way that was not possible before. And yet even with the coming of Jesus, we will see that God continues to desire his holy people—now united together through Christ and the Spirit—to be a blessing as they pursue justice and righteousness for others.

In today's world we're quite familiar with "bilateral" agreements that stand only so long as both parties hold to their end of the bargain. The same is true of bilateral covenants; if the conditions are broken by either party, the covenant ends. In contrast, God initiates a covenant with Abram that is completely unconditional and unilateral. By doing so, Abram and all of his descendants can know God's faithful, steadfast, unwavering, and everlasting *hesed* love. No matter what Abram, his children, his children's children, their neighbors, and all future generations do, no matter how unfaithful or sinful any of us are, God is faithful. Even though there will be consequences for disobedience, no consequence can go so far as to break God's promise in his covenant.

God's covenant promises reflect what God had already intended to do because of who God is—a loving, faithful, righteous Creator and Redeemer. In the covenant God makes with Abram, God tells Abram to leave his country, his people, and his father's household and go to the land God will show him. God's promise to the newly renamed Abraham renews his original vision for creation (Gen. 17). Abraham and his wife, Sarah (formerly Sarai), who have been barren up to this point in their lives and are past childbearing age, are told they will be given the gift of fertility just as Adam and Eve were given this gift. They are promised a land of their own to live in and steward. They will be called, as God's covenant people, to create, cultivate, and steward a society that is full of justice and righteousness. As God says of the covenant he made with Abraham, "For I have chosen him, so that he will direct his children and his household after him to keep the way of the LORD by doing what is right and just" (Gen. 18:19).

The blessing God gives to his people is never solely for the benefit of one community but always connects to God's desire for others to be blessed as well.

Abraham's descendants eventually became known as the people of Israel, named after Abraham's grandson (Gen. 35:10). They were nomadic until a severe famine forced them to move to Egypt where food had been stockpiled. In Egypt they became "exceedingly fruitful" (Exod. 1:7), in partial fulfillment of God's covenant with Abraham, but Egypt is also where God's people became slaves for many generations, until God took action on their behalf.

In Egypt Israel laments to God in their captivity, and God hears them. They "groaned in their slavery, and cried out, and their cry for help because of their slavery went up to God. God heard their groaning and he remembered his covenant with Abraham, with Isaac and with Jacob" (Exod. 2:23–24). In biblical language *remembering* is synonymous with *acting*.[8] It was not that God had forgotten his covenant with his people but that, in response to the lamenting groans and cries of his people, he put his faithful love into action.

God called Moses to lead the Israelites out of slavery into the land promised to Abraham, a land that the Bible describes as flowing with milk and honey—that is, full of God's abundant provision and delight. As God acts to deliver his people through Moses, God reaffirms the heart of the covenant promise, saying to the Israelites, "I will take you as my own people, and I will be your God" (Exod. 6:7). Once the people of Israel are delivered from slavery in Egypt, they are led into the desert, where God gives them laws to form them more intentionally into his people, in keeping with his covenant promises.

> *In biblical language* **remembering** *is synonymous with* **acting.** *It was not that God had forgotten his covenant with his people but that, in response to the lamenting groans and cries of his people, he put his faithful love into action.*

In the law, God regularly asks Israel to remember that they themselves were once slaves and that God rescued them, calling them to love God and others in light of this remembrance. It is a call to act with gratitude toward God for his gracious rescue. It is a call to act with justice and righteousness toward those in their midst who are in a foreign land, as well as those who are suffering or oppressed. God's rescue of his people from oppression and slavery was meant to shape the very core of Israel's identity and practices as they moved into their own land.

When Israel fails to live according to the law, they are failing to honor the God who rescued them and called them to live his way of justice and righteousness. As Jewish theologian Abraham Heschel writes, "Israel was the vineyard that the Lord had planted. . . . He looked for it to yield justice, but it yielded perversion of justice; for righteousness, but it yielded outrage (Isa. 5:2)."[9]

God's people often fail to live into their identity as God's set-apart people, marked by justice and righteousness. Israel laments in prayer to God when injustice and unrighteousness abound because they have not followed God's law. The law is given by God as a reminder of God's promises, intended as a gift to point them in the way of life they are called to live.

God's Gift of the Law

Through the exodus God led his people out of Egypt into the desert. At Mount Sinai, God made another covenant with Israel when he gave them the law to help them live as God's redeemed people, the people God had rescued from slavery. Obedience to the law was to enable them to live the way of justice and righteousness and be a blessing to others, always remembering they were once slaves and that the God they are following is the one who rescued them. Recognizing that the world is broken and that things are not what they are supposed to be, the law is meant to help God's people, yet full of sin, to live the way of life God intended for them. The word that we translate "law" comes from the Hebrew *torah*, which means instruction or teaching; the law instructs God's people in the way of God or, put another way, what it means to live as God's holy people. When we look at the content of the law, it becomes clear that God's holy people are to be set apart by God dwelling with them and by their active love and pursuit of justice, righteousness, and the flourishing of all.

The covenant that God makes with Israel in giving them the law does not replace or undermine the unconditional, unilateral covenant God made with Abraham. God promised Abraham and his descendants—and therefore the people of Israel now receiving the law unilaterally and unconditionally—that he would be their God and they would be his people and that he would always make a way for them to know him and be blessed in knowing him. In providing the law, God is not laying down requirements that Israel must fulfill *if* they want to be his people. Instead, God begins with who they are *as* his chosen and rescued people and then shows them how to live in light of this identity. The law is not a way for them to reach God but rather the way to live because they already belong to God.

God is essentially saying, "I am the Lord your God, who brought you out of Egypt, out of the land of slavery, so that you might live as my people.

> *The law . . . is offered to the people after the exodus to help them live the way of justice and righteousness, in turn enabling them to bless others.*

Therefore, in keeping with who you are as my people, live according to my way. Have no other gods before me, do not make any idols, do not misuse my name," and so on. Connected to these first Ten Commandments, God gives his people the rest of the law in Exodus, Leviticus, Numbers, and Deuteronomy. God promises that his people will be blessed if they keep the law, but if they fail to follow it they will be cursed (Lev. 26; Deut. 27–28). These curses include severe consequences, such as being exiled from the land that God gave them. Yet even as they face the consequences that come as a result of their disobedience, they will still be God's covenant people because their relationship with God depends not upon their faithfulness but upon God's loving kindness (*hesed*).

How the Law Functions

Many Christians perceive the law as largely negative in its purpose, primarily intended to show the Israelites that they were not able to keep God's commands on their own and therefore needed God's grace. In this sense, the law is seen as the opposite of grace. But to pit law and grace against each other is to risk missing the truth that God's giving of the law is a gracious act.

John Calvin's work is helpful in understanding the law as a gift that, inextricable from grace, strengthens us toward lives of justice and righteousness. He identifies three functions of the biblical law that come through Moses: the law convicts, restrains, and strengthens. First, the law offers a reflection of God's righteousness and what God's righteousness requires of his people. In so doing it serves as a mirror that shows us how far short we fall of God's righteousness on our own. This in turn helps us to "flee to grace" as we see how much we are in need of a savior.[10]

The second function of the law is connected to civil law in its function of restraining evildoers and protecting the community from injustice. The laws of society play an important role in preventing people from committing crimes by setting out consequences and punishments for the breaking of laws. As Calvin notes, this function of the law does not transform people into those who love justice and righteousness. Instead, it plays a more limited role in restraining those "who are untouched by any care for what is just and right unless compelled by hearing the dire threats in the law."[11] This function of the law is a gift that God provides to help societies function, but it does not come close to what Calvin calls the "proper purpose of the law."[12]

The third and principal function of the law, as Calvin sees it, is to instruct God's people in the nature of God's will and strengthen them in their obedience to God's will and ways. It serves a positive function, even "among believers in whose hearts the Spirit of God already lives and reigns."[13] While the Bible promises that the law is engraved on the hearts of those who know Christ (Jer. 31:33; Heb. 10:16), Calvin insists that the written law contained in Scripture itself also benefits Christians.

> *To pit law and grace against each other is to risk missing the truth that God's giving of the law is a gracious act.*

The laws given to Israel involve instructions for sacrifice and worship so that the Israelites could be reconciled to God and honor their union with him. The laws include guidelines for how humans can live with justice and righteous treatment of one another, instructions to make sure all who live in their midst are looked after (especially the most vulnerable, such as migrants, widows, and orphans), and rules to govern their interaction with the land. Simultaneously wide-ranging and specific, the laws address everything from how to plant and harvest the land to how to make sure poor people are treated fairly in the judicial system and how the high priest can make atonement on behalf of the people one day a year.

The law of the Old Testament, or Hebrew Scriptures, embodies "the rule of perfect righteousness." This "perfect teaching of righteousness" possesses what Calvin calls "a perpetual validity."[14] Scriptures like Psalm 119 draw us deeply into the fruit of meditating on the law. When we open our eyes to see "wonderful things" (119:18), longing for the law and treasuring it like "great riches" (119:14), we learn more fully the nature of God's righteous will and ways, which in turn awakens and strengthens us to draw near to God even in the midst of injustice and suffering, to follow God's will and ways.

Jesus and the Ten Commandments

We can long for the law and long to follow its ways because the law reflects the character of God, the lawgiver, which is the very character that we today (as the people of God) are still called to reflect. In meditating upon the law, we are able to see more clearly and fully the justice and righteousness of God that we are called to reflect. Furthermore, because Jesus Christ fulfills the law, he is both the best interpreter of what the law is intended to teach and the way in which we gain power to obey the law.[15] As theologian Todd Billings points out, Christ is the embodiment of justice, the embodiment of the law of love.[16]

Jesus did not come to abolish the law and the teachings of the prophets, but to fulfill them (Matt. 5:17–20). In the New Testament (new covenant) teachings Jesus asks us to continue to look at these commands from the Old Testament (old covenant) to learn what it means to live with love toward others. While Christ's fulfillment of the law and the prophets means we don't have to worry about seeking our own righteousness through the keeping of these commands, this doesn't mean the law is no longer relevant. Jesus's fulfillment of the law is in harmony with God's desires for creation; the law given to Moses is a reflection of God's ongoing desires for his people and creation to live in justice and righteousness. Billings writes, "God's law . . . is the fulfillment and restoration of God's created purposes, a fulfillment that configures the love of neighbor, and the neighbor's wounded body, as part of a restoration of communion with God."[17]

> *In meditating upon the law, we are able to see more clearly and fully the justice and righteousness of God that we are called to reflect.*

When the Pharisees ask Jesus to name the greatest commandment in the whole of the law, Jesus answers, "'Love the Lord your God with all your heart and with all your soul and with all your mind.' This is the first and greatest commandment. And the second is like it: 'Love your neighbor as yourself.' All the law and the Prophets hang on these two commandments" (Matt. 22:37–39; Lev. 19:18; Deut. 6:5). The Ten Commandments in Exodus 20:1–17 and Deuteronomy 5:1–22, as well as the whole of the Torah, correspond to these two great commandments. The first four commandments offer instructions on how to live in a loving and honoring relationship with God (the basis from which Jesus teaches the "greatest commandment" to love God). The next six are the basis from which Jesus teaches the second-greatest commandment, as these are each concerned with loving our neighbor and give guidelines for living well with one another.

Jesus's fulfillment of the law through his life, atoning death, and resurrection confirms God's ongoing desire for his people to love both God and neighbor, which is made possible by the grace of God in Christ. True faith implicates us in loving our neighbor. As Paul writes, "It is by grace you have been saved . . .

not by works" (Eph. 2:8–9); in the same breath he
continues his argument by emphasizing that we
were "created in Christ Jesus to do good works"
(Eph. 2:10). Good works flow from faith—the two
were never meant to be separated. Love of God
and conformity to God's law are connected to a
way of life that provides the most fruit for our
neighbors. Moreover, Christ shows us that our
neighbors are not limited to the people in our im-

> *The law makes clear that love of God and love of neighbor are deeply interconnected.*

mediate vicinity but include "the whole human race without exception."[18] The
law makes clear that love of God and love of neighbor are deeply interconnected.

Laws of Justice

The Ten Commandments show that love of God is connected to love of
neighbor. We can see more specifically how God calls his people to love others
when we look closely at the laws that relate to treating others justly. These
laws give content to the way of justice and righteousness that God calls his
people to live.

Biblical scholar Bruce V. Malchow places these laws regarding the treatment of others in three broad categories. One kind of law opposes the
mistreatment of others (such as orphans and widows) and instructs Israel
to love and treat fairly the foreigners in their midst.[19] For example, God
tells his people, "When a foreigner resides among you in your land, do not
mistreat them. The foreigner residing among you must be treated as your
native-born. Love them as yourself, for you were foreigners in Egypt. I am
the LORD your God" (Lev. 19:33–34). For the Israelites, loving their neighbors
had tremendous social and economic implications because it meant treating
those in their midst as they would have wanted to be treated when they were
foreigners in Egypt.

A second kind of law more specifically governs actions that could result
in the poor being *deprived*. These laws include regulations that ensure
clothes used as collateral for a loan are given back before sundown so that
everyone has a way to stay warm overnight, prohibitions against collect-
ing interest on loans given to the poor, and guidelines for fair treatment
in courts of law.[20] God's careful attention to the needs of the poor in such
laws is striking:

If the neighbor is poor, do not go to sleep with their pledge in your possession. Return their cloak by sunset so that your neighbor may sleep in it. Then
they will thank you, and it will be regarded as a righteous act in the sight of
the LORD your God. Do not take advantage of a hired worker who is poor and
needy, whether that worker is a fellow Israelite or a foreigner residing in one
of your towns. Pay them their wages each day before sunset, because they are
poor and are counting on it. Otherwise they may cry to the LORD against you,
and you will be guilty of sin. (Deut. 24:12–15)

The final group of laws calls for *positive actions* toward the impoverished.
Deuteronomy 15:7–11 tells the people not to be hard-hearted or tightfisted
but to freely give whatever a poor person needs, while other passages tell
farmers to leave gleanings in the field so that the poor can have food.[21] The
Sabbath-year practice of allowing the fields to lie fallow (which occurred
every seven years) also falls in this category, although the practice was also
encouraged for the good of the farmland and to remind the people of their
dependence on God, who owns and provides the land.[22] Other positive laws
include distributing the annual tithe of produce
to the needy every third year (Deut. 14:22–29);
including servants and foreigners in the command to keep the Sabbath so that everyone had
the opportunity to rest (Exod. 20:8–11); and
keeping the practice of the Jubilee year, in which
land was to be returned to its original owners
and Israelite bondservants were to be released
(Lev. 25; scholars are not in agreement about
whether the Jubilee was actually observed).[23]

*When God's
people honored
the Sabbath, left
gleanings in the
field, let the land lie
fallow, and looked
out for the good of
others, they were
trusting that God
would provide.*

These laws were intended to form Israel into
a community that lived in keeping with God's
way of justice and righteousness. They spelled
out in specific ways how God's people could
use the power God had given them to seek the
flourishing of everyone in their midst. Israel's
obedience to these laws required them to live in
a relationship of dependent trust on God. When God's people honored the
Sabbath, left gleanings in the field, let the land lie fallow, and looked out for
the good of others, they were trusting that God would provide. As a justice-
seeking community, they were to live in trust that pursuit of God's justice

and righteousness would result in justice and righteousness—the flourishing of shalom—for all.

God's Prophets

Given the fall and the subsequent pervasion of sin throughout humanity, it is not surprising that Israel did not faithfully live the way of justice and righteousness to which God had called them through the law. As N. T. Wright reflects, "The body of the Old Testament carries the deeply ambiguous story of Abraham's family—the people through whom God's solution was being taken forward, composed of people who were themselves part of the problem."[24] In keeping with the unconditional nature of his covenant with Abraham, God did not abandon his people, no matter how far they strayed. But God certainly anticipated Israel's inability to live the way of justice and righteousness, which is evident in the system of offerings and sacrifices that God built into the law to atone for sins and to reconcile the people to himself. Moreover, God provided judges and then kings whose God-appointed task was to promote and maintain justice and righteousness for the sake of the community and the glory of God.

Judges were raised up by God to help God's people when they fell into trouble and suffered oppression for failing to live the way of God outlined in the law. These judges did not regularly rule the entire nation as a king would but were called by God when there was a particular need for God's people to be saved "out of the hands of their enemies" (Judg. 2:18). Eventually God's people asked for a king so that they could be like other nations. Though they were warned from the start that these kings would not rule with the justice God had in mind for his people, Israel nevertheless begged for a king, and God conceded (1 Sam. 8). So began the time of the kings within Israel's history; Saul was the first to be anointed (1 Sam. 10) and then David, with whom God made a special covenant (2 Sam. 2 and 7). Generation after generation of more or less corrupt, unjust kings followed until Jerusalem fell, the temple was destroyed, and the people of God were sent into exile in Babylon as a curse for failing to live the way of justice and righteousness that God had laid out for them in the law (1 and 2 Kings).

Throughout this time, God sent prophets to the judges, the kings, and the people to call them to live God's way of justice, righteousness, and love. Prophets such as Samuel, Nathan, Isaiah, Amos, Hosea, Micah, Jeremiah,

Ezekiel, and Habakkuk were called by God to speak God's words of rebuke and repentance—words filled with righteous anger and dismay over how the people of God were living. As Jewish theologian Abraham Heschel writes, "The fact that filled the prophets with dismay was not the absence of adequate Laws, but the absence of righteousness."[25] We see this reflected in the words of the prophet Isaiah:

> See how the faithful city
>   has become a prostitute!
> She once was full of justice;
>   righteousness used to dwell in her—
>   but now murderers!
> Your silver has become dross,
>   your choice wine is diluted with water.
> Your rulers are rebels,
>   partners with thieves;
> they all love bribes
>   and chase after gifts.
> They do not defend the cause of the fatherless;
>   the widow's case does not come before them. (Isa. 1:21–23)

Prophets beckoned and even berated Israel's rulers and God's people to live as set apart and holy according to God's law. They pointed God's people to the way of justice and righteousness. They reminded kings of their calling to uphold and restore justice and to live with righteousness. But the kings and the people of God consistently defied God.

God, in his active loving-kindness (*hesed*), steadfastly sought to be reconciled to his people again and again.[26] Yet even as God pursued reconciliation with his people, the reality of judgment did not fall to the wayside—a reality that the prophets make clear. As we read in 2 Chronicles, "The LORD, the God of their ancestors, sent word to them through his messengers again and again, because he had pity on his people and on his dwelling place. But they mocked God's messengers, despised his words and scoffed at his prophets until the wrath of the LORD was aroused against his people and there was no remedy" (2 Chron. 36:15–16). The consequences that resulted from the people's failure to pursue justice were severe: the temple was destroyed; the promised land was overtaken by foreign powers; and all of God's people were driven into exile as strangers in enemy territory. Even the prophets themselves—the very ones who had been warning the people to repent, lest these things come to pass—cried out in lament and questioned the severity of God's actions.[27]

And yet *again*, God's faithfulness propels him to right the wrongs of the world, even when those wrongs are being inflicted by the people he calls his own. The end goal of God's action is justice—the restoration of life and flourishing among God's people and through God's people to the entire created world.

> *God's faithfulness propels him to right the wrongs of the world, even when those wrongs are being inflicted by the people he calls his own.*

Waiting on the Messiah

In the midst of their prayers of lament and their calls for the repentance of God's rulers and people, the prophets were ultimately waiting for God to act to redeem and reconcile that which was broken and ruptured. The prophets believed and promised the people of God that God was coming, giving them hope in the midst of injustice, brokenness, and even exile. Among these promises was the anticipation of a Messiah who would

> reign on David's throne
>   and over his kingdom,
> establishing and upholding it
>   with justice and righteousness
>   from that time on and forever. (Isa. 9:7)

The promises included hope for "the day of the LORD" (Joel 2:1, 11, 31), a day of judgment anticipated by the prophets in which God would judge and save, consuming evil and ushering in a day of glory.[28] This judgment was considered a good thing, for it would offer God's deliverance and salvation; God would do everything needed to right all of the wrongs committed by and against his covenant people.

As Christians we believe that Jesus Christ was the Messiah promised by the prophets, the king who God had promised long ago would rule with justice and righteousness. We believe that in and through Christ, God answered every lament and set right all the wrongs of the sinful world, bringing his judgment against evil and sin and offering deliverance and salvation to all the people of the world.

Indeed, Christians believe that each of the covenants made by God is fulfilled in and through Jesus Christ. In fulfillment of God's covenant promise to Abraham, we believe that Christ ushered in God's kingdom for all the earth and all peoples of the earth, that all people might be blessed as they come to know God as their God. In fulfillment of God's covenant with Moses, we believe that Jesus Christ perfectly embodied and fulfilled the justice and righteousness of the law. In fulfillment of God's covenant promise to David, we believe that Jesus is our Messiah and King, delivering us from our captivity to sin and bringing his kingdom of justice and righteousness to all the world.

By taking the full weight of sin and all lament upon himself, in fulfilling all of these covenant promises, Jesus ushered in a new covenant in which God promised that his people would be renewed and transformed (Jer. 31:31–34; Ezek. 36:24–28; Heb. 9:15).[29] Because of the saving work of Jesus Christ and the gift of the Holy Spirit, the new covenant has a transforming power that the old covenant never had (2 Cor. 3:7–18). Through Jesus Christ and the Holy Spirit, we can finally be formed into the holy people of God, living God's way of justice, righteousness, and love.

Following the Prophets

As we follow Jesus Christ today, seeking to live God's way of justice, righteousness, and love, one of the great gifts we receive from the story of Israel is the witness of Israel's prophets. The writings of the prophets blaze a trail forward for us as we pursue the justice calling and grapple with a world full of suffering and injustice. They open the door wide for us to lament—to mourn and to wrestle with the pervasiveness of corruption and the overwhelming range of needs in our world. They invite us into prayers and cries and promises that can guide us as we wrestle with God. They remind us that even in the deepest times of lament we can know with certainty that all has been and will be made right through Jesus's ultimate victory.

Like Israel, we fail to follow as God leads. Again and again, the call to know God and to live God's justice goes unanswered as we whirl about in the chaos of our lives and the suffering that surrounds us. Our neighbors know loneliness far more than they know our love. Our enemies know our vengeance far more than mercy. The vulnerable in all corners of the planet—whether in our backyard or on a distant continent—know violence far more than healing. Even in our own lives, many of us know a depth of pain to which we can hardly bring words.

As in the time of the prophets, we see pervasive corruption and negligence in public justice systems. Though good laws have been made all over the world to combat slavery, rape, police abuse, and the destitution of widows, these laws are not enforced, especially in regions populated by the very poorest people. Those with the mandate to enforce laws and protect the most vulnerable members of their communities all too often use their clout to shield lawbreakers or reinforce a status quo that favors those in power.[30]

When Israel's suffering increased and injustice festered as the people failed to listen, over and over again the prophets responded by lamenting before God. As we see suffering and injustice and fail to listen today, there is just as much cause for us to lament. Reading the laments of the prophets, we need to keep in mind that these ancient prophets can show us how and why we need to face the brokenness of sin head-on. The lamenting into which the prophets invite us is an invitation to a way forward. To lament is to wait upon the Lord for him to act, but it is a waiting that moves—a waiting that is also a seeking, a longing, and a pursuit. As King David sings,

> I waited patiently for the LORD;
>   he turned to me and heard my cry.
> He lifted me out of the slimy pit,
>   out of the mud and mire;
> he set my feet on a rock
>   and gave me a firm place to stand. (Ps. 40:1–2)

Habakkuk Teaches Lament

Calling out to us across thousands of years, the prophets show us that asking "why"—the core question of lament—is not a betrayal of faith. Directing our cries of lament to God can become a bold demonstration of faith, an acknowledgment of who God is and a determination to draw near to God rather than pull away. Habakkuk is a prophet whose writings open a deeper

> *To lament is to wait upon the Lord for him to act, but it is a waiting that moves—a waiting that is also a seeking, a longing, and a pursuit.*

understanding of the life-giving, oxygen-rich reality that God is far bigger than our questions and that questioning God is not fundamentally an act of distancing ourselves from God. Even in the midst of Habakkuk's anguish, his questions stand alongside his declaration of the glory of God's person. Habakkuk's conversations and pleadings with God show that God invites our questions and pleas. Rather than enveloping ourselves in despair and silence, locking ourselves in hidden hurt and questions we are too ashamed to ask, we can unabashedly draw near to God and ask "why."

Our best understanding of the timing of Habakkuk's prophecy dates the text's authorship right around the turn of the sixth century BC. In Habakkuk's day the people of Israel were living in the midst of horrible violence and injustice—neighbor fought against neighbor, town against town, nation against nation. In hindsight, we know that the pain Israel was experiencing in the days of Habakkuk's prophecy was only the beginning of even greater darkness and suffering to come. Even as Habakkuk pleaded with God about the suffering all around him, even as he proclaimed the promise that God would come with healing and restoration, even as he rejoiced in the midst of misery, the worst was yet to come.

> *Asking "why" of God is not a betrayal of faith. Directing our cries of lament to God can become a bold demonstration of faith—a determination to draw near to God rather than pull away.*

Habakkuk's prophecy came just as Israel was about to be ransacked by the Babylonians; Jerusalem would soon be conquered, and the people of God would be forced into what we now know as the Babylonian captivity—a period in the life of Israel in which they were deported from the promised land and made to live in exile for seventy years. Habakkuk offers a picture of what it looks like and means to cry out to God in the midst of suffering and violence and to persevere in crying out to God even when the suffering and violence increase.

Habakkuk questions God at a deeper level than many of us would be willing to go, and in doing so he opens the door for us to follow. When he asks, "LORD, are you not from everlasting?" (Hab. 1:12), he borders on sarcasm, asking a rhetorical question that is best understood as an outright accusation of God. As Tim Keller explains, it's as if Habakkuk is saying, "I thought you were infinite, but clearly you're not."[31] But even as Habakkuk contends with

God and protests God and even accuses God of not being who God says he is, Habakkuk *never stops talking* with God or seeking to hear God. Habakkuk never walks away. In his anger and anguish and confusion and tears, Habakkuk keeps moving *toward* God.

Look at what emerges in Habakkuk's cries as he moves toward God in the midst of his railing anger at God: "My God, my Holy One," and then again, "my Rock" (1:12). Habakkuk claims God as *his* God.

Habakkuk shows us that when we call out to God as *our* God rather than treating him as some distant deity who we want to "do stuff" for us (a "cosmic butler," as Gary Haugen often quips), we are drawing near. We are moving into the reality of what God has been telling us about ourselves all along: that *we are his*; that he pulls us out of the muck and mire; that he is our rock.

Even as Habakkuk declares who God is, he does not soften his words as he lobs his complaints:

> How long, LORD, must I call for help,
>   but you do not listen?
> Or cry out to you, "Violence!"
>   but you do not save?
> Why do you make me look at injustice?
>   Why do you tolerate wrongdoing?
> Destruction and violence are before me;
>   there is strife, and conflict abounds.
> Therefore the law is paralyzed,
>   and justice never prevails.
> The wicked hem in the righteous,
>   so that justice is perverted. (1:2–4)

Habakkuk shows us how to cry out to God in the midst of suffering and violence, to persevere in prayer even when we cannot see any way forward.

Habakkuk's Three Moves

As Habakkuk fights to persevere in drawing near to God (when he was likely tempted to curse God instead), he makes three critical moves that buttress

> *In his anger and anguish and confusion and tears, Habakkuk keeps moving* toward God.

him against being swallowed by anger and despair. When the pain and suffering seem too much to bear, Habakkuk *laments*, he *stations* himself, and he ultimately *rejoices*.

LAMENT

Habakkuk opens his writing with lament, and his questions pervade the book (paraphrased):

> How long, Lord?
> Where are you?
> Why are you letting this violence continue?
> Why do I have to see this?
> Why are you tolerating any of this at all?
> Do you even hear me when I cry to you?
> Do you see any of this?
> Do you care at all?
> Where is all the power I thought you had?

Habakkuk asks deep, haunting questions that are not answered in the space of his lifetime. We too have deep, unanswered questions for God and one another. Some questions will become clear in our lifetime, and others will not. But whether we experience God's answers in the ways we long to experience them does not change who God is, and neither does it change the unshakable reality that God is good and that his love for us endures forever.

Emmanuel Katongole and Chris Rice describe biblical lament as wholly distinct from despair and nothing akin to whining, grumbling, arguing, or shouting into nothingness. What makes lament distinct from other forms of complaint or despondency is the intentional direction of lament, the subject to which lament points. Lament is "a cry directed *to God*. It is the cry of those who see the truth of the world's deep wounds and the cost of seeking peace. It is the prayer of those who are deeply disturbed by the way things are."[32]

Together, we need to learn the language of lament before rushing to try to find solutions for the problems we see. Lament opens the way for us to name the brokenness, to truly sit and mourn with those who mourn. Lament helps us to become aware of ways that we might be contributing to the problems we see, and it prepares the ground for the long-lasting but slow-going work of transformation.[33]

STATION

After crying out to God a second time in rage and doubt, Habakkuk stations himself on a rampart to await God's response concerning his complaint. Habakkuk leaves behind all the distractions that surround him and plants himself in a place where his sight is elevated—an act that is both a sign of Habakkuk's eagerness to hear from God and his confidence that God will respond to his complaint.

And God does respond, but not as Habakkuk might have hoped.

God replies, "Keep waiting." God reiterates that he will bring a vision to Habakkuk but prepares him to know that it may not seem to come quickly enough: "Though it linger, wait for it"; "If it seems to tarry, wait for it" (2:3 NRSV); "If it seems slow, wait for it" (ESV).

You might be familiar with this kind of response; in certain seasons of our lives, many of us feel like we've received nothing more than a "keep waiting" admonition from God. It can be deeply frustrating and confusing. Like Habakkuk perched on his rampart, waiting on God even as the fall of Israel to Babylon was still to come, thundering over the horizon, we rarely know how long the wait will be for God to answer our prayers, or what we might have to endure in the meantime. But what we do know is that the Lord promises to meet us in our waiting. For all of their bold exhortations and lamentations, the prophets were deeply aware that justice and the ultimate coming of the Messiah would not be realized by their own efforts. What marked their ministry was their obedience to God's call to wait. The prophets actively waited for God to move, for God to redeem and reconcile everything that was broken and ruptured through injustice.

Some of the most powerful lessons I (Bethany) have learned about what it looks like to persevere in prayer, with a waiting that moves, have come from my colleagues at IJM who serve in the most violent and poverty-ridden regions of the world. They know what it's like to go into places where justice is warped and the fall seems to prevail. They know what it means to dig themselves out from the discouragements and distractions of the pervading reality, to get to a high place, and to station themselves as they wait for God's justice to be made known. But even for those of us who are not on the front lines facing the most brutal forms of injustice firsthand, we are invited to stand together with those who are suffering, to station ourselves with those who are putting their own lives in the balance to intervene, and to wait on the Lord together.

In Habakkuk 2 we see that, as Habakkuk waits, God eventually begins to speak. God asks Habakkuk to write down the vision that he receives from

God. In response to Habakkuk's first complaint (that the injustice within Israel is taking place at the hands of their own leaders), God tells Habakkuk that he has been watching what is happening and has been preparing a response. God will send the Babylonians to Israel, and he will use the Babylonians to bring judgment on Israel for their unjust living. But this answer does not in any way satisfy Habakkuk because the Babylonians themselves are an unjust people. So Habakkuk offers a second prayer of lament; he complains that God would send such a wicked people to execute judgment and questions how a holy God who cannot tolerate wrongdoing could allow his own people to be punished by people who disregard God altogether.

God responds to Habakkuk again, assuring him that the wickedness of Babylon will not ultimately prevail. God promises that his reign is over all people, including Babylon, and that his final victory will extinguish all injustice. God's ultimate victory may be hard for Habakkuk to see as he waits on his rampart, but whether or not Habakkuk can see beyond the destruction to come, he knows that he can wait in hope and trust that God's justice will reign. God's glory will be made known to all the earth as God sets all things right.

We rarely know how long the wait will be for God to answer our prayers, or what we might have to endure in the meantime. What we do know is that the Lord promises to meet us in our waiting.

Ramparts are few and far between in most societies today. But what could it mean for us to "station" ourselves? What could a rampart represent in our own lives, and what would be the point of getting up on top of it? What is the role of waiting when everything around us begs for action? Can waiting itself be an act?

International Justice Mission founder Gary Haugen and I taught on the book of Habakkuk at a recent Global Prayer Gathering. In his own grappling with the somewhat abstract idea of "stationing," Gary came to understand that a "rampart" can be any place that we go to see reality more clearly. And *unlike* Habakkuk, as a body of Christ more often than not our ramparts need to be places that we go to with others. Gary called each of us first to *know where* the rampart is that we will run to, to *guard* that rampart, and to find *strength* and stability as we stand together before the Lord and allow him to help us see more clearly. Every time we return to our rampart to station ourselves and wait on the Lord, we will see more clearly that our prayers do matter. Why God has so determined that our prayers matter is a mystery. The God of the universe, who called all things into being, does not need our prayers. But God has chosen to invite us into his work, and he has determined that our prayers do and will matter.

REJOICE

Habakkuk begins his writing in lament and anguish, but that's not where he ends. Considering his circumstances, Habakkuk culminates his lamenting and his stationing—almost inexplicably—with rejoicing.

> LORD, I have heard of your fame;
>   I stand in awe of your deeds, LORD.
> Repeat them in our day,
>   in our time make them known;
>   in wrath remember mercy.

> I heard and my heart pounded,
>   my lips quivered at the sound;
> decay crept into my bones,
>   and my legs trembled.
> Yet I will wait patiently for the day of calamity
>   to come on the nation invading us.
> Though the fig tree does not bud
>   and there are no grapes on the vines,
> though the olive crop fails
>   and the fields produce no food,
> though there are no sheep in the pen
>   and no cattle in the stalls,
> yet I will rejoice in the LORD,
>   I will be joyful in God my Savior.

> The Sovereign LORD is my strength;
>   he makes my feet like the feet of a deer,
>   he enables me to tread on the heights. (Hab. 3:2, 16–19)

God's ultimate victory may be hard for Habakkuk to see as he waits on his rampart, but whether or not Habakkuk can see beyond the destruction to come, he knows that he can wait in hope and trust that God's justice will reign.

No matter how much violence and suffering we may encounter—even, or especially, when things seem only to get worse, even if it looks like we have lost everything that matters to us—we need to follow Habakkuk's lead. In the midst of his lament, in the midst of waiting upon God without hearing what he longed to hear, Habakkuk still proclaimed trust in God; he still sought strength in the faithful love of the Lord. Habakkuk chose to rejoice. We can "tread on the heights," going to the places of suffering and hardship that take our breath away and vie to snare our feet and leave us fallen on our faces, and find that by trusting the Lord we yet have the sure footing of a deer.

God has chosen to invite us into his work, and he has determined that our prayers do and will matter.

When we choose to rejoice we choose to remember who God is, remember what God has done, and remember what God will do. To rejoice is to receive grace; we cannot rejoice in lament of our own accord. The psalmist knows this truth. Even as he was in the muck and mire, he knew it was God who would not only pull him out and set his feet on a rock but also be the one to *give* him the song of rejoicing:

> He put a new song in my mouth,
>   a hymn of praise to our God.
> Many will see and fear
>   and put their trust in him. (Ps. 40:3)

The invitation from God to rejoice, even as we tremble, comes as we wait. It comes as we move toward God rather than away. While doing so we trust the sure hope that Jesus is working in and through us and will fully and finally overcome the evil and injustice in this world.

Invitation for Today: Lament

> So you, by the help of your God, return,
>   hold fast to love and justice,
>   and wait continually for your God. (Hosea 12:6 ESV)

Lament is a gift. In the midst of everything going wrong around us—whether in the world at large or in the lives of people whose names and faces we know and hold dear—lament is a gift given to help us hold fast to God. God invites lament because he knows our temptation to turn away rather than toward him in the heat of hardship. Some of us turn away by not talking to God when we experience pain in our lives or see the suffering and evil of oppression at work in the world. Others turn away by pretending they can simply press on with their lives and shelter themselves from the pain they feel or see, seeking to avoid the tension of wrestling with a good God who reigns over a world that is festering in grief. Lament is only the beginning of our journey toward God in hope, but it is a beginning that we can hardly plumb too deeply. Even as we *station* ourselves to wait upon the Lord and determine to *rejoice* in the midst of trembling, in the face of injustice we need to return again and again to lament.

> *Lament is a gift given to help us hold fast to God.*

The more we probe Scripture to see how prophets and leaders and ordinary people lamented their circumstances, the more it becomes clear that God invites our questions and pleadings rather than our despair and silence. God can handle the questions we bring; no question is too shocking or big for God. In the midst of the enslavement of God's people, Moses shows us faith that laments: "Why, LORD? Why have you brought trouble on this people? Is this why you sent me?" He even goes so far as to accuse God of not doing what God has promised, crying, "You have not rescued your people at all" (Exod. 5:22–23).

The psalmists accuse God of not being present in the midst of suffering: "Why, LORD, do you stand far off?" (Ps. 10:1). They show impatience with God's timing, frustration at having to wait, and the pain of feeling forgotten:

> My soul is in deep anguish.
> How long LORD, how long? (Ps. 6:3)

They admit that the ultimate victory of the Lord is not always clear, that defeat often feels much more near: "How long will my enemy triumph over me?" (Ps. 13:2). They argue that suffering and injustice make God look like a fool and ask why God does not show the world the truth of his power: "How long will the enemy mock you, God? . . . Why do you hold back your hand?" (Ps. 74:10–11).

The books of Job[34] and Lamentations echo harrowing questions directly accusing God of being the one who not only allows but also intentionally inflicts vicious suffering. The following excerpt from Lamentations 3:1–18 is one example of the laments found throughout Scripture. Take a few moments to read this slowly—perhaps even out loud—and allow the painful depth of what is being said of God to sink in:

> I am the man who has seen affliction
>   by the rod of the LORD's wrath.
> He has driven me away and made me walk
>   in darkness rather than light;
> indeed, he has turned his hand against me
>   again and again, all day long.
>
> He has made my skin and my flesh grow old
>   and has broken my bones.
> He has besieged me and surrounded me
>   with bitterness and hardship.
> He has made me dwell in darkness
>   like those long dead.
>
> He has walled me in so I cannot escape;
>   he has weighed me down with chains.
> Even when I call out or cry for help,
>   he shuts out my prayer.
> He has barred my way with blocks of stone;
>   he has made my paths crooked.
>
> Like a bear lying in wait,
>   like a lion in hiding,
> he dragged me from the path and mangled me
>   and left me without help.
> He drew his bow
>   and made me the target for his arrows.
>
> He pierced my heart
>   with arrows from his quiver.
> I became the laughingstock of all my people;
>   they mock me in song all day long.
> He has filled me with bitter herbs
>   and given me gall to drink.

> He has broken my teeth with gravel;
>> he has trampled me in the dust.
> I have been deprived of peace;
>> I have forgotten what prosperity is.
> So I say, "My splendor is gone
>> and all that I had hoped from the LORD."

The prayers of lament in Scripture give us the gift of anguished language when we can't find words of our own. And we need to speak; we need to speak aloud to one another during those times when we feel we *are* continuing to talk to God—we're clinging and crying out to him, moving toward him, praying, worshiping, seeking him—and yet we don't experience any response on his part. Just as the passage from Lamentations describes, it can seem that not only is God turning a deaf ear, but he is no longer even present.

Lindsey, a dear friend of mine (Bethany), has been living through a season of excruciating loss, one after another. As difficult as it has been for me to watch her undergo seemingly relentless waves of grief, it is exponentially more difficult for her to endure them. And yet she clings in lament—through anger and confusion—to the very same God whose ways are confounding her. Recently she read the above passage from Lamentations out loud as a handful of us who have been walking with the Lord together since college sat together in quiet witness to her tears. After she read the raw accusations from the passage in Lamentations, she then read Psalm 77:

> I cried out to God for help;
>> I cried out to God to hear me.
> When I was in distress, I sought the Lord;
>> at night I stretched out untiring hands,
>> and my soul refused to be comforted.
>
> I remembered you, God, and I groaned;
>> I meditated, and my spirit grew faint.
> You kept my eyes from closing;
>> I was too troubled to speak.

> Will the Lord reject forever?
>> Will he never show his favor again?
> Has his unfailing love vanished forever?
>> Has his promise failed for all time?

Has God forgotten to be merciful?
Has he in anger withheld his compassion? (77:1–4, 7–9)

When we are brutally honest with God in the midst of true lament, we may find that "rock bottom" does not seem to exist; there can appear to be no end or limit to the grief, no enduring relief for the pain. We need to know that we are not alone in this sense of fathomlessness.

Jesus shows us what prayers of grief look like when the bottom has fallen out. Quoting Psalm 22:1, Jesus utters the ultimate protest of lament. Hanging on the cross in the fullness of his humanity and deity Jesus cries,

My God, my God, *why have you forsaken me?* (Matt. 27:46, emphasis added)

Like Jesus, we can and should turn to the desperate cries of the psalms and the prophets as we grapple for words in our lament. In his own recent book on lament, my (Kristen's) friend Todd Billings, suffering from incurable cancer, reminds us that the book of Psalms was given by God to be the prayer book of God's people, and there are more psalms of lament than any other type of psalm. He encourages us to receive the gift that God has given us through the psalms as "companions in our current sojourn to the heavenly city."[35]

What pain in your own life leaves you raw? What grief would you prefer to avoid altogether rather than face it through lament? Where does the suffering of others intersect with your own heart in such a way that you are tempted either to run or close your eyes? As we allow the laments of Scripture to guide us toward finding words for our own confusion and lament, our prayers might sound something like these:

God, I know you have full power and authority to heal and to rescue and to restore. Why haven't you healed my friend's babies? Why did they each die at birth? What is your plan for her?

Why do you seemingly stand by while children and even entire families are trapped and beaten and sold?

Why didn't you heal my mentor (or my mother, my best friend, my child, my sibling) from cancer? I thought you were the God who can heal all sickness and take away all disease. Why haven't I seen you heal the people I so love?

Why do millions of girls spend their childhoods in brothel dungeons?[36]

Soldiers are using rape as a weapon of war against women and children[37]—why don't you "break the arm of the wicked" as your Word says? How could you allow people to bring this kind of terror on one another?[38]

Why do you stand far off while people who proclaim your name are lined up and beheaded for all the world to see? Aren't you powerful enough to stop the sword?

Why do they have to fear being hurt by those who are supposed to protect them? Why are some people forced to live in fear of violence from the police and other government authorities?

Why are innocent people accosted and rounded up by corrupt authorities, detained without evidence or trial, just because they are poor and vulnerable?[39]

If your perfect love casts out fear, why am I still so afraid? Why don't I have the courage to rise up and follow as you lead? When will I stop faltering in believing you?

Why Lord? We know who you are—we know your promises. You say that you command your angels to guard and protect; you say that through fire and storm and flood you are with us; you say that even though the mountains crash into the sea you are still God, that you will uphold your people and your creation with your righteous right hand. You say that you have loved us with a love that is everlasting, a love from which we can never be separated. Why are there times when we don't see you or feel that love?

Habakkuk cried out "My God, *why*?" Jesus too cried out, "My God, my God, *why*?" In Jesus's cries from the depths of suffering and violence on the cross—the deepest grief ever known—he carried our *whys* with him. And we can continue to carry our questions to the foot of the cross, knowing that through the Holy Spirit Jesus himself is praying with and for us (Rom. 8:26–27).

The psalm Lindsey read to us, Psalm 77, does not end with despair, even as it seems like the psalmist is so close to abandoning hope. Despair causes us to believe that redemption is impossible, but the psalmist knows there is a new song on the horizon. He intentionally moves himself to remember who God is and what he has done: this is the same God who freed his people from slavery in the exodus, who parted the Red Sea and made a way when all seemed utterly impossible.

Then I thought, "To this I will appeal:
>   the years when the Most High stretched out his right hand.
I will remember the deeds of the LORD;
>   yes, I will remember your miracles of long ago.
I will consider all your works
>   and meditate on all your mighty deeds."
Your ways, God, are holy.
>   What god is as great as our God?
You are the God who performs miracles;
>   you display your power among the peoples.
With your mighty arm you redeemed your people,

Your path led through the sea,
>   your way through the mighty waters,
>   though your footprints were not seen. (77:10–15, 19)

Cry out to God with the prophets and the psalmists. Even when you don't see his footprints amid the mighty waters, stand firm. Remember who God is even when you cannot see the truth of who he is in your midst. Rejoice that he is the God who fulfills all that he has promised, the God who saves, the God whose love for us and all of his creation is everlasting, never-failing. All glory will be revealed (Isa. 40:5; Rom. 8:18). Darkness will never be the final word.

5

Live as Saints (Not Heroes)

Justice and Jesus

When I (Bethany) met little Kunthy and Chanda in Cambodia, they were eleven- and twelve-year-old girls living as children should live—going to school, playing, laughing. They were free. But only months earlier, these young girls were living as chattel, kept prisoner by the adults in their lives who profited from their daily rape.

The girls were beaten if they tried to go outside of the brothel in which they were held. They were beaten if they cried while men were having their way with them. To help the customers feel they were getting the most out of the cash they had forked over, the traffickers injected Kunthy and Chanda with narcotics, blunting their resistance and their tears.

Kunthy and Chanda are just two out of millions whose lives have been forcefully and fraudulently converted into a commodity sold to the highest bidder. While their mothers participated in a one-time exchange of money when they sold their daughters into sexual slavery, the traffickers were able to sell and use the girls' bodies virtually without limit.

By now it's probably clear that you don't have to crack a history book to know what slavery is like. Very much alive and festering today, slavery is one of the deep wrongs of the world that needs to be set right. The people of Israel and the prophets of the Old Testament cried out to God to address the

111

injustices of the world. God came to set things right in a more powerful way
than the prophets and the nation of Israel could have imagined; the holy and
faithful God of Israel put his love into action as he came *himself*. In the person
of Jesus Christ, God entered fully into this broken world and in the midst of
the brokenness and injustice showed what holiness, faithful loving-kindness,
and righteousness look like. God in Christ demonstrated the full extent of his
hesed and his righteousness when he gave his life to condemn evil. Through
the saving work of Christ on the cross, God condemned every injustice that
has kept God's world and God's people from God's shalom. Through Christ's victory over sin
and evil, God set and is setting all things right.

> *One thing is clear: Jesus is not calling us to be justice heroes.*

But hearing a story like that of Kunthy and
Chanda, we are quickly reminded of how per-
vasively corrupt the world continues to be. We
hear the call to move toward the darkness, and
we want to grieve for specific people who are
suffering; we are committed to lamenting the existence of slavery and all the
injustice and unrighteousness in this world. But what more can we do as we
wait for God in Christ to make all things new? What more should we do?

One thing is clear: Jesus is not calling us to be justice heroes. Personally,
I (Bethany) recognize that part of my draw to the justice calling is the hope
that I might be a hero, and I've met scores of well-meaning Jesus followers
who have this same hope. We are constantly asking "What can *I* do?" but the
deep reality many of us need to admit to ourselves is that no list of possible
"action-steps" will satisfy us short of the opportunity to show up, in person,
on a rescue mission. Until we get the chance to feel a brothel door being kicked
down with our own feet, witness the police rushing in, and hug the little girls
as we usher them to safety while their slave masters are taken to jail, we will
not be satisfied with any other response so long as our hero-impulse goes
unchecked. While some of the people reading this book *will* be the ones to
go with local authorities in countries across the world and rescue victims of
violence or will play a tangible role in a survivor's road to healing, most of
us will not, and our call to justice is no less strong and resounding than the
call upon frontline justice professionals. And none of us are heroes.

We need to admit the hero impulse to ourselves if we're going to be able to
move beyond it and step wholeheartedly into the unique ways that God has
created each of us to respond to the justice calling. But the hero impulse runs

deep, particularly for those of us who have grown up within American culture. From a young age, our imaginations are shaped by heroes like Superman or Spider-Man, who fight for truth and justice.[1] I (Bethany) can't help but admit the quickening pulse I felt as I heard the wisdom whispered by Peter Parker's uncle from beyond the grave: "With great power comes great responsibility."[2] While there's nothing overtly wrong with these superhero callings to truth, justice, and power wielded with responsibility, our response to God's calling in Jesus Christ to truth, justice, and power will not ultimately make us heroes. Our calling is even better. We are called to be saints.

On the surface, asserting we're called to seek justice as saints might sound even more preposterous than saying we want to be heroes, summoning up as it does all manner of negative connotations in terms of self-righteousness. But in and through Jesus Christ, the calling to be saints is truly not about self-perfection or being better than others, and neither is it a pipe dream you'll futilely spend your life trying to attain. Through the saving love of God in Christ, each of us has been adopted into the family of God (Rom. 8:14–17; Gal. 3:26–29). This means that you are *already* a saint, because all of us who follow Jesus are already part of God's holy and much-loved people. Throughout the New Testament—in Acts, Romans, 1 Corinthians, 2 Corinthians, Ephesians, Philippians, and Colossians through Revelation—we read over and again that we *are* God's holy people in Christ Jesus, holy and dearly loved (Phil. 1:1; Col. 3:12).[3]

> *Our response to God's calling in Jesus Christ to truth, justice, and power will not ultimately make us heroes. Our calling is even better. We are called to be saints.*

As saints, we don't just occasionally fight for truth and justice. By the grace of God, we live the way of truth, justice, and righteousness. As saints, we don't need to rely on our own powers, our own strength, or our own impeccable timing to save the day—lest the victim go unsaved, the train crash proceed unimpeded, or the evil mastermind reign victorious. We do not need to feel the weight of saving the world on our shoulders because we are not the ones who save. We are not the ones who ultimately sets things right. Thanks be to God that Jesus Christ is the one who has set, is setting, and will set all things right. And we get to join him.

The saving love of God in Christ has already set all things right, "for God was pleased to have all his fullness dwell in him, and through him to reconcile to himself all things, whether things on earth or things in heaven, by making peace through his blood, shed on the cross" (Col. 1:19–20). This good news means that through Christ humanity has been reconciled to God. It means that through Christ all the broken things of the world have been overcome. We are still waiting for the fullness of Christ's work to be revealed; this world will one day be made new and will finally reflect God's justice and righteousness. But the work of setting things right nonetheless rests safely and securely with Christ.

As we respond to the justice calling today, we do so not as heroes operating alone, driven by a passion for justice and relying on our own faltering good intentions as we draw on our own strength in an attempt to set things right. Instead we seek justice together as beloved saints. We are God's reconciled and holy people—empowered by Christ and the Holy Spirit, rooted in Christ's victory over sin and evil, and ignited by God's passion for justice, incarnate in his Son.

> As saints, we don't just occasionally fight for truth and justice. By the grace of God, we live the way of truth, justice, and righteousness.

Kunthy and Chanda are living testimonies to the work of redemption and restoration that God desires to bring to all of creation through Jesus Christ. While I remember their laughter and joy as I met them in the security of their aftercare home, I also carry with me the reality that their bodies will always bear the memory of the injustice they were made to suffer: the beatings, the scars from narcotics forced into their veins, and the nightmare of watching money exchange hands as they were thrust into the arms of strangers. But these wounds and scars are not the final word. Kunthy and Chanda have new lives.

The freedom Jesus offers girls like Kunthy and Chanda isn't limited to literal, physical freedom. Jesus offers freedom for tangled and broken spirits, as well as hearts, minds, and bodies. Through his transforming power, Jesus offers freedom from all forms of sin and evil. And the truth is, those of us who desire to seek justice also need to experience for ourselves the freedom and transformation that come in and through Jesus Christ. Each of us needs to be set right with God. Each of us needs to receive the gift of salvation, becoming a part of the family of God.

In *The Dangerous Act of Loving Your Neighbor*, Mark Labberton explains the critical truth that we can't change the world without changing the heart. Citing Martin Luther King Jr., Labberton says, "Jesus didn't tell Nicodemus to keep commandments but said to be born again."[4] Nicodemus's whole being needed changing. Throughout the biblical story thus far, we have seen that God has always cared about righteousness and justice; God has always called his people to seek righteousness and justice. But we have also seen God's people consistently fail in this pursuit. In Jesus, we can finally receive the transformation we need to live as the beloved saints of God, set apart by the love, justice, and righteousness that God gives us in and through Christ.

> *Those of us who desire to seek justice also need to experience the freedom and transformation that come in and through Jesus Christ.*

As we look at the needs of the world more closely and take steps toward darkness in faith, we need the transforming love of Jesus in our lives so that we can be set free to live with righteousness and love with justice. We need the transforming love of Jesus in this world so that our pursuit of justice depends not on ourselves but on the saving work of God, who in Christ sets all things right.

Jesus: Priest, Prophet, and King

How is it that the saving work of Jesus Christ can have such profound ramifications for setting all things right in this world? How can proclaiming what Jesus Christ did through his life, death, resurrection, and ascension two thousand years ago be essential for our lives and for the pursuit of justice today?

One way to try to capture the world-altering ramifications of Christ's ministry is to better understand Jesus as priest, prophet, and king. Locating Christ in all three of these offices helps us to get a bigger picture of the salvation and reconciliation that God accomplished through him. *Messiah* in Hebrew and *Christ* in Greek are both translations of the same word—*anointed*—which refers to the belief that God would anoint this anticipated person to redeem God's people. In the time of the Old Testament, three roles required anointing: priest, prophet, and king. Christ as the Anointed One is the fulfillment of all three. As priest, prophet, and king, Jesus condemned evil and set things right in this world. As the image of the invisible God, Jesus was the embodiment of God's loving-kindness, holiness, justice, and righteousness. What's more, we are invited to become the holy and righteous children of God,

> *How can proclaiming what Jesus Christ did through his life, death, resurrection, and ascension two thousand years ago be essential for our lives and for the pursuit of justice today?*

transformed and called to love and seek justice by the grace of God.

Moving forward, we encourage you to slow down and take time to enter into the significance of Jesus's three roles as priest, prophet, and king. There's a common tendency among Christians across the theological spectrum to emphasize certain parts of Jesus's life and ministry and pay less attention to other parts. Those who are passionate about justice, for example, often focus on our justice calling in light of the language Jesus uses to talk about his new kingdom. Others focus on Jesus the prophet, who embodied a new ethic over the course of his life and continues to provide an example for justice work today. Some strands of the Christian church spend the most time focusing on Jesus's sacrifice on behalf of

our sins, thereby prioritizing his priestly role. All three roles are inextricably connected, however, and it is critical that we hold them all together as we pursue Jesus and respond to his calling upon us as his beloved saints.

Priest

In Jesus Christ the justice of God was at work setting all things right. Through Christ, the judgment of God against all that injures and distorts God's creatures, God's world, and God himself was executed. Evil was condemned and judgment was passed, but upending all expectations, the Righteous Judge displayed the full extent of his righteousness by becoming the one judged in our place. In an unprecedented move, Jesus Christ became the great high priest who offered himself on the cross as the sacrifice of atonement (Heb. 9–10). "The Righteous One" became the atoning sacrifice for our sins and the sins of the whole world (1 John 2:1–2). In so doing, God in Christ vanquished all sin, set right everything that had gone wrong, restored peace and wholeness, and reconciled all things (Col. 1; 2 Cor. 5). Jesus demonstrated God's justice and righteousness and became the one who justifies so that those who believe in him might themselves become the righteous people of God (Rom. 3).

The significance of Jesus's sacrifice on the cross connects to a larger biblical tradition rooted in the Hebrew priesthood. In the Hebrew Scriptures, God set apart certain men to serve as priests, which meant that they served as mediators between God and humanity (Exod. 28–29). While there were a number of different kinds of offerings in which priests represented the people of Israel to God and then represented God back to the people (Lev. 1–6), once a year the priest who was designated the high priest was called to make atonement for all the sins of the Israelites. On the Day of Atonement the high priest performed an elaborate ritual of cleansing and sacrificial offerings in the most holy place (where God dwelled) to atone for the sins of Israel on behalf of the Israelites. After the sacrifices had been offered, blood sprinkled, and a scapegoat sent into the wilderness carrying the sins of the people to a faraway place, the priest offered forgiveness to the people of Israel on God's behalf (Lev. 16).

The book of Hebrews offers a rich exploration of Jesus Christ as our great high priest. In Hebrews we read that since God's children have flesh and blood, Jesus became flesh and blood, sharing in their humanity (2:14). Jesus was "made like them, fully human in every way, in order that he might become a merciful and faithful high priest in service to God, and that he might make atonement for the sins of the people" (2:17). In other words, Jesus's humanity made it possible for him to represent the people to God as the priests had in former generations—for all of humanity. Unlike the priests who offered animal sacrifices day after day or year after year, Jesus made a sacrifice "once for all" (7:27) by offering himself as the perfect sacrifice for the sin of the entire world. Through his resurrection and ascension, Jesus rose victorious over death and all the consequences of sin; the power of God triumphed over evil, setting right all that had gone wrong in the fallen world, even though we have yet to see that fully realized (2:8–9).

Upending all expectations, the Righteous Judge displayed the full extent of his righteousness by becoming the one judged in our place.

As both God and human, Jesus is able to be the high priest who on behalf of humanity gives his own self as the atoning sacrifice for the sin of the world and on behalf of God offers the forgiveness of God to humanity. This connects us to the cosmic victory that Christ has over every power and authority that enables us to depend upon Jesus as we pursue justice (Eph. 1:20–23). Moreover, he enables us to receive the forgiveness and the transforming love of God; we have been forgiven and made holy through the sacrifice of Christ once for all (Heb. 10:10).

> *As we are made clean by Jesus Christ, we are drawn into the family of God and compelled to urge one another on to lives that reflect the love, justice, and righteousness of God.*

Even today, Jesus continues to serve as our great high priest. He has "a permanent priesthood," which means that "he is able to save completely those who come to God through him, because he always lives to intercede for them" (Heb. 7:24–25). Whereas the priests of old entered into God's presence in the most holy place once a year, through Christ's sacrifice of himself *and* his ongoing role as our mediating priest, we can dwell with God in the most holy place—in the very presence of God—as part of the family of God all the time, wherever we are. As theologian Julie Canlis writes, "Our adoption is a true participation in Christ and his Sonship, a Sonship that is part of his ongoing ministry to us at his Father's right hand."⁵ Let's look at the words of Hebrews directly:

> Therefore, brothers and sisters, since we have confidence to enter the Most Holy Place by the blood of Jesus, by a new and living way opened for us through the curtain, that is, his body, and since we have a great priest over the house of God, let us draw near to God with a sincere heart and with the full assurance that faith brings, having our hearts sprinkled to cleanse us from a guilty conscience and having our bodies washed with pure water. Let us hold unswervingly to the hope we profess, for he who promised is faithful. And let us consider how we may spur one another on toward love and good deeds, not giving up meeting together, as some are in the habit of doing, but encouraging one another—and all the more as you see the Day approaching. (10:19–25)

Cleansed and washed clean by the atoning sacrifice of Christ, we can enter the most holy place, living in the very presence of God, with full assurance of our forgiveness. This is not a call to individuals but to all of us in community: as we are made clean by Jesus Christ, we are adopted into the family of God and compelled to urge one another on to lives that reflect the love, justice, and righteousness of God.

Note that our work and good deeds do not come first. We do not become children of God by what we do or by earning our way into the presence of God. Because of the sacrifice of Christ our great high priest, as we are united to Christ by the Spirit we are cleansed and transformed into the holy and beloved children of God. Then we can pursue the things of God by the grace of God, as his people. Through Jesus Christ and the Holy Spirit we have become God's dearly loved children; we cannot become any more beloved based on our actions or efforts. But from our transformed identities and our ongoing sanctification, the Spirit will empower us to do works that reflect who we are as God's children. As Paul says to the church at Ephesus, we are not only saved by faith and not by works, but we are also Christ's workmanship, created to do good works (Eph. 2:8–10). Our identity as God's children comes first and is based on what Jesus has done for us; this, in turn, shapes how we live by the Spirit. Who we are shapes what we do, not the other way around.

> *As we are justified by God through Christ, we receive from God the righteousness we need to live the way of justice and righteousness to which God calls us.*

The Reformed tradition has a term for this truth that who we are shapes what we do: *double grace*. In Christ we receive grace as both forgiveness of our sins (linked with justification, or how we are made right with God) and new life, which enables us to live as the set-apart children of God here and now (linked with sanctification, or how we are made holy). The reconciling work of God in Christ includes both: as we are made right with God in and through Christ, we receive the gift of new life by the Spirit so that we can be transformed into God's holy people who live the way of justice and righteousness. As we read in Paul's second letter to the church at Corinth, "We implore you on Christ's behalf: Be reconciled to God. God made him who had no sin to be sin for us, so that in him we might become the righteousness of God" (2 Cor. 5:20b–21).

Justification connects to the "past" part of our salvation. Our sinful selves are dead because of the saving work of Jesus Christ, which means that because of Jesus Christ's atoning sacrifice, we have been justified before God, declared righteous, pronounced innocent, freed from the consequences of sin, and accounted just. Sanctification connects to the "present" and ongoing part of our salvation; the saving work of Jesus Christ also enables us to be transformed into the holy people of God here and now. Paul acknowledges the importance of both receiving forgiveness and becoming a part of the sanctified people of God when he describes the ministry that God gave him to the gentiles, "that they may receive forgiveness of sins *and* a place among those who are sanctified by faith in [God]" (Acts 26:18, emphasis added). We also see this in one of Peter's letters when he quotes the book of Isaiah: "'He himself bore our sins' in his body on the cross, so that we might die to sins *and* live for righteousness" (1 Pet. 2:24, emphasis added).

> *In Christ we have been both justified and sanctified so that as we are made right with God, we are simultaneously set free to rightly love others.*

In Christ we have been both justified and sanctified so that as we are made right with God, we are simultaneously set free to rightly love others. As theologian Todd Billings writes, "Our life of justice is *inseparable* from our incorporation into Christ's life, a consequence of receiving the double grace in Christ. The new life received in Christ by the Spirit bears fruit in acts of justice in our lives, yet the new life is a gift."[6]

Just as we are given the gift of righteousness and set free to seek righteousness in Christ, so we are given the gift of peace and set free to seek peace in Christ. Paul writes in Romans, "Since we have been justified through faith, we have peace with God through our Lord Jesus Christ" (Rom. 5:1). Before his death, Jesus draws on the standard Hebrew word used for both greeting and farewell, *shalom*, to say farewell to his disciples: "Peace I leave with you; my peace I give you" (John 14:27).[7] After his resurrection, Jesus greets his disciples by saying, "Peace be with you!" (John 20:19)—a common Jewish greeting still used today. With these words, Jesus is not only greeting his disciples but also declaring God's promise of shalom, which is fulfilled in him, the Prince of Peace (Isa. 9:6): "For God was pleased to have all his fullness dwell in him, and through him to reconcile to himself all things, whether things on earth or things in heaven, by making peace through his blood, shed on the cross" (Col. 1:19–20). As William H. Van Doren writes in his nineteenth-century commentary on John,

By sin man is at war with himself, his neighbor, and his God. The only peace therefore which sinful man can ever receive is that which flows from the Lord's death. It is *the peace* which cost Jesus His agony and bloody sweat, His Cross and passion. But it is *perfect peace*; for His mediatorial work is complete, finished, everlasting.[8]

Because Jesus Christ is our peace (Eph. 2:14), we can live at peace with God as the children of God and seek God's wholeness and flourishing for others, ourselves, and this created world.

Prophet

If looking at Jesus the priest helps us see *how* Jesus set things right, then looking at Jesus the prophet helps us see what "right" *is*. Without Christ's life, death, resurrection, and ascension on our behalf, it would not be possible for us to be the reconciled children of God, living with and seeking God's justice, righteousness, and shalom. But it's equally true that without Jesus's life and teachings, we would not know what God's justice, righteousness, and shalom look like. Jesus is the image of the invisible God (Col. 1:15), which means that when we look to Jesus, we see more clearly who God is. Jesus is also the first human to fully live his life as God calls each of us to live, and this means that when we look to Jesus we see more clearly who we are called to be and how we are called to live.

Jesus is not only greeting his disciples but also declaring God's promise of shalom, which is fulfilled in him, the Prince of Peace.

Throughout the biblical story God calls his people to be set apart by their lives of justice and righteousness as they put love in action by seeking shalom and the flourishing of God's world. Each of these calls upon God's people—to holiness, to justice, to righteousness, to *hesed*, and to shalom—is a reflection of God's character. Through the life and witness of Jesus Christ, we can gaze deeply into this character. We must hold up whatever we thought we knew about holiness against what we see in Jesus, the exact representation of God's being (Heb. 1:3). The same is true for justice, righteousness, loving-kindness, and flourishing wholeness. By doing so, we get a picture of how God wants us, the saints of God, to live today because Jesus, while being God, is also the Son of the Father, showing us what it means to live as children of God.

As we explore Jesus as prophet and what that teaches us about who God is and who God calls us to be as his saints, it's critical to emphasize that Jesus did not show us what it looks like to live as God's children and then throw us back on ourselves, leaving us to struggle by our own strength to live up to his example. That is not what it means to be saved by grace. The "hero" approach to life assumes that everything is left up to us and that we depend only on ourselves. Jesus came as the much-anticipated Savior; while he was a prophet preaching repentance, he also came in fulfillment of God's prophecies, offering repentance by the grace of God.

Without Jesus's life and teachings, we would not know what God's justice, righteousness, and shalom look like.

If prophets of the Old Testament revealed God and God's will for his people, then the divine-human Jesus can be considered "the prophet of prophets," revealing not just certain parts of God or the words of God but revealing God himself, the Word made flesh (John 1:14). Jesus did not just point the people to their need for repentance, freedom, and reconciliation; he also made their repentance, freedom, and reconciliation possible.

As we learned in the previous chapter, the Hebrew Scriptures teach that prophets were called by God and anointed with power through the Spirit to speak God's words to his people. They were sent to call God's people to repentance for failing to live with justice and righteousness. Guided by the Spirit, the prophets called God's people to love God wholeheartedly, with a love that manifested itself in loving others rightly and justly. We can see all of these marks of the prophets reflected in the life of Jesus.

Jesus began his prophetic ministry after receiving the gift of the Holy Spirit in baptism "to fulfill all righteousness" (Matt. 3:15). Like the prophets, he preached repentance, declaring that the kingdom of God is at hand (Matt. 4:17). Luke records Jesus in the temple explicitly placing himself in the prophetic tradition by echoing Isaiah's words:

> The Spirit of the Lord is on me,
>   because he has anointed me
>   to proclaim good news to the poor.
> He has sent me to proclaim freedom for the prisoners
>   and recovery of sight for the blind,

to set the oppressed free,
to proclaim the year of the Lord's favor. (Luke 4:18–19)

After reading these words, Jesus boldly proclaims, "Today this scripture is fulfilled in your hearing" (Luke 4:21). Jesus declares that he has been anointed as a prophet to proclaim God's good news to the people.

If prophets were known for proclaiming the words of God to the people of God through the Spirit, what did Christ proclaim through his prophetic ministry? The shorthand answer is "the kingdom of God." The long answer is found by looking at the entirety of Jesus's life and ministry. All of Jesus's life and teachings help us to answer that question.

God's love is put into action when Jesus enters the fallen, broken, unjust world in human form. His willingness to become flesh and enter this world shows us that God's holiness does not keep him separated from the sinful, suffering world. Instead, he draws near, bringing his light into the darkness. Over the course of Jesus's life he drew near to offer healing and flourishing life to the physically and spiritually ill (Matt. 8:1–17, 28–34; Mark 10:46–52). He entered the homes of sinners and tax collectors and shared fellowship at the table with them (Matt. 9:9–13; Luke 19:1–10). He touched lepers (Luke 5:12–16). He showed compassion to prostitutes and adulterers (Luke 7:16–50; John 8:1–11). He forgave sins (Mark 2:1–12; Luke 7:44–50). He prayed, and he worshiped in the temple (Mark 14:32–42; Luke 5:16; 21:37–38). He kept the Sabbath while reclaiming its God-intended purposes (Matt. 12:1–14; John 5:1–18). He healed Jews and gentiles (Mark 7:24–30; Luke 7:1–10). He shared conversation with those who were supposed to be his cultural enemies (John 4). He welcomed little children (Mark 10:13–16). He multiplied food so that everyone could have their fill (Matt. 14:13–21; 15:32–39). He lamented over the sinfulness of Jerusalem, and he cried in the face of his friend's death (Matt. 23:37–39; John 11:32–44). He became angry when the temple was being used for unjust economic practices (Matt. 21:12–17). He demonstrated his power over the

> *Jesus did not just point the people to their need for repentance, freedom, and reconciliation; he also made their repentance, freedom, and reconciliation possible.*

water and the wind (Matt. 8:23–27; John 6:16–21). And he used his power to serve rather than dominate others throughout his life, which culminated in his death on the cross (Luke 23; John 13:1–20).

Throughout his life we see Jesus provocatively addressing the wrongs of the world, whether physical or spiritual. He turned cultural norms upside down in order to seek the flourishing of those he encountered, intentionally seeking out the poor and the marginalized over the rich and the established. His teachings reflect this same commitment: Jesus declares that the poor, the meek, and the mourning are to be considered especially blessed (Matt. 5:3–5). Through his teachings, Jesus declares that he came not to abolish the law or the prophets but to fulfill them, so that through his life and teachings we can see the depth of the justice and righteousness that God longed for us to have when he gave the gift of the law (Matt. 5:17–20). As Paul writes in Romans, "Now apart from the law the righteousness of God has been made known, to which the Law and the Prophets testify" (Rom. 3:21).

The law given through Moses pointed to the justice and righteousness to which God called his holy people, but the teachings that Jesus gives us show even more fully the justice and righteousness we are called to embody and seek as God's holy people today. The law given to Israel told the people of God not to murder, but Jesus tells us that we ought to be so deeply reconciled with our brothers and sisters that we don't even harbor any anger against them (Exod. 20:13; Matt. 5:21–24). The law says that we can take an eye for an eye and a life for a life as a way to seek justice when things go wrong, but Jesus teaches that his economy of justice would have us give generously, share, and go the extra mile (Exod. 21:24; Matt. 5:38–42). As the holy people of God, Jesus teaches us to hunger and thirst for justice and righteousness; to be merciful (think *hesed*); to seek peace (think shalom); to be pure in heart; and to expect persecution as a result of seeking righteousness in this world (Matt. 5:6–12).

Reading the Sermon on the Mount can sometimes feel like an inspiring call to live God's way of justice and righteousness, but it can just as easily feel like an impossible ethic that we can never live out. However, understanding Jesus as the prophet of prophets enables us to receive these teachings as a gift of God's grace to the saints of God rather than a burden we must bear. As a prophet, Jesus already fulfilled each stroke of each letter of the law (Matt. 5:17–18). He embodied every beatitude, from his material and spiritual dependence on God (being poor and poor in spirit) to being insulted and persecuted and having all kinds of evil falsely said against him as he made his way to the cross (Matt. 5:1–12). Jesus turned the other cheek instead of striking back when he was arrested and beaten (Matt. 5:39; 26:47–56; 27:27–31); he went to hell and back on our behalf (Matt. 5:41; 1 Pet. 3:18–20); and he loved his enemies and prayed for those who persecuted him when he prayed from the cross, "Father, forgive them, for they do not know what they are doing" (Luke 23:34; see also Matt. 5:43–48). Jesus demonstrated, through the power of the Holy Spirit, how a human can be righteous and live for justice.

Rather than receiving Jesus's prophetic teachings as a millstone that drags us down because we can't possibly "be perfect . . . as your heavenly Father is perfect" (Matt. 5:48), we can receive the invitation into Christ's perfect way of life through his life, death, and resurrection. Having been justified and sanctified in Christ, we have received the gift of God's righteousness so that we can hunger and thirst for righteousness in this world; we have received the gift of God's peace so that we can be peacemakers (Matt. 5:6, 9).

The grace we have been given through Jesus Christ—and only this grace— enables us to seek first the kingdom of God and his justice and righteousness (Matt. 6:33). Likewise, it is only the grace of Jesus Christ that enables us to follow Christ free of worry as we depend upon and trust in the sufficiency of God's provision (Matt. 6:25–34). As Jesus was teaching that God's will is for us to seek God's kingdom and righteousness above all else, and to live without worry, he was living each moment of his life in full and intimate communion with God the Father through the Holy Spirit. In so doing, Jesus Christ lived out the faithful, trusting, receiving, and dependent life to which God calls all of humanity. Though Adam and Eve were created to live in trusting dependence on God as they stewarded this world, they took for themselves the one thing forbidden to them instead of receiving with gratitude all the good gifts God had given. That began a cycle of humanity seeking their own good over the good of others (like Cain and Abel) and depending on their own strength and seeking their own glory (like those who built the Tower of Babel) instead of relying on God and seeking God's kingdom.

Jesus Christ overcame all of this when, on behalf of all humanity, he offered back to God the love and trust that Adam and Eve failed to offer and the people of Israel failed to offer; and that every one of us fails to offer. Jesus gratefully received from God and the Holy Spirit all the strength he needed to live the way of justice and righteousness faithfully in this world, which culminated in offering his own life as the atoning sacrifice for our sin and the sin of the world (1 John 2:2). Because of his life, death, resurrection, and ascension on our behalf, we can be drawn into the communion that the Father and the Son share as we ourselves become the children of God by the power of the Holy Spirit (Rom. 8:14–17). In and through Jesus Christ and the Holy Spirit, we are restored to right relationship with God so that we might be set free to offer, in gratitude, every part of ourselves as instruments of justice and righteousness (Rom. 6:13). Living as saints instead of heroes means relying not on ourselves but depending together on the grace and power of God as we seek first the kingdom of God and his justice and righteousness.

King

As saints of God, we are children of God, fully loved by him. But there's more: this new identity brings with it a new citizenship. As those of us who were outside of God's covenant relationship with Israel are invited into God's family through the reconciling work of Christ, we become "fellow citizens with God's people and also members of his household, built on the foundation of the apostles and prophets, with Christ Jesus himself as the chief cornerstone" (Eph. 2:19–20). Being a member of God's household is accompanied by a political component as our chief allegiance is transferred to the kingdom of God. Our identity as citizens of God's kingdom is to be more formative than our identity as citizens of a particular place. We are united as citizens of the kingdom of God under Christ our King, the one with the power and authority to set all things right. In reconciling us to God, Jesus sets us free to seek the justice and righteousness of God's kingdom in this world.

During the time of Jesus Christ's life on earth, the covenant people of God were waiting for God to fulfill his promise to send the Messiah to deliver them from foreign rule, since the Roman Empire had invaded Israel. Their expectations for the Messiah had a political shape, not least because God had promised Israel a king in the line of David (2 Sam. 7:12–16). Kings, as God intended them to function, were to restore and protect right relationships within God's kingdom.[9] Within the context of a broken world,

> *Living as saints instead of heroes means relying not on ourselves but depending together on the grace and power of God as we seek first the kingdom of God and his justice and righteousness.*

God expected kings to uphold justice and restore righteousness, although rarely did the kings of Israel faithfully fulfill this role. As they waited for the Messiah, God's people were hoping for a king who would live out this God-intended calling of setting things right by bringing freedom, peace, justice, and righteousness to the kingdom of Israel.

Through God's provision of Jesus as the promised Messiah, God delivered freedom, peace, justice, and righteousness in and through Jesus Christ in ways that went beyond what anyone was expecting in scope and possibility. Christ the King set things right in all the world. Christ the King made it possible for God's justice, righteousness, and shalom to be available to all people. The scope of God's saving work was not limited to the kingdom of Israel (located in a specific time and place), but in Christ was expanded to the kingdom of God, meaning the entire world, over which Christ reigns.

> *When we look at Christ our King we see power used to promote justice, authority used to overcome evil, and personal privilege sacrificed so that all might have the privilege of becoming the children of God.*

The kingdom that Christ ushered in was also marked by an entirely different kind of rule than the kingdoms of this world had known. Jesus used his power to enter the world as a servant, serving others throughout his life and then giving his very life for the sake of others (Phil. 2:6–8). In using his power to bring about justice and righteousness, he took the just judgment of God upon himself, demonstrating that his kingdom is marked by an altogether different understanding of justice and power from the kingdoms of this world. When we look at Christ our King we see power used to promote justice, authority used to overcome evil, and personal privilege sacrificed so that all might have the privilege of becoming the children of God, equal before God through grace and the forgiveness of sins.

God has always been king of all that he created, since he is above and ultimately sovereign over creation. And yet, that kingship has not been acknowledged by humans or visible to the fallen human eye. The kingdom that Jesus proclaims is, as one biblical scholar writes,

> the promised redeeming kingdom of God, where he restores his rule and delivers people from a fallen creation. Such a redeeming kingdom, whose authority and

blessing reaches into all nations, is what Old Testament saints anticipated as far
back as God's promise to Abraham to bless the world through the patriarch's
seed (Gen. 12:1–3), even though they believed that in one sense God ruled over
all nations already.[10]

In bringing the kingdom, Jesus fulfills the promise made long ago through
Abraham that God intended to bless the whole world. As the King who ushers
in this kingdom, Jesus demonstrates that he has the authority and power to
bring justice (as he delivers this world from evil) and uphold righteousness (as
his saving grace enables his followers to live in right relationship with God,
others, themselves, and the created world). In calling us to be citizens of his
kingdom, Jesus calls us to join him in seeking the justice and righteousness
that mark the kingdom that he ushered in.

Anticipation of the kingdom marked the ministry of Jesus Christ before it
began. As John the Baptist prepared the way for Jesus, he proclaimed, "Repent,
for the kingdom of heaven has come near" (Matt. 3:2). Likewise, when Jesus
started his preaching ministry, he "began to preach, 'Repent, for the kingdom of
heaven has come near'" (Matt. 4:17). In Mark the kingdom of God is equated
with the good news of the gospel: "Jesus went into Galilee, proclaiming the
good news of God. 'The time has come,' he said. 'The kingdom of God has
come near. Repent and believe the good news!'" (Mark 1:14–15). In Luke,
proclaiming the kingdom of God is considered central to the ministry given
to the disciples (see Luke 9:59–62; 10:8–12). When Jesus teaches his disciples
to pray, he tells them to pray that God's kingdom will come (Matt. 6:10; Luke
11:2). And at the end of Jesus's life, he is accused of claiming to be Messiah
and King, which ultimately leads to his excruciating death on a cross.

Mary, the mother of Jesus, offers our first real glimpse into the kingdom of
God. After being told she will give birth to the Messiah, who will reign on the
throne of David, she sings a song of praise, which anticipates the deliverance
that God will bring about through this king. She sings of God in his mercy
and holiness scattering the proud and bringing down rulers while lifting up the
humble and filling the hungry with good things but sending the rich away empty
(Luke 1:46–55). Through Mary we see that the kingdom of God connects to
political dynamics as well as the material realities of this world. She believes
without a doubt that God cares about how people actually live and eat and
are treated. Introduced through Mary in the first chapter of Luke, this teaching about the kingdom appears again and again throughout Luke's Gospel.[11]

Looking at the early church in the book of Acts, we see that part of what it means to follow Jesus is to become part of a new people who are unified under the reign of Christ rather than the reigning emperors and kings of the day. We see these political ramifications reflected in the use of the term *ekklesia*, the Greek word that we translate as "church" to refer to the earliest Christians (Acts 5:11). At that time it was a term used to refer to groups of citizens called to assemble for political purposes. The political implications of this new collective identity are also evident in the use of the word *Christian* to refer to the early followers of Jesus (Acts 11:26). While the word literally means "follower of Christ," it implied that those who followed Christ did not follow the emperor and that they viewed Christ, rather than Caesar, as their King and Lord. In this way it was widely acknowledged that the kingdom of God is not separate from the realities of life in this world—that is not merely "spiritual" but also possesses material and social consequences.[12]

As Lord and King, Jesus's life, death, resurrection, and ascension have power to save that includes the forgiveness of human sin and healing all of the ruptures that resulted from the fall. When Jesus sets things right, he addresses all of the broken things of the world that are not the way they are supposed to be. His victory over evil includes every ruptured layer of shalom—from the broken relationship between God and humanity to the brokenness between people, within people, and within the material and cultural realms. Jesus connects forgiveness of sins with the healing of those who are sick; casts out demons; calms a raging storm; and teaches his disciples to love their enemies, share belongings with those in need, focus on being the least rather than the greatest, and avoid the hypocrisy of being clean on the outside and full of greed and wickedness on the inside (Luke 6:20–49; 9:46–50; 11:37–52).

> *More than just acknowledging these layers of brokenness, Jesus (as King) has authority and power to heal them.*

More than just acknowledging these layers of brokenness, Jesus (as King) has authority and power to heal them. Looking closely at the miracles in Luke 8, this authority is particularly evident. When Jesus rebukes the wind and raging waters that caused his disciples (who were seasoned fishermen) to fear for their lives, we see that he has authority over the created world (8:22–25), which places him in continuity with the Old Testament understanding that God has power over the wind and the seas.

When Jesus heals the woman who had been bleeding for twelve years, we see Jesus's authority over disease (Luke 8:42b–48). Her condition made her a social and religious outcast, unable to participate in the religious life of her people. Through her healing she is returned to health and simultaneously restored to relationship with others and God. When Jesus brings back to life the twelve-year-old daughter of Jairus, the synagogue ruler, we see that God can overcome death, that his power is more absolute (Luke 8:49–56).[13]

When Jesus cast out the evil spirit from a man who had been demon-possessed for years, we see Jesus's authority over spiritual principalities and powers that had turned away from the goodness of God (Luke 8:26–39). Jesus's interactions with demons and evil spirits throughout the Gospels give glimpses of these fallen powers, entities that often recognize Jesus and are afraid of the power he possesses over them. Moreover, Jesus's resurrection and ascension solidify his triumph over them.

This passage from Paul's Letter to the Ephesians gives us a sense of Christ's ultimate victory over the spiritual realm, which is not visible to the human eye:

> I pray that the eyes of your heart may be enlightened in order that you may know the hope to which he has called you, the riches of his glorious inheritance in his holy people, and his incomparably great power for us who believe. That power is the same as the mighty strength he exerted when he raised Christ from the dead and seated him at his right hand in the heavenly realms, far above all rule and authority, power and dominion, and every name that is invoked, not only in the present age but also in the one to come. And God placed all things under his feet and appointed him to be head over everything for the church, which is his body, the fullness of him who fills everything in every way. (Eph. 1:18–23)

The suggestion here is that a spirit of darkness had authority within the earthly realm prior to the death and resurrection of Jesus Christ. In Colossians, salvation is described in terms of rescue "from the dominion of darkness," so that we can be brought into "the kingdom of the Son he loves, in whom we have redemption, the forgiveness of sins" (Col. 1:13–14).[14] Paul teaches that through Christ's resurrection and ascension all things have been placed under Christ's feet, including all power, rule, and authority found within the spiritual realms.

While Christ has ultimate authority over the fallen powers that have turned away from God, Paul instructs that until the return of Christ, we need to remember the battle is ongoing: "Finally, be strong in the Lord and in his mighty power. Put on the full armor of God, so that you can take your stand against the devil's schemes. For our struggle is not against flesh and blood, but against the rulers, against the authorities, against the powers of this dark world and against the spiritual forces of evil in the heavenly realms" (Eph. 6:10–12).

Spiritual forces that work for evil rather than good still have power in this fallen world, and we see evidence of the darkness, brokenness, and injustices every day. We want to acknowledge these realities as we work toward justice, which is yet another reason why we seek justice as saints rather than heroes. On our own, we do not have the power that is needed to stand up to the evil at work in the world, but Christ's victory over these fallen powers is sure and secure. Jesus Christ created all authority and power, and he has supremacy and victory over them, no matter how twisted they have become. In Colossians, Paul assures us that Christ's authority is greater than any fallen power because God in Christ both created and reconciled all things (Col. 1:15–20).

While Christ has ultimate authority over the fallen powers that have turned away from God, Paul instructs that until the return of Christ, we need to remember the battle is ongoing.

As the people of God who live in hope of Christ's return, we are reminded that the story is not over. We still see brokenness and injustice in this world even while we believe that Christ has redeemed and reconciled the world. This is often referred to as the "already/not yet" tension within the biblical story: Christ has *already* set things right through his life, death, resurrection, and ascension and *already* reigns as King in this world, but we do *not yet* see that fully realized. When Christ returns, he will fully usher in his kingdom of justice and righteousness. Living as saints of God through the reconciling work of God in Christ and waiting for Christ's return, we are summoned by God to be ambassadors of reconciliation (2 Cor. 5:20), but we are also reminded that the outcome of the story does not depend upon our heroic actions. We are called as God's holy people to join in the story through Christ and the Spirit, but we are not responsible for its outcome. We are to seek the kingdom of God in this world, but we do not need to be the ones to usher it in. That work is in God's hands; he will fully and finally bring his kingdom to this earth when Jesus the King returns.

Invitation for Today: Live as Saints, Not Heroes

"Be holy, because I am holy" (Lev. 11:45). Spoken by God to the covenant people of Israel, these words are rightfully daunting. How can we possibly be holy as God is holy? And yet even after Jesus calls us into the new covenant, Peter reaffirms the importance of these words: "Just as he who called you is holy, so be holy in all you do; for it is written, 'Be holy, because I am holy'" (1 Pet. 1:15–16).

> *How can we possibly be holy as God is holy?*

From the very beginning of the biblical story we see God creating and calling a holy people to be set apart for a special purpose—to love God and one another and to care for this world in keeping with God's vision of justice, righteousness, and shalom. In God's covenant relationship with Israel, we see God's ongoing faithful loving-kindness and ongoing commitment to be in relationship with a holy people who will seek justice, righteousness, and shalom. We see it in the person of Jesus Christ, who embodies God's loving faithfulness, holiness, justice, righteousness, and shalom. And we see it as God ushers in the new covenant, transforming the people of God through the forgiving, cleansing work of Christ so that they can finally live as the holy people of God (Jer. 31:31–34; Heb. 8).

Because of Christ, holiness is not something we have to achieve but something we receive. As Peter puts it:

> You are a chosen people, a royal priesthood, a holy nation, God's special possession, that you may declare the praises of him who called you out of darkness into his wonderful light. Once you were not a people, but now you are the people of God; once you had not received mercy, but now you have received mercy. (1 Pet. 2:9–10)

Because of the merciful loving-kindness (*hesed*) of God in Christ, we *are* the people of God, a holy nation set apart to declare the praises of our redeeming God. Paul's letters remind us again and again: we are already saints because of the saving love of Christ.[15]

The salvation offered in and through Christ is more wide-ranging and all-encompassing than we are often capable of imagining. It is not just freedom from our sin so that we can "get into heaven" after we die; we are saved *into* the family of God here and now. Through the reconciling work of God in

Christ, we are set apart to be saints and freed to live in intimate union with God, in harmony with one another, at peace with ourselves, and in loving stewardship of the created world. In Christ we, the beloved saints of God, are finally set free

> to act justly and to love mercy
>> and to walk humbly with [our] God. (Mic. 6:8)

This is why Jesus Christ is absolutely essential to our pursuit of justice.

In and through Christ, the embodiment of God's faithful love in action, we are finally able to live as God's holy people, living in right relationship with God and out of that relationship loving others and this world as God intended. Jesus is the righteous one, setting right what went wrong in the garden of Eden and sharing his righteousness with us. Restored to right relationship with God, we can now live with justice and righteousness in this world. But we are utterly dependent on Christ, who is "our righteousness, holiness and redemption" (1 Cor. 1:30).

The salvation offered in and through Christ is more wide-ranging and all-encompassing than we are often capable of imagining.

As we live and love with righteousness and justice, we bear witness to God's kingdom. Shattering our conception of righteousness as having to do with individuals self-righteously living morally perfect lives, Jesus tells us that the righteous feed the hungry, offer drink to the thirsty, invite in strangers, offer clothes to those in need, look after the sick, and visit the imprisoned. He says that as we do these things, we are serving God himself and living in anticipation of the kingdom of God, which he will finally and fully bring about upon his return (Matt. 25:31–46).

A friend of mine (Kristen's) who is a professor at a Christian college told me that he takes a quick survey of his freshman students at the start of the semester; he asks them why they think people are Christians. About 80 percent of students respond that people are Christians because they will receive eternal life with God when they die. While this perspective connects with part of the biblical truth about salvation, it fails to recognize our calling to life in Christ here and now. It misses what it means to live as the holy people of God in the kingdom of God today. Jesus did not save us from our sins and then leave us alone, withdrawing from this world to while away his days in the clouds as we pass the days waiting for eternal life. God calls us to seek justice and righteousness here and now as his holy people.

As Latin American minister and theologian René Padilla notes, salvation in Christ is past, present, and future.[16] We have been justified by Christ; our sinful selves are dead, and the eternal consequences of sin have been overcome. But through Christ and the Holy Spirit we have received new selves—"created to be like God in true righteousness and holiness" (Eph. 4:24)—so that we can live and bear fruit as God's children in the present. We also wait in hope for the future when Christ will come again to bring about his full reign on this earth, enabling us to live in full and complete union with God and in harmony with others and the created world for eternity.

> *Salvation in Christ is past, present, and future.*

In my own life, even when I've tried to remember that salvation involves how I live here and now, I default into thinking that it's up to me to learn how to grow in faith, pursue holiness, and seek justice. Or I think that *before* I can be properly considered a child of God, I have to learn how to grow in faith, pursue holiness, and seek justice. This simply does not correspond with what we learn from the Bible about God's saving grace, which is God's gift to us for the past, the present, and the future. God created us to live in dependent trust upon him, gratefully receiving all that we need to live as God's people in this world.

How can the seemingly lofty notion of being saints possibly intersect with the injustices we find in the world today? How can it be good news for girls like Kunthy and Chanda, living as slaves within the sex industry? Don't we need heroes who can rush to their rescue rather than a company of set-apart saints?

Consider the role of the hero. Entering the story at a time of crisis, the hero provides the decisive action that changes everything for the good. The hero becomes the center of the story by virtue of heroic action, involving some combination of impeccable timing, strength, courage, and wisdom that changes everything for the good. The hero can take all the credit for the rescue because without the hero's decisive action, the story will not end well. But this also means that the hero must take responsibility for the failure. If the day has not been saved, it is the hero's fault for not acting with the right timing or enough strength, courage, and wisdom.

This hero vision is different in every way from the portrait of the saint. As minister and theologian Samuel Wells notes, the word *hero* does not appear anywhere in the New Testament. But the word *saint*? It appears sixty-four times.[17]

Saints, according to the true meaning of the word, do not save the day. They don't provide the decisive action that changes everything for the good—because Jesus Christ already has. Saints are not defined by their holiness or abilities but rather are declared saints because of the perfect holiness of Jesus Christ. Saints do not have to depend on their own timing, strength, courage, and wisdom to provide the heroic action that saves the day. Saints are not the center of the justice story because God is the center of the justice story; God is ultimately responsible for the way the story ends.

Who of us, on our own, could heroically rescue all the victims of injustice in this world? Who of us could bear the weight of that? It would crush us.

It might be tempting to use hero language to motivate ourselves and others to respond to the justice calling, but that tactic always backfires. The "hero calling" is not sustainable. While it might arise from one's initial passion for justice, the hero calling does not allow that passion to be transformed into a perseverance that permeates our lives for the long haul. The hero calling is discarded when one encounters too much brokenness, too much darkness, and too many failures. What's more, the hero calling is lonely.

> *The word* hero *does not appear anywhere in the New Testament. But the word* saint? *It appears sixty-four times.*

In contrast, the justice calling is not undertaken alone. Every single one of the sixty-four references to *saints* in the New Testament is plural.[18] In Paul's first Letter to the Corinthians he writes, "To the church of God in Corinth, to those sanctified in Christ Jesus and called to be his holy people, together with all those everywhere who call on the name of our Lord Jesus Christ" (1 Cor. 1:2). "Saints" and "holy people" are different translations of the same word, linked to God's call for his people to be set apart for a special purpose. Each of us is one member of the larger body of Christ. We need to depend on this community and on God, not ourselves, as we persevere in the justice calling. This is a true gift.

Reconciled and transformed through the grace of God to be righteous and to do justice, we are not set apart to receive glory for our works but to bear witness to the kingdom. Just as important, we are not set apart by our flawless witness—that would only put us back in the center of the story. Saints are imperfect people who are nonetheless set apart by the grace of God. It is the Holy Spirit who enables us to grow in holiness as we are drawn further into union with Christ. To live as God's holy people is to depend on God's ongoing grace and forgiveness. As saints, we ought to be brutally honest about our failures and shortcomings, pointing not to ourselves (as heroes would) but to Jesus Christ as the only one who fully embodies justice and righteousness in this world. Failure is an opportunity to bear witness to the grace and faithfulness of God, who never abandons his people or his kingdom mission.

While it might arise from one's initial passion for justice, the hero calling does not allow that passion to be transformed into a perseverance that permeates our lives for the long haul.

Christ sets us free not only from sin but also from the weight of being heroes who pursue justice on their own. The grace of God in Christ through the Spirit frees us to be God's holy people. Only by the ongoing grace of God can we do the good works that God prepared beforehand to be our way of life (Eph. 2:8–10). It frees us to remember with great joy that in our justice calling we rely on the ongoing sanctifying work of God through Christ and the Spirit, for it is God who works in us that we might will and act to fulfill his good purpose (Phil. 2:13). As saints we are free to offer our lives and our callings—our loaves and fishes—to Jesus Christ, knowing that God is the only one who can turn our humble offerings into rich and plentiful food.

Kunthy and Chanda's country, Cambodia, has long been a hotbed for human trafficking, and certain parts of the country are notorious for providing the youngest of children to sex tourists. But through the quiet, faithful work of God's saints, the tide is turning. Many of these saints come from churches, both within Cambodia and throughout the world, churches committed to seeking justice in a way that is central to their worship of God, understanding that time and prayer are critical gifts they can give. Many of these saints lead and serve with organizations that have been responding on the ground in Cambodia for years, diligently making the investment of specialized training, willing sacrifice, and years of cultivating relationships with government and other institutions. Some of these saints offer financial support, enabling those who do frontline work to get the training they need, move with their families, and invest in local institutions and relationships. Other saints work to connect people on the ground in Cambodia with Christians in other countries who are looking for ways to respond to the needs of others even if they are in a different region of the world; these saints work to provide updates and prayer requests so that others can discern what actions they will take as they are formed by Christ in their passion for justice.

In the case of Kunthy and Chanda, some of the saints on the ground were Cambodian and expat professionals with IJM who pursued a tip that young girls were being sold for sex at a certain brothel in Phnom Penh. Strategically making entry into the brothel, they collected evidence of the ages of the girls and the prices given for their sale.

The professionals took the evidence to the local police. Because of IJM's sustained presence in Cambodia, the relationships carefully built, and the robust training provided to the police force (which had formerly been known for taking bribes to shield the brothels), the Cambodian National Police agreed to conduct a rescue operation at the brothel.

Kunthy and Chanda were not only rescued but were also brought into the safety and love of an aftercare home, receiving close attention from social workers, including opportunities for counseling, art therapy, education, and vocational training for living independently once they become adults. The girls themselves bravely testified in a tiny Cambodian courtroom, standing just feet away from those who had brutalized and enslaved them. The courage these young girls mustered was astounding, their testimony so powerful that the judge convicted the traffickers and sentenced them to prison.

Rescue operations, ensuing criminal prosecutions, and partnership with the government in Cambodia have continued to grow over the years; from 2003 to 2015 alone more than a thousand girls were rescued from sexual exploitation in Cambodia.[19] There are still significant needs throughout the country, and the public justice system in Cambodia needs sustained investment. However, in regard to the rampant impunity with which child sexual exploitation formerly existed in Cambodia, a remarkable transformation has been under way since the early 2000s, and it is a transformation that will grow in beauty as the body of Christ continues to draw near.[20]

Cambodia is becoming a remarkable example of saints in the body of Christ coming together with kingdom focus and vision to transform justice systems and begin the dismantling of an entire industry of exploitation.

God's people are mobilizing in response to the biblical command to seek justice; as a result, young girls like Kunthy and Chanda are being rescued from lives of sex-trafficking and serial rape, and many thousands more are being protected from ever being exploited in the first place.

The transformation in Cambodia is a signpost of the kingdom of God and the flourishing our God brings to places that were once broken. There are many key players dedicated to this work, to seeing this transformation unfurl, but none of these key players are lone ranger heroes. The beauty we are beginning to glimpse in Cambodia is the work of a whole communion of saints, moving toward darkness, building relationships even in hotbeds of corruption, and fully living in dependence on God to move and make his beauty known.

6

Be Sanctified and Sent

Justice and the Church

Consider this: the words to one of the most globally known, frequently sung, and universally beloved songs in all of Christian history, "Amazing Grace," were written by a human trafficker. And not a trafficker who had turned from his ways, but a trafficker still fully living and profiting from the transport and sale of slaves.

John Newton fits the definition of a "saint" in every sense of what we learned from Scripture in the last chapter. Newton, refined by the Holy Spirit and set apart by his love for justice, poured out the latter years of his life fighting the slave trade, mentored key leaders in abolition such as William Wilberforce, and was utterly humbled by his need for the grace of Jesus Christ. But there abides a certain amount of folklore regarding the circumstances under which Newton penned his famous hymn. If we operate from the folklore version of Newton's life, we risk being distracted from the deeper realities of Newton's life, from which so much can be learned.

Newton did indeed write "Amazing Grace" while captaining a slave ship. In the middle of the Atlantic Ocean, the hull of his ship full of slaves purchased from the west coast of Africa, he came to a profound realization of his sin and need for the grace of God. But renouncing slavery—his buying, transport, vicious beatings, and sale of human beings—was not part of his repentance. According to his own journals, even Newton himself "could not consider himself a true believer" until many years after this initial conversion.[1] The abiding folklore version of Newton's story has him coming to his point of conversion, penning "Amazing Grace," and then immediately turning around his ship full of slaves and *returning to Africa*, where he promptly *sets all of the slaves free*.[2]

It's a powerful story. But it's not true.

The truth about much of Newton's life is far more disturbing than the folklore versions known to most. And yet, there is great power in knowing the true story, because in the real story of Newton's life we see truth that is archetypal for the church as a whole throughout history and today: conversion is only the beginning. From the point of Newton's conversion, God was not finished with him in the least. God's work of sanctification in Newton's life unfolded over many decades, just as God's work of sanctification is ongoing in every one of us and within his church as a whole. To be clear, it wasn't that Newton was "saved" and then "saved again" and then "again" but rather that Newton shows us what it looks like for the Holy Spirit to take hold of a life and sanctify it year by year, making that life holy as God is holy, continually forming that life into the image of Christ, no matter how heinous that person's brokenness had once been.

> *Newton shows us what it looks like for the Holy Spirit to take hold of a life and sanctify it year by year, continually forming a person into the image of Christ, no matter how heinous that person's sins.*

If we tell carefully scrubbed redemption stories of our heroes in the faith rather than understanding them as saints in whose lives God's ongoing grace is actively at work, we'll miss the fullness of what redemption holds and the beauty of God's work to refine and sanctify the members of his body over time. As the church—the body of Christ all over the world—today seeks to live God's justice calling, if we take a moment to open our eyes and know the truth of Newton's life we'll find an opportunity to be formed and encouraged all the more by the deep and pervasive ways in which the Holy Spirit works through broken and redeemed followers of Jesus Christ.

The truth is that, following his conversion to faith in Jesus Christ (during which he did *not* free slaves, and neither did he repent of his slave trading),

Newton was known to walk the decks of his ship talking to God in prayer and even *thanking* God for the good fortune of his opportunity to be in the lucrative slave trade, which afforded him ample time for introspection: "I never knew sweeter or more frequent hours of divine communion, than in my last two voyages to Guinea . . . reflecting on the singular goodness of the Lord to me."[3] As Newton walked the decks in prayer to the God to whom he had given over his life through Jesus Christ, slaves lay chained below his feet in fetid quarters. While Newton certainly did have dramatic spiritual experiences throughout his life—including during his time as a slave trader—none of these moments of conviction and spiritual transformation were catalyzed by the fact that he was captaining a ship filled with bound and beaten slaves whom he had personally worked to extract from Africa.

If it is true that God has consistently cared about justice and righteousness and consistently called his people to seek justice and righteousness, then we have to ask what has kept the church from faithfully responding to this call.

It was not until nearly a decade after he left the slave trade that Newton wrote "Amazing Grace," and there is no evidence in his journals or in his public life that the song was a response of repentance in regard to the brutal business of captaining a slave ship. The hymn was written a decade *before* Newton even began to speak out publicly against the slave trade.

For obvious reasons, many Christians are unable to reconcile Newton's active pursuit of godliness with his torture and sale of human beings. Perhaps this disconnect is the reason why most Christian commentators skim over the detail that for a full eight years after his initial conversion to faith in Jesus Christ, Newton continued not only to buy, sell, and transport slaves in the transatlantic triangle between England, the west coast of Africa, and North America, but he also continued to sadistically abuse slaves. His personal journal details his torture of slaves alongside his gratitude to God for enabling him to be in such a trade. In fact, Newton left the slave trade only because it became too physically taxing.

It's disturbing that Newton sought Jesus and at the same time was complicit in such atrocities. But taking an honest look at Newton's own story could help us to make sense of the church's journey today. If it is true that God has consistently cared about justice and righteousness and consistently called his people to seek justice and righteousness, then we have to ask what has kept the church, in large part, from faithfully responding to this call. If we are right that being saved by Christ means becoming saints who seek the kingdom of God in this world, then we have to consider the ways in which the body of Christ has not lived into its new identity and be encouraged that, despite previous shortcomings, the church is continually being sanctified and sent on a kingdom mission.

Like Newton, the church's manifold and deep faults are concurrent with its claim to follow Jesus, and yet by the power of the Holy Spirit the church can live more and more faithfully as God's holy people, set apart by the pursuit of justice and righteousness. Like Newton, who did not acknowledge the sinfulness and tragedy of slavery until decades after his initial conversion to Christ, large swaths of the Protestant and evangelical church in recent generations have failed to heed the mandate in Scripture to seek justice, rescue the oppressed, defend the orphan, and plead for the widow (Isa. 1:17). Even as the modern church awakens to this ancient biblical call, we are often quick to speak while still slow to act.

All of us who follow Jesus are invited into what missiologist and theologian Darrell Guder calls a "continuing conversion"[4]—that is, to be continually formed by the Spirit so that we can see, with increasing clarity, the world and others as God sees them. While in a very real sense we are sanctified in and through Christ as we are saved into the holy people of God, the Spirit's unfolding sanctification of our lives is lifelong. It took years of formation in the faith for Newton to see that loving God, loving neighbor, and supporting the slave trade were incompatible. It will take time, but the church today is being likewise transformed into the holy people of God by the ongoing grace of God in Christ. We too must seek God's justice, righteousness, *hesed*, love, and shalom in this world.

God's Church Sent on a Kingdom Mission

In some respects, we are at the most exciting part of the biblical story. This is where we get to explore the "so what" of all that's gone before—so what does this mean for who we are and how we live today?

For thousands of years, God has consistently cared about justice and righteousness and consistently called his people to seek justice and righteousness. At long last, those of us who live by the saving grace of Jesus Christ can live with justice and righteousness in this world. Having been justified in and through Jesus Christ, we have been set right with God. Having been sanctified in and through Jesus Christ, we have been set apart to be the holy people of God. As the sanctified saints of God living by the Spirit in utter dependence on the grace of God, we are sent by God on a kingdom mission: we are to actively and intentionally seek the kingdom of God and his righteousness and justice in all that we do in this world.

When we are saved into the family of God we are simultaneously called to mission. As biblical scholar and theologian Richard Bauckham writes, the mission of the church "takes place between the highly particular history of Jesus and the universal goal of God's coming kingdom."[5] This is where we are living right now within the biblical story—between the first coming of Jesus and our anticipation of his return, between the inauguration of the kingdom of God and its universal realization. As we live in this "already/not yet" time of waiting and hope, we are called to live in mission, to receive the same mission that Jesus gave to his first disciples after his resurrection: "Peace be with you! As the Father has sent me, I am sending you" (John 20:21).

Through the particular people of Israel, God had universal intentions. We see this in the covenant that God made with Abraham, that is, the promise that all nations would be blessed through Abraham's descendants (Gen. 12:1–2). God called the people of Israel to bear witness to his justice and righteousness so that other people and nations might be drawn to him. God wanted all people to know him as their God and King, but the ancient expectation was that the nations would be drawn to Jerusalem to worship God. This made sense, since the temple of Jerusalem was considered God's home. While hints of the word of God going forth to the nations can be found in the Old Testament, it is not until the incarnation of Christ that God's people understood their calling to move toward others in mission, with Jerusalem no longer at the center.

Through the person of Jesus, God's universal intentions are made even clearer.[6] In Christ, God makes his presence manifest not only in the temple but also throughout the world. The curtain of the temple is torn in two when Jesus dies (Matt. 27:51), symbolizing that in Christ we are able to live in God's holy presence at all times and places. Through Christ's resurrection and ascension, we see the power and scope of God's victory over death, evil, and injustice. The entire world lies under the reign of God in Christ, and it is the lordship of Christ that inspires the new missional reality for God's people. At its heart, Christian mission is a Spirit-generated response to the conviction that Christ is Lord over everything in this world, including everything fallen and broken.[7]

The impetus to move outward in mission does not arise from human creativity or initiative. Christian mission, as New Testament scholar C. Kavin Rowe puts it, "exceeds dramatically all human possibilities of creation and initiation. It not only is but must be the *missio Dei*."[8] God is the one who calls and sends us through Jesus Christ in the power of the Holy Spirit. In both its origin and its execution, the mission of the church relies on the activity and presence of God.

We see this clearly in the final words Jesus speaks to his disciples (known as the Great Commission) before his ascension as relayed in the Gospel of Matthew: "All authority in heaven and on earth has been given to me. Therefore go and make disciples of all nations, baptizing them in the name of the Father and of the Son and of the Holy Spirit, and teaching them to obey everything I have commanded you. And surely I am with you always, to the very end of the age" (Matt. 28:18–20). With these words Jesus gives the disciples a mission with the assurance that he (as King) has been given all authority and that he empowers his disciples in light of that authority. Jesus promises that he will be with his disciples as they undertake this mission so that they are never acting on their own or by their own strength.

> *The impetus to move outward in mission does not arise from human creativity or initiative. . . . God is the one who calls and sends us.*

Christians understand the Holy Spirit to be the fulfillment of Jesus Christ's promise that he will be with them always, which corresponds with the promise recorded in the Gospel of John that Jesus will give his disciples the Spirit of truth to be with them and help them after Jesus leaves them (John 14:15–18). This is the beauty and gift of the Holy Spirit for the holy people of God. Like the disciples, we are sanctified and sent by the Holy Spirit and continue to receive the gift of the Spirit as we respond to God's missional call.

The presence of Christ with us is further reinforced in Jesus's commissioning of his disciples as recounted in the book of Acts: "You will receive power when the Holy Spirit comes on you; and you will be my witnesses in Jerusalem, and in all Judea and Samaria, and to the ends of the earth" (Acts 1:8). On the day of Pentecost the Holy Spirit came upon the disciples, fulfilling Jesus's promise that he would be with them as they moved forward in mission. By his power they proclaimed the good news of the kingdom of God, and many responded by repenting, being baptized, and receiving forgiveness of sins and the gift of the Holy Spirit. These earliest converts were drawn into the family *and* the ongoing mission of God, united in what came to be called the church.

Just like the earliest saints, we receive and depend on the gift of the Spirit as we are drawn by the Spirit into the ongoing mission and family of God. We believe that Jesus continues to be alive and active in this world as our ongoing priest, prophet, and king. This changes everything when it comes to being sanctified and sent—what we could call "living the Christian life."

Looking at what Jesus did thousands of years ago and then guessing what I should do today isn't the answer.

It's often hard to understand how exactly Jesus fits in to the everyday reality of the Christian life. He died for our sins, but how does that really help us as we try to live? When I (Kristen) first encountered the question "What would Jesus do?" I found it to be a helpful framework for my life. It pushed me to think about each decision I made in new and challenging ways. While the fad of the WWJD movement has since faded, I have noticed that many Christians continue to think that the most important role Jesus plays in our daily lives is that of moral exemplar. One of the shortcomings of this approach is that we think and act as if we are on our own—lone individuals trying to make faithful moral decisions based on an example that Jesus left two thousand years ago in a time and place far removed from our own. Through the years my students and I have come up with other acronyms that more fully and faithfully invite us into the Christian life and the ongoing mission of God. "WIJD" is my favorite—What is Jesus doing in this world, in his people, in my life? Looking at what Jesus did thousands of years ago and then guessing what *I* should do today isn't the answer. By the grace of God in Christ through the Spirit, I am invited to participate in what *God* is doing today to bring justice and righteousness to this earth and to our lives. Through the Holy Spirit, I can discern where God is at work and join in the ongoing mission of Jesus in this world as a member of the body of Christ, joined by my brothers and sisters in Christ near and far.

The Church's Call to Mission in Word and Deed

The book of Acts gives a beautiful, multifaceted picture of how the earliest church understood its missional calling to "be my witnesses in Jerusalem, and in all Judea and Samaria, and to the ends of the earth" (1:8). The mission of the early church involved verbal proclamation of the good news of Christ: Peter proclaims the gospel again and again (2:14–39; 3:12–26; 4:8–12); Stephen speaks (7:2–53); Philip preaches (8:4–13); and Paul and Barnabas are commissioned and sent to share the gospel with Jews and then gentiles (8:13–14). The proclamation of the gospel moves from Jerusalem to Judea, Samaria, and out toward the ends of the earth.

The early church did not have separate categories for evangelism and justice. They seamlessly lived James's conviction that "faith without deeds is dead" (James 2:26).

The book of Acts also makes it clear that the mission of the early church involved attending to material needs. As the gospel is proclaimed and received, it connects directly with the social and economic realities of people's lives, which are intertwined with their spiritual needs.[9] This seamless connection between the proclamation of the gospel and concern for material realities—between word and deed—permeates the book of Acts. In the earliest description of the church after Pentecost, meetings for prayer and worship flowed naturally into making sure the material needs in their community were met (2:43–47). Distributing food daily to widows became a regular practice of these early Christians and was considered so significant that seven disciples were commissioned to oversee this part of the church's mission and to ensure that no one was neglected (6:1–6). Paul returns to the church in Jerusalem from a missionary journey in part to bring money for the poor in support of the church's mission (24:17). Scholar Helen Rhee writes that "early Christians consciously and intentionally constructed their self-definition revolving around their understanding and practice of wealth and poverty," which manifested itself in the "common use of resources for common flourishing," in generous almsgiving and remarkable hospitality.[10]

The Great Commission was fulfilled not only as the disciples moved into new geographic locations but also as they intentionally addressed the social and economic realities at home and abroad. As they engaged those who were marginalized, impoverished, and neglected, they bore witness to the upside-down nature of God's kingdom in Christ (Acts 17:6–7 NRSV). The early church did not designate separate categories for evangelism and justice. They seamlessly lived James's conviction that "faith without deeds is dead" (James 2:26). What we today call evangelism and justice together make up the kingdom mission of the church. Biblically, the pursuit of justice, righteousness, and shalom includes mission in word and deed.

Theologian René Padilla has spent a lifetime demonstrating how both evangelism and social involvement are integral to the mission of the church. He understands the mission of the church to be an extension of the mission of Jesus—that is, a manifestation of the kingdom of God, a new reality ushered in by Jesus Christ that "affects human life not only morally and spiritually but also physically and psychologically, materially and socially."[11] Just as Jesus's mission manifested the many layers of the kingdom through his preaching and his acts of justice and mercy, so should the church's mission. Good works are not an optional add-on to the proclamation of the gospel; only together can they point to the fullness of the kingdom of God that Jesus Christ inaugurated. In an exhortation to the church today, Padilla writes: "Both word and deed are inextricably united in the mission of Jesus and his apostles, and we must continue to hold both together in the mission of the church, in which Jesus's mission is prolonged until the end of the age."[12]

The deep biblical connection between evangelism and justice has been a key component of the witness and teachings of John Perkins as well. After experiencing a conversion to the gospel in his late twenties in California, he became deeply committed to sharing the gospel through evangelism. He then sensed a call from God to return with his family to his home state of Mississippi to bring the good news to the black community he had left. As he entered further into ministry there, he became increasingly convinced of the significance of holistic mission that attends to spiritual and material needs. As Perkins writes,

> I want to be clear that there is no competition between evangelism and social responsibility. If I were to spend all my time teaching my children the Bible, but not lift a finger to see that they are fed, that they are educated, that they are job-prepared, that they learn to give to others, I could justly be called an irresponsible parent. In the same way, our love for others is questionable if either spiritual or social concern is lacking. Jesus never put evangelism and social action at odds with each other, so neither should we.[13]

As we are sent by Jesus to love God and love others, our mission must involve both evangelism and justice.

Throughout Scripture God consistently cares about human flourishing on every level; neat and clean divisions between spiritual and physical well-being do not exist. Likewise, the early church proclaimed a holistic gospel in word and deed. This is the same gospel that the church proclaims today. This holistic mission does not minimize the fact that "the widest and deepest human need is for a personal encounter with Jesus Christ, through whom the kingdom is mediated."[14] We each need to be restored to right relationship to God through Christ.

At the same time, God's vision of justice and human flourishing is relational on every level; we need to be restored to union with God in order to rightly love others and the rest of God's created world. When we love others with justice and righteousness in the name of Christ by addressing both physical and spiritual impoverishment, we are bearing witness to God's kingdom. Padilla casts a vision for the church that teaches "every human need . . . can be used by the Spirit of God as a beachhead for the manifestation of his kingly power."[15] Understanding and pursuing the mission of the church in light of the kingdom of God enables us to see that everything we do to address spiritual and physical human need witnesses to the kingdom and ultimately to the King. Because the King is the one who sends and empowers our mission, we can trust the Spirit to use what we offer, in word and deed, to make God known.

Marks of God's Sanctified and Sent People

When we talk about mission and the kingdom, it can be tempting to focus the conversation entirely on what we do. While what we are called to do is an important part of this chapter of the story, the more fundamental part is who we are in Christ. What we do flows from who we are; therefore, our identity as beloved saints shapes our activity in this world. The heart of mission entails the *living out of who we are as God's people* by the grace of God in Christ and the power of the Holy Spirit.

From the beginning of the biblical story, God has been calling his people to live the way of justice and righteousness, which is now possible because of the justifying and sanctifying work of Jesus Christ. As we discussed in chapter 5, this does not mean that we need to live the way of justice and righteousness perfectly in order to qualify as saints. While many Christians and non-Christians think that living the Christian life is primarily about what we do or don't do, such lists of moral behaviors miss the deeply relational core of righteousness. Our ongoing sanctification is the Spirit's work in helping us to live more and more into our new identity as God's beloved saints, so that our lives increasingly reflect the justice, righteousness, and holiness that have been given to us by the grace of God.

From our new identity flows our new way of living; from our "being" flows our "doing." The New Testament consistently describes our "doing" in this way.[16] Consider this example from Colossians:

> As God's chosen people, holy and dearly loved, clothe yourselves with compassion, kindness, humility, gentleness, and patience. Bear with each other and forgive one another if any of you has a grievance against someone. Forgive as the Lord forgave you. And over all these virtues put on love, which binds them all together in perfect unity. (Col. 3:12–14)

Who we are, as God's holy and dearly loved people, comes first. That identity cannot be earned by our actions, though our identity ought to increasingly be reflected in our actions as we live with compassion, kindness, humility, gentleness, patience, forgiveness, and love.

So being sanctified and sent does not mean that we are already perfect, but that by the ongoing grace of God we are living more and more into our new identity as God's beloved saints. As theologian Julie Canlis notes, "From this transformed identity flows all the imperatives of grace, which are not mere commands that we are suddenly empowered to do. No, they are signs of sonship, harbingers of our new identity."[17] The fruit in our lives—our love for God and others in word and deed—is a manifestation of who we are as God's beloved children. Jesus tells us, "I am the vine; you are the branches. If you remain in me and I in you, you will bear much fruit; apart from me you can do nothing. . . . This is to my Father's glory, that you bear much fruit, showing yourselves to be my disciples" (John 15:5, 8). This call to bear fruit in word and deed as we live in Christ is an important mark of God's sanctified and sent people.

Every human need . . . can be used by the Spirit of God as a beachhead for the manifestation of his kingly power.

As we live the way of life that God has prepared for us (the way of justice and righteousness), we can do so with deep gratitude for the grace of God that enables us to *be* God's holy people and to *do* what God calls us to do. "And whatever you do, whether in word or deed, do it all in the name of the Lord

Jesus, giving thanks to God the Father through him" (Col. 3:17). The unending grace that God has lavished upon us through Jesus Christ and the Holy Spirit calls for this gratitude—which is another mark of God's holy people. By gratitude we mean an active, all-encompassing, Spirit-empowered response to God. As we receive the grace that God has offered us with thanksgiving, by the Spirit we offer our entire lives back to God in pursuit of the things that God cares about the most.

Recognizing that all we have been given comes from God, we offer our gifts, our relationships, our time, our paid and unpaid callings, and our money back to God so that we can seek God's kingdom and God's justice and righteousness wherever we are and whatever we are doing. Being "sanctified and sent" doesn't mean we have to go to a faraway place to seek the kingdom. By offering our lives to God with gratitude and by living lives suitable for God's people, we can seek the kingdom of God right where we are, which means loving others and seeking the flourishing of those around us in whatever ways we can. As Bauckham puts it, "The church is those people who, so far, acknowledge God's rule as he is implementing it in Jesus and live for others in the light of the coming of his kingdom in all creation."[18]

What we do flows from who we are; therefore, our identity as beloved saints shapes our activity in this world.

I (Kristen) was reflecting on our call to offer our lives for others in light of Christ when my family went to a children's ministry event on Good Friday. To help the children contemplate the significance of Christ's death on our behalf, our kids were each invited to make a wooden cross. We helped our two-year-old daughter make a cross, and for the rest of the evening she proceeded to hold it up to anyone and everyone and say, "Mine, mine, mine." At that stage in her life, she regularly claimed all sorts of things as "mine," but it was jarring to see her do this with the cross. Of course we long for her to know that God's saving love is for her, but we also long for her to know that she is not saved just for her own sake. As she encounters the saving love of God in Christ, we hope she will see that the cross represents God's love for all of humanity and all creation. We hope that, empowered by the Spirit, she will take up her cross in order to deny herself and follow Christ for the sake of others. We hope that she will give her life back to God with gratitude and that she might love God and love others in word and deed wherever she is and whatever she is doing.

In chapter 3 we saw that living with gratitude is connected to living in dependent trust on God. Offering our entire lives to God through the Spirit in order to seek the shalom flourishing of others and God's world requires trust that God will provide and guide us even when we don't make ourselves the top priority. It requires us to trust that the way of life God sets before us is the best way, even when we are tempted by seductive voices suggesting that other ways of living are better.

Jesus demonstrated that his kingdom is marked by altogether different understandings of justice and power from the kingdoms of this world. As we are sanctified and sent, we are likewise called to use our power in the pursuit of justice—yet another mark of God's holy people on a kingdom mission. By the power of the Holy Spirit, we can offer our entire lives to God in gratitude, trusting God's sufficiency as we use our power to seek the kingdom of God and God's justice and righteousness wherever we are and whatever we are doing.

The Importance of Worship

Another important mark of God's sanctified and sent people is worship. Broken and unholy as they often seem, the worshiping lives of our local churches can still be used by the Holy Spirit to sanctify us into kingdom people who enter this world with kingdom vision. The Spirit can also use the worship of our local churches to bear witness to the kingdom of God. As missiologist Benjamin T. Conner writes, "There is no such thing as true worship that is not missional, just as there is no such thing as true mission that is not worship."[19]

God has always longed for a people to live in union with him and from that union to live with justice and righteousness. Through Christ and the Spirit, the church *is* that body of people—and we are most ourselves, most who God created and redeemed us to be, when we come together in worship and praise of God. Coming together in worship and inviting people to see and experience this as a foretaste of the kingdom of God are just as much a part of our mission as proclaiming and doing works of justice outside the church's walls. As we gather together in worship and share life together, we bear witness to God's presence in our midst and God's lordship in our lives.

Mission in the early church included forming communities of salvation, centered in Jesus Christ and empowered by the Holy Spirit.[20] The same is true today. As Bauckham states, "The church's mission requires both the individuals and groups who, authorized by God to communicate his message, go out from the community to others, near or far, and also the community that manifests God's presence in its midst by its life together and its relationships to others."[21] In other words, we don't want to focus so much on the "doing" and "being sent" part of mission that we miss the significance of our local communities of worship. Worship does not just serve a utilitarian function to prepare us to be sent in mission.[22] Worship itself is a mark of the missional people of God.

The church is a lot like Newton: even as it acknowledges the amazing grace of God to save and sanctify, it needs continuing sanctification in order to bring flourishing to all the layers of shalom that were broken in the fall, to live into its new identity as the holy people of God. This is another reason why we need to worship: it includes our collective repentance and confession. When we repent of our ongoing failure to faithfully live as the holy children of God, we are confessing that we need the grace and mercy of God to live with and to seek justice, righteousness, and shalom. When we confess in our worship that Christ is Lord, we are confessing that we are not the ones who save; we are God's people living in continual dependence on the Spirit's sanctification.[23] As we repent and reaffirm our dependence on Christ, we are bearing witness to the faithful loving-kindness and generous sufficiency of Christ our King.

Barriers to Biblical Mission

As we think back to the life and witness of Newton, we are reminded not only of our need for ongoing sanctification but we are also given hope that God's sanctifying Spirit is indeed at work in our lives and in our churches. Despite the ways in which God's people and the church fall short, like Newton we can increasingly manifest the righteousness and justice of God's kingdom. Part of the church's "already/not yet" existence is that it continues to be full of flawed but redeemed children of God who are united in Christ, not through perfection but through God's grace and merciful loving-kindness.

With the advantage of time, distance, and a different cultural perspective, we can look at Newton and easily critique him for not immediately seeing that slavery is wrong. We don't want to focus so much on the speck in Newton's eye that we don't take time to address the planks in our own (Matt. 7:3–5).

Where has the church not yet lived into its calling to seek God's kingdom of justice and righteousness? What barriers stand in the way of the church being sanctified and sent on its kingdom mission? Much could be said in response to these questions. Focusing specifically on the American Protestant church, we suggest that the church has allowed itself to become defined by false dichotomies that separate social engagement from evangelism and physical concerns from spiritual ones.

One hundred years ago, much of the church in America was steadily building toward a major rift in belief about what constituted the best ways for Christians to live out the gospel. This rift is known by historians as the fundamentalist/modernist controversy.

Modernists were associated with the development of what became known as the "Social Gospel," a movement that developed out of a desire to address the desperate poverty and injustice of the day by applying Christian ethics to social problems. Those who called for this new Social Gospel were committed to reclaiming the significance of the kingdom of God within Jesus's teaching, but they tended to focus almost entirely on how *they* could usher in God's kingdom in this world by addressing institutional sin and the tangible needs of society.

Proponents of the Social Gospel tended to operate under the assumption that sin is a result of societal structures rather than a fallen condition that marks each human person. They focused on changing society in light of the ethics of the kingdom of God, believing that this type of social

The church has allowed itself to become defined by false dichotomies that separate social engagement from evangelism and physical concerns from spiritual ones.

reform could eradicate the impact of sin. The Social Gospel downplayed the need for each person to encounter the forgiveness offered through Jesus Christ.

A subsequent "fundamentalist" backlash focused on the salvation of individual souls and rejected commitment to social reform. Verbal evangelism and personal piety became the focus of the fundamentalist movement. By 1920 a divide had developed between evangelism and social action in the American Protestant church.

In the late 1800s and into the early 1900s, evangelically minded Christians had been known for their involvement in society, particularly in regard to issues such as temperance, health, poverty, and even forced labor and prostitution.[24] In a shift so dramatic that historians call it "the Great Reversal," these Christians came to see social engagement as peripheral to the heart of the gospel.[25] Neglect of social action became an opportunity for evangelicals to clearly distinguish themselves from the liberal modernists and demonstrate their commitment to a particular understanding of salvation—namely, the salvation of souls. Preaching against the Social Gospel, fundamentalist followers of Jesus rallied around a compelling "us versus them" narrative concerning the truth of the gospel.

Much has changed since the original divisiveness of the fundamentalist/ modernist controversy. After World War II in particular, evangelical leaders began forging the frontiers of relief and development work. Bob Pierce, an evangelist who began his ministry with Youth for Christ in the 1940s, sought to meet the immediate physical needs of orphans in Korea, which gave birth to World Vision, a billion-dollar mercy ministry serving communities across the globe. Carl Henry wrote *The Uneasy Conscience of Modern Fundamentalism* in 1947, calling the evangelical American church and its leaders to deeper engagement with the social and cultural problems of the day.

In addition, World Relief, Compassion International, Habitat for Humanity, Opportunity International, and hundreds of other organizations have risen up and effectively drawn previously disengaged evangelicals into engagement with the more physical, tangible needs of their neighbors both near and far.

More recently, Christians have become increasingly involved in ministries that address not only tangible needs but also matters of violent injustice, rising up to intervene where abuse against the poorest of the poor goes unchecked. Slavery in all of its forms, as well as police abuse, unprosecuted rape, torture, illegal detention, and land exploitation, are beginning to appear on the radar of the church, and God's people are beginning to mobilize on behalf of the most vulnerable and voiceless in our world.

Echoes of the fundamentalist/modernist controversy, however, can still be heard, as a significant degree of wariness toward justice ministry can be found among much of the evangelical church. Questions of "primacy" continue to arise, particularly in regard to whether the rescue of souls is being subverted by emphasis on the rescue of bodies.

In addition to the dualism between evangelism and social concerns, the American church has been marked by a dualism between the spiritual and the physical realms. Often without realizing it, when the American church gives in to the ancient gnostic temptation to segregate our souls and our bodies, the American church is likewise tempted to segregate our understanding of Christian salvation and mission into spiritual and physical realms.

Greek philosophy first introduced the idea of the immortality of the soul apart from the body, and "Christian" gnosticism builds upon this idea with the belief that physical matter is evil while spirit is good. The implication is that we can and ought to pursue spiritual things at the expense of attention to physical matters. Robustly biblical, orthodox Christianity has never formally tolerated this dualism, but it easily creeps in. Irenaeus of Lyons, one of the early fathers of the Christian faith, emphasized this point as he argued against the heretics of his day. Scholar Wayne Meeks writes, "It was doubtless in his struggle against the Gnostics, with their exaltation of 'spirit' and contempt for the body, that Irenaeus concluded that the whole Jewish and Christian tradition taught that soul and body alike are objects of God's creation and salvation. Therefore faith entails care for all our embodied relationships, and affects them."[26]

Operating with a false dichotomy between the soul and the body is like trying to convert an enslaved girl's soul without attempting to rescue her out of the brothel. But the kingdom of God is concerned with both material and spiritual realities, as the saving and redeeming love of God in Christ makes clear. Jesus's saving work includes the reconciliation of all things, from the forgiveness of the sins of humanity to the redemption of the created world itself. Therefore, the mission of the church is to bear witness to the justice and righteousness of God through word and deed, through evangelism and justice, through attention to the soul and the body. Our souls are inextricably linked to our bodies; our lives are inextricably linked to the lives of others around us; and our discipleship is inextricably linked to the way we treat this world.

Matters of justice are matters of salvation. We cannot be faithful in our mission as the people of God unless we continue to retool our thinking to align with the whole of the biblical witness to salvation. As the late mission theologian David Bosch so helpfully instructs:

> The moment one regards mission as consisting of two separate components one has, in principle, conceded that each of the two has a life of its own. One is then by implication saying that it is possible to have evangelism without a social dimension and Christian social involvement without an evangelistic

dimension. What is more, if one suggests that one component is primary and the other secondary, one implies that the one is essential, the other optional.[27]

Thankfully, a growing portion of the American church is moving deeper into its biblical calling to seek justice and righteousness. As the church increasingly rejects false dichotomies between evangelism and justice and between the physical and spiritual realms, people's entire lives—physical, mental, and spiritual—are being transformed around the globe. Seeing ministries of justice and mercy as central to the church's mission acknowledges Scripture's consistent teaching that seeking the kingdom of God is a matter of justice and righteousness.

The work of the church and the gospel encompasses spiritual reconciliation with God as well as physical rescue, healing, and restoration—God through his people alive in the world. In his book *Called*, Mark Labberton teaches that our calling, above all, is to follow Jesus; the work of justice, healing, and restoration is at the very heart of so much of what Jesus is up to in our world.[28]

Invitation for Today: Be Sanctified and Sent

Each time my (Kristen's) family sits to eat dinner together at the table, we light a candle, and the kids join us in saying: "Christ is the light of the world. In him there is no darkness at all. The light shines in the darkness, and the darkness cannot overcome it *at all*!" When our son was two, he added the last "at all," and we've said it ever since. We hope that our children will never forget that no matter where they go, no matter what kind of darkness they encounter, the light of Christ can never, ever be overcome. We pray that our children will not hover in the safe, comfortable, seemingly light places of the world but rather will choose to offer their lives and gifts, allowing God to send them into the dark places of the world with the inextinguishable light of Christ.

But we also pray that they know they will not enter those dark places alone. God sends his chuch to respond to injustice together as the body of Christ united in our own communities and across the globe. As we respond together, we do so out of the grace given to us in Jesus through the Holy Spirit, not from our own abilities. We rely on the powerful light of Christ that shines in each dark place. As one of my (Kristen's) students has said, there are no God-forsaken places, only church-forsaken places. God asks his people to take up their crosses and follow him into these places, as it may be through them that God works to set things right.

In our own pursuit of the justice calling, both of us have been encouraged by the sanctification we see happening in churches all over the world. Followers of Jesus are increasingly living into their identities as God's saints, opening their eyes to the enormity of need, and responding with humble hearts to the commands of Scripture to be sent on a kingdom mission of justice and righteousness. Furthermore, we relish the many different forms that the work of justice takes as more churches understand that their mission inextricably weaves together proclamation of the gospel *and* social engagement.

Operating with a false dichotomy between the soul and the body is like trying to convert an enslaved girl's soul without attempting to rescue her out of the brothel.

Being sanctified and sent involves whole churches working together in mission as they pursue justice and righteousness both locally and globally. Being sanctified and sent also involves each of us personally pursuing justice and righteousness right where we are. Jesus's commission to go into all the world to make disciples (Matt. 28:18–20)—to be God's witnesses in Jerusalem, in Judea and Samaria, and to the ends of the earth (Acts 1:8)—can be understood as a geographic call to seek God's kingdom as well as a call to engage the cultures in which we currently live.[29]

Pursuing justice and righteousness means actively longing for people to enter into the family of God *and* for those who are suffering as a result of injustice and oppression to be freed from their suffering. We can and ought to use whatever influence we have been given in whatever places we live and work to strive toward both. This means that we care about sharing God's good news because we believe that union with God through Jesus Christ and the Holy Spirit enables us to live in right relationship with God, others, and the larger world. This also means that we care about sharing the gospel as we work toward justice through social, cultural, and institutional engagement, believing that God's vision of shalom requires that everyone is given the opportunity to flourish—both in their personal relationship with God and in their daily, physical lives.

Wherever we are, whatever we are doing, whatever responsibilities have been entrusted to us, we are called to live as God's holy people, seeking God's justice, righteousness, and shalom. This is not something we do only at church, in Bible studies, as part of a justice team or mission trip, or when we leave our "normal" lives and responsibilities behind. Every part of our ordinary, daily lives can be offered to God with gratitude as we seek the kingdom of God in this world.

God's vision for justice and righteousness is meant to shape each of our callings and commitments and all of our practices within those callings and commitments. In this way, we can better understand every one of our callings as a kingdom calling, as Amy Sherman so helpfully puts it.[30] If we use the language of *calling* at all, we tend to equate it with the idea of our career. We might ask what career or profession God is calling us to. Connecting our faith in God to our working lives is an important and needed thing, and this is where Sherman's work is so very helpful. She invites us to consider how each of our professions can and ought to be pursued in light of God's kingdom vision for this world.

> *Every part of our ordinary, daily lives can be offered to God with gratitude as we seek the kingdom of God in this world.*

But even beyond career, we each have a number of other callings at the same time, such as our callings to be spouses, family members, parents, and community members. When we engage with our physical neighbors or get involved in our local communities and schools, when we seek marriage and nurture our families, when we tend to our homes and pursue our careers, we do so as kingdom people. All of these callings need to be understood in light of our most formative calling—the calling to be God's holy people. As God's sanctified and sent people, we are to love God and others in ways that foster justice, righteousness, and shalom in all the rest of our callings.

In his recent work, James Davison Hunter casts a vision for how we in the church can carry shalom into all of our callings. Calling it *faithful presence*, Hunter believes that we need to be deeply formed through our local churches into people who see the world in light of God's vision of shalom and then are sent into each of our callings guided by and working toward this vision. Wherever we have been given power and responsibility, we are to use that power and responsibility to "challenge, undermine, and otherwise diminish oppression, injustice, and corruption, and, in turn, encourage harmony, fruitfulness, and abundance, wholeness, beauty, joy, security, and well-being."[31]

Living each of our callings in ways that engage the realities that lead to injustice and oppression requires hard work and imagination. Because the sinfulness of the world manifests itself in personal brokenness and in cultures and institutions that prevent people from living as God intended, we need to engage in conversation with others who can dream and imagine with us. This does not mean that culture is bad or that institutions are inherently evil but rather that culture and its institutions become twisted and distorted as a result of the wide-ranging implications of the fall. Both James Hunter and Andy Crouch highlight the degree to which many Christians today either ignore the importance of institutions or are deeply suspicious of them. And yet, as Crouch writes, "Institutions are essential for flourishing."[32] If we believe we are called to care about justice, then we need to enter into each of our callings thinking about the people we encounter and the larger institutional realities that impact how those people are treated.

> *Living each of our callings in ways that engage the realities that lead to injustice and oppression requires hard work and imagination.*

This kind of multilayered kingdom thinking can apply to every institution and every calling. As you consider your own callings in light of the kingdom vision we are casting here, we invite you to be open to the Spirit's leading and prompting. Ask God to enable you to be receptive to the ways your local church can form and shape you to engage your callings in light of a biblical vision of justice, righteousness, and shalom. We encourage you to be in conversation with others in the family of God as you intentionally seek God's kingdom and righteousness in the different callings with which he has entrusted you.

Remember: just as we have sometimes underestimated God's determination to rescue *others* from lives of oppression, we have also underestimated God's determination to rescue *us* from lives of perceived comfort and safety so that we can be led into lives of courageous trust and hope in God's kingdom.

When I (Kristen) think about people I know who have been "sanctified and sent," I almost always think of a group of friends from college who have consistently sought to pursue their callings in light of the kingdom of God. Concerned about the segregation they noticed within the Christian fellowship groups of our college campus, these friends, from an array of ethnic backgrounds, took a spring break trip to John Perkins's Voice of Calvary Ministry in Jackson, Mississippi. Here they caught God's vision for racial reconciliation and Christian community development. After graduation they married, discerned God's paid callings upon their lives, and pursued graduate school to prepare for those callings. Mary Kay completed her master's degree in education. Romesh and Danny went to medical school. Sarah pursued nursing, while her husband, Corey, went to seminary to prepare for ministry. Matt became a financial adviser. Then they returned to the dream they believed God had formed in them during their college years—to be faithfully present in a specific neighborhood and in their respective callings for the long haul.

As they found themselves able to move to the Richmond area, they began to discern where specifically they should live. It was important to them that they be invited into a neighborhood rather than imposing themselves upon it. They deeply believed that they would not be the ones to bring God into the neighborhood to which they moved. Instead, they would join Jesus's ongoing kingdom mission as they connected with others from that neighborhood who were already faithfully engaging in God's kingdom work.

God opened doors to a specific neighborhood through a community member who invited them to move onto her street and a local pastor, Don, who sensed that God was sending them to the very neighborhood in which he had been born, raised, and continued to minister. Don began his life in one of the public housing developments in the Church Hill neighborhood in the East End of Richmond. Through a foster care program, he and all four of his siblings were eventually removed from the home of their biological parents and welcomed into the home of a godly family in the community. After attending college in a nearby part of Richmond, Don returned to the neighborhood. He and his wife, Florence, have been laboring faithfully in Church Hill their entire marriage. Don continues to serve the neighborhood through his involvement as lead pastor of a local church while also serving the larger city as the chair of the Richmond School Board.[33]

Based on his reputation as a respected pastor who was active in the community, Don was sought out by a couple members of this group of friends. They learned from Don that he had been praying for years for a movement of God's people in his neighborhood. His prayers were for a movement focused on racial reconciliation and Christian community development. Just like this group of friends, Don had been influenced by John Perkins and his vision for

Christians to commit to living and investing in underresourced neighborhoods. Don believed that this group was a direct answer to the prayers that he and others had been offering. When he invited them to move into the neighborhood, they prayerfully accepted the invitation. He has been a faithful and significant mentor since these friends moved into Church Hill, as their hearts have become increasingly troubled by issues that had long been burdening many of those who lived there long before they arrived.

After moving into the neighborhood, Mary Kay taught in the local elementary school before having children and serving the neighborhood by nurturing her family and regularly opening their home to house and feed people in the community. Her husband, Danny, is a pediatrician with a master's degree in public health who works as Richmond's deputy director of public health, helping to improve the medical options available to low-income residents. In conversation and discernment with others, Corey and Don eventually began a local church in the neighborhood that draws people to worship together from all walks of life. As they raise their children, Corey and his wife, Sarah, also regularly open their home to welcome and house others in need.

Catherine and Matt seek the flourishing of God's children through their commitment to the local public schools, which involves both relational and institutional engagement.[34] Romesh is a pediatrician at Virginia Commonwealth University, where he studies holistic health care for those from lower socioeconomic backgrounds, access to quality health care for Spanish-speaking patients, and childhood obesity (a problem that disproportionately impacts urban children). His wife, Lawson, began a nonprofit committed to helping urban youth experience the outdoors through year-round outdoor educational activities and summer camp scholarships, including a range of partnerships with inner-city schools, community organizations, churches, and tutoring groups.[35]

As this group of friends is continually drawn by the Holy Spirit into God's kingdom mission, they have found that they must live in dependent trust on God. During a recent visit, one of them shared with me that she has learned more than anything else that she alone can't change a thing, but that she can rely on God, who is always at work. Another shared that for every small need that they've seen met during their time in this neighborhood, they have become aware of hundreds that have gone unmet. He and his wife have learned that to persevere in hope, they have to depend on the help of their friends and neighbors and the grace of God.

While they face daily struggles and hard decisions, and they navigate the expectations and hopes of their parents (who pictured very different lives for their children and grandchildren), the Holy Spirit is with them in the journey, strengthening and leading them further into their identity as God's saints. With gratitude for God's grace, they offer their lives, their time, their money, their relationships, and their callings to God. They use the power and privilege that have been given to them in their callings as neighbors, mothers, fathers, friends, doctors, social entrepreneurs, and pastors to seek personal and structural justice, righteousness, and shalom for others. They worship together, and they confess together. Abiding in Christ, by the grace of God they are trying to seek first God's kingdom, justice, and righteousness with hope that their lives are bearing kingdom fruit in word and deed, although that fruit can sometimes be hard to see in the short term.

When I (Bethany) think about churches and organizations that are humbling themselves to be "sanctified and sent" in response to God's kingdom calling, I am especially encouraged by those I've come to know who have been pursuing the work of justice for years through prayer and the earnest study of Scripture, stepping out in small and large ways as God leads. Through the Spirit, their labor is bearing fruit beyond what they imagined when they started out, and countless more churches and organizations are planting seeds for fruit to be born in years to come.

Jason Butler once grabbed a copy of International Justice Mission's free downloadable resource—the Community Justice Assessment Tool—and took it with him to the church he pastors in Milwaukee. Using the tool as a guide to look at their community through the lens of justice, his church made a huge impact within just a couple of years, joining with other churches in the city to confront the multinational banks responsible for rampant foreclosures in the community. They also discovered a human trafficking operation and confronted it together with the local government. Once they learned that high-quality safe houses for rescued girls was one of the most critical needs in the work to fight human trafficking, the church partnered with other churches throughout the city and built a safe house. Jason and others in this coalition continue to uncover and find ways to meet needs in their own city as well as encourage leaders, pastors, and church communities in other cities all over the United States.

Rather than building a new facility for their own gatherings, a church community in California donated their building fund to build an aftercare safe house in the Philippines for girls who otherwise could not have been rescued.

House of Refuge meets the critical needs of safety and ushers former trafficking victims into lives where they can flourish.

Grace Farms in New Canaan, Connecticut, has forged an exquisite action-oriented cultural center situated on seventy-five acres of carefully preserved historic farmland. Free and open to the public year-round, Grace Farms provides space for reflection and prayer; exceptional performance, athletic, and library facilities; and regular lectures from top scholars and practitioners in the fields of justice, community development, and the arts.

Crossroads Community Church in Cincinnati, Ohio, saw the stark and crushing needs in Kolkata, India, home to some of the darkest exploitation of women and children on the planet. The work they've done in partnership with organizations local to Kolkata is meeting the deep recovery needs of rescued trafficking survivors in that city.

Another Crossroads Church, in Woodbury, Minnesota, took on an ordinary yet catastrophic problem of court file disorganization in Uganda. Members of this church flew to Uganda and met with widows and orphans who had been left crippled and destitute from the illegal seizure of their land (often by their own relatives after the death of their husband or father). After meeting with these women and children, the church learned that the reason so few of them receive justice is because their files are lost in massive stacks of papers crammed in attics full of bats and rodents, never to be seen by the court officials who have the power to protect them. At the end of their two-week trip—which consisted of twelve-hour days in hot, infested, cramped quarters—church members organized more than one hundred thousand files and created a sustainable filing system. Each file, representing the life of a woman and her children, can now see the light of day and radically help transform lives through basic protection of the law.

So many more stories could be told. Living into our justice calling as the church can take countless shapes. Where might God be calling you to join his kingdom mission? Who in your church and community could you link arms with to scout out the needs in your neighborhood, your city, or in a city across the world? What obstacles seem too big? How might you bring those needs and obstacles before God in prayer, inviting him to make a way and lead you to the next step?

As we pursue the justice calling, God invites each of us to consider what gifts and callings he has given to us that can be used in service of his kingdom. Rather than pursuing the use of these gifts in isolation, we need to join together, propelled by the work of the Holy Spirit in our midst. As we are sanctified and sent, we can offer our entire lives with gratitude to God, who so deeply loves us that he graciously gives us all we need to live as his children, seeking first his kingdom, justice, and righteousness.

7

Persevere in Hope

Justice and All Things Being Made New

Mala was trafficked into one of the most brutal brothels that International Justice Mission (IJM) had ever encountered.[1] The lead trafficker was powerful, wealthy, and deeply connected to a wide network of other traffickers in the underground world of rape for profit. He stopped at nothing to keep the girls in his brothel under his power. Some of his victims witnessed him murdering another girl simply to give a warning, lest they resist his will. If ever I was tempted to call another human being a monster, it would be this man. If ever there was a human being I would be tempted to believe was unreachable by the grace of God, by the redemption and new life offered in Jesus Christ, it would be this man, Mala's trafficker.

Loosely disguised as a hotel located just off a major freeway, the brothel where Mala was held was a frequent stop for truck drivers and men who wanted to buy sex. The front door led to a bar and restaurant, but if a customer asked for more, he was taken to a back room—the viewing room—where Mala and other girls were lined up. Trapped in this brothel for nearly a year, Mala had lost hope of escape. At the age of fifteen she was faced with the reality that so many victims of human trafficking have learned, that there were only two ways out: either be sold to another brothel or die.

Like all of the new girls, Mala was raped by the trafficker as her initiation into what she would be required to endure every day. The trafficker made his power clear to each of the girls in his brothel. Years later Mala explained to our staff, "He was the owner. No one could stop him."² Indeed, he believed he was invincible. One of the victims in his brothel recounted him saying, "I'll never be convicted because that is my power. I'll pay out on every level."

Mala and the other girls worked around the clock, raped by ten to twenty men every day. If they tried to refuse a customer, they were tortured. When Mala attempted (and failed) to run away, she was viciously beaten. After a few months in the brothel, Mala became pregnant, but her trafficker beat her even then, using a metal pipe and kicking her stomach. Mala lost her baby.

> *The idea of hope can begin to appear as nothing more than just that—an idea, fleeting and nebulous, like a vapor that appears for a moment and then evaporates.*

What hope could we possibly hold on to for Mala? Where do we even begin to look for hope in the face of what she suffers? In the face of the *millions* of lives her own suffering mirrors?

And what about Mala's trafficker? What hope could we possibly hold for him? And what would compel us to even attempt to hope for him?

The closer we get to suffering, the more the idea of hope can begin to appear as nothing more than just that—an idea, fleeting and nebulous, like a vapor that appears for a moment and then evaporates. But the author of Hebrews claims that hope is tangible, that hope is an anchor for our souls (Heb. 6:19). Hope is not a fleeting idea; we can "hold unswervingly to the hope we profess" (Heb. 10:23). Paul writes that hope is certain: "Since we have such a hope, we are *very bold*" (2 Cor. 3:12, emphasis added). Peter proclaims that through Christ we have been birthed into a "living hope" (1 Pet. 1:3). We can hope with certainty and boldness "for he who promised is faithful" (Heb. 10:23).

Our hope is not based on our own abilities to act or to change the world, and neither is it based on our ability to dredge up the capacity for hope. Our hope is entirely grounded in the reality that God has always cared about justice and has always called us to join him in seeking justice. God promises not only that his justice will be made known but also that he will hear and redeem and fully usher in his kingdom of justice and righteousness. Our God is faithful to the end. Because of what God has done, is doing, and will do in and through Jesus Christ and the Holy Spirit, we can enter a fallen world of suffering and heartache rooted in a persevering hope.[3]

A Night of Prayer

I (Bethany) will never forget seeing the jarring images from the brothel where Mala was held. I'll never forget the wry smiles captured on the faces of those who wielded their violent power against her and so many other girls. We first shared Mala's case with those those gathered for IJM's annual Global Prayer Gathering. We sensed the need to spend one night of our gathering focused on the most impossible situation our field staff was currently facing. That year, nothing seemed more impossible than shutting down that brothel.

Months prior, my colleagues serving in Mala's country had built a case documenting clear evidence of trafficking at the roadside "hotel" and presented it to a special force within the state-level law enforcement. This special force agreed to lead an operation to rescue Mala and the other underage girls who were trapped with her. But someone tipped off the brothel, letting the owner know a rescue operation was at hand. Months of meticulous planning were thwarted.

The team regrouped with the local law enforcement unit and prepared for another rescue operation. On the second attempt, the brothel owner was tipped off again.

And again.

. . . And again.

Seven times over six months they attempted rescues. Seven times they were thwarted by tip-offs coming from within the police force. Each time they moved forward with a rescue operation Mala's trafficker was successful in evacuating the brothel before the rescue team arrived.

But the body of Christ continued to pray. Early in these attempted rescue operations, we went to our prayer partners—thousands of committed intercessors all over the world—and asked them to pray. Recalling Paul's words, we asked them to boldly petition our God of justice to make a way in an impossible city where the darkness and brokenness of the fall were palpable. We used a temporary blog to post real-time updates, and in response our partners used the comments section of the blog to post their prayers for these girls and for the team and police seeking their rescue. Hundreds of prayers poured in through the blog, and thousands more believers prayed from wherever they were in the world.

Early in the year following the initial attempts at rescue, IJM worked closely with the local law enforcement team to prepare yet another rescue operation (the eighth attempt); police officers of goodwill were determined to stop the plan from getting leaked to the brothel owner. Strengthened by prayer from around the world, the rescue team went back to the brothel. While there was no tip-off this time, the brothel managers saw the cars coming into the area and began to scatter.

When the team of police and IJM staff reached the building, just a few girls were locked in their rooms, asleep. The brothel managers had chased most of the girls and women from the brothel with clubs.

IJM helped the authorities to bring the girls who had been left behind out into freedom. Three girls were rescued, but Mala, the girl from whom our team had gained the most evidence, was not among them.

The "People Who Care about These Girls"

Our staff had images of Mala's trafficker and others in the brothel, including photos of Mala and some of the missing girls. Tired and frustrated by all of the tip-offs, one of IJM's lawyers pulled out Mala's picture and showed it to a police officer. Beginning with Mala, she was hoping the officer knew someone who could help find out where the missing girls had been taken. The local police officer was surprised that our staff lawyer had a picture of a girl from the brothel. He asked why she wanted to find this girl. The lawyer calmly told the officer: "There are people who care about these girls." Little did this officer know just how many people across the world were praying and longing for these girls to be free.

Even though many police officers were still beholden to the brothel owner's power, these officers, by no small miracle, agreed to search for Mala in the area. The law enforcement community in Mala's country was so corruptly connected with the trafficking networks that they found Mala *within an hour*. From there forward, the scales of power in this case began to tip.

Mala and the other survivors were taken to a safe home for aftercare where they started to process the trauma and pain they had endured in the brothel. She shared with one of my colleagues that she is glad she will never again have to watch other girls her age being beaten to death with a club. I cannot begin to imagine carrying the burden that leads to this kind of relief.

Bringing Justice

While IJM social workers spent years building trust with Mala and helping her to move through her trauma into restoration, IJM lawyers spent years supporting a legal case against her trafficker and another brothel manager who had been arrested with him.

The first challenge was locating the trafficker, who had disappeared after his brothel was ordered closed. The man who once thought he was invincible was on the run. It took nine months, but he was finally arrested and could be charged for his crimes.

Our staff never knew what day this trafficker might be up for bail; the bail postings were announced on tattered sheets of paper hung on the wall at the courthouses each day. One of our staff members needed to be ready to contest the bail hearing on whatever day his case came up. Otherwise, he could be set free, and the pursuit of arrest would start all over again. If this man gained his freedom, more girls' lives would be endangered.

We asked them to boldly petition our God of justice to make a way in an impossible city where the darkness and brokenness of the fall were palpable.

Mala's trafficker applied for bail more than fifty times and in multiple courts. It took nearly three years of this relentless perseverance to ensure that he never got out on bail before the first court hearing could even take place. Three years, day after day of dogged perseverance.

After many more nearly debilitating delays, the trial was under way and three of the survivors, including Mala, had decided to testify. The decision to testify was incredibly courageous, not only because of the pain that arises fresh in the process of retelling the details of the abuse they had endured but also because testifying meant they would have to face—in the courtroom—the man who had raped and tortured them and profited from their exploitation. One of the survivors said she only dared to dream about a day when their trafficker would be convicted for his crimes. But if that day ever came, she said, "I also feel that the punishment should be announced, so that all the people doing the wrong things should get scared or frightened about doing these things."

God often reveals his justice in ways that we do not get to witness in our lifetime. But in this case of impossible obstacles too numerous to recount, we were able to see justice carried out in the here and now. In March 2013, Mala's trafficker and his manager were convicted and sentenced to ten years of hard labor. Her trafficker was also found guilty of rape—the first time this particular court gave a conviction for both trafficking and rape in the same case.

> *"All it takes is one conviction of [one trafficker] to keep hundreds of girls safe."*

One of my colleagues explained what the conviction means for the larger community in Mala's nation: "All it takes is one conviction of a man like [Mala's trafficker] to keep hundreds of girls safe." This has proven to be the case in the entire region where this particular trafficker once operated with impunity; the tables are turning, and great change is under way. The brothel where Mala was held was ordered closed and still remains closed. The local police force has also closed several other brothels in the same area that were once notorious for selling underage girls for sex.

Early in 2015 our director of South Asia reflected on how this case has spurred unprecedented change in the region since the first successful rescue back in 2009:

> What's so exciting about the incredible momentum we're seeing is the driver behind it. Six years ago [when Mala was rescued], just about every rescue operation depended on us gathering evidence and building a case. But now, police are regularly coming to us with solid cases and simply asking for our assistance in the operation.

The Church's Witness of Hope

The scourge of injustice across the globe gives us an opportunity to be a living testimony to the hope we have in Christ. Perhaps in more than any other era of human history, we have the opportunity to proclaim the persevering hope we have in the face of the overwhelming brokenness of this world. No other generation has been exposed on such a global scale to so many different

forms of horrific violence and abuse taking place or the desperate needs in
every country and continent. This is not to say that injustice has only recently
become a widespread phenomenon—not in the least. However, living in the
information age means we have unfettered access to knowledge about our
world, for better and for worse.

These new frontiers of knowledge can foster unprecedented hopelessness. As we are exposed to the abuse taking place in our neighborhoods
and across the globe, as we learn about children being sold into brothels
and families locked in slavery, as we realize that
authorities assigned to protect innocent citizens
are sometimes corrupt, we risk sliding into cynicism and despair.

But this unprecedented knowledge also gives
us the tremendous opportunity to give "an ac-
counting for the hope" that is in each of us (1 Pet.
3:15 NRSV). Why can we hope in the midst of
brutal injustice? Because the story is not over
yet. Because we serve a God who in Christ has
entered into this broken world and conquered
sin and evil, who reigns with justice and righteousness over this world, and who will not rest
until his kingdom has finally and fully come to
this earth.

*Perhaps in more
than any other
era of human
history, we have
the opportunity
to proclaim the
persevering hope we
have in the face of
the overwhelming
brokenness of
this world.*

This is not a cheap hope; our hope is often
broken, bloodstained, and costly as was Christ's
sacrifice on the tree at Golgatha. This is not a trite hope; in the midst of our
hope we still need to acknowledge and lament the places in this world that fall
short of God's kingdom vision. This is not a passive hope; this active hope
intentionally joins God in his ministry of reconciliation. It is a hope rooted
in the power of the light of Jesus Christ to finally and fully overcome all the
darkness of the world in his perfect timing.

At every point of the biblical story, God's faithful, steadfast love is made
manifest in God's ongoing commitment to this world as a place of justice,
righteousness, and shalom. God consistently calls his people to be set apart
by their loving pursuit of justice, righteousness, and shalom. Yet as prophets
like Habakkuk and others throughout the millennia know, our mission to
fight the evils of injustice is not safe, comfortable, or easy. Justice can be

scary, dangerous, and despair-inducing work. But it is work to which we are all called, and it must be rooted in the hope of Christ if we want to persevere. As we come to the end of the Scripture story (which is yet only the beginning), we are given biblical glimpses of how Christ our King will return to this earth to fully and completely usher in his kingdom of love, justice, righteousness, and shalom. As we move toward a deeper grasp of these biblical truths, mere glimpses though they may be, the Holy Spirit can profoundly ground us in persevering hope.

The Return of Christ the King

We are not the only ones who long for a day when healing and new life will reign. When God looks at this broken world and the suffering we still experience, God longs for the day when he will fully dwell with us in a redeemed creation that has no more death, mourning, pain, or tears (Rev. 21:4). When this happens, Christ the King will have finally and fully overcome all the brokenness in this world.

Throughout our exploration of the biblical story we have repeated this consistent and defining conviction: Jesus Christ will come again. In fulfillment of all the promises of redemption made by God to his people throughout Scripture, this coming will complete all that Jesus started when his reign as King began with his ministry on earth. The "already/not yet" dynamic of the kingdom in which we've been living will turn to full consummation.

Jesus himself promised to return to bring the kingdom to its full realization and creation to its full redemption. Because of God's faithful love (*hesed*), which is evident throughout Scripture and embodied in Jesus Christ, we can trust God's promise that he will be faithful to the end. When he comes we will see the realization of shalom as all things are fully and finally set right. In this new creation, God's people will live in complete union with God and in restored relationships with one another and the created world. God will dwell with us as all of creation lives and flourishes together. Righteousness and justice will have finally and fully prevailed.

When Christ returns to consummate his kingdom of righteousness and justice, there will be a final judgment against all that is not right and just. It is critical to remember that God's judgment against unrighteousness is *good* news because it is God's condemnation and victory over the evil and injustice of the world. Christ the King will not allow any evil or suffering to remain in his kingdom as he brings his final condemnation of all that prevents his people and his creation from flourishing. This final judgment is not meant to induce fear; as we live in Christ "we know and rely on the love God has for us," a "perfect love" that "drives out fear" (1 John 4:16, 18).

As Christ the King ushers in this new age of justice, righteousness, and shalom, he is not merely turning this world back into the original garden of Eden. As theologian Michael Horton writes, "The new creation is not an *ex nihilo* creation. It is not a return to the beginning, but the everlasting Sabbath that was forfeited by the first Adam. The Spirit is associated throughout Scripture with bringing about the *fulfillment* of God's plans: in creation, redemption, and the consummation. Every gift we receive through union with Christ here and now is a morsel of the age to come."[4] Christians throughout the ages have believed that the age to come involves a transformation of creation in which God's original vision for creation will be realized even as the new creation goes beyond what it was before and anything we could imagine here and now.[5]

> *God will dwell among his creation as all of creation lives and flourishes together. Righteousness and justice will have finally and fully prevailed.*

Scripture gives us glimpses of this transformation. Paul writes that our bodies will be transformed in the age to come in ways that we can't yet imagine as our perishable bodies become imperishable (1 Cor. 15). Jesus himself was not immediately recognizable after his resurrection (Luke 24:15–16; John 20:14), and yet neither did his body return to an unmarked condition; he kept his scars after his resurrection from the dead even as he was transformed (John 20:24–28). This suggests that our condition in the age to come does not represent a return to innocence, as if sin and suffering had never occurred. The scars we acquire in this broken world will remain with us in the age to come, but Christ makes us whole and wipes away the tears that came with those scars. Throughout the Bible, the images of our life with God shift quite dramatically as well—from living in a garden in the opening pages of Genesis to dwelling in a city with God and one another in the closing pages of Revelation 21.

There is a lot we don't know about the age to come. N. T. Wright has dedicated considerable effort and energy to exploring the nature of Christ's return, and even he acknowledges that "all Christian language about the future is a set of signposts pointing into a mist."[6] The Bible points us in a certain direction, but it does not give us a detailed picture of what the age to come will look like. And yet, as Wright points out, signposts are worth paying attention to because they point you in the right direction.[7]

Signposts of the Kingdom

One of these significant scriptural signposts is found in the book of Isaiah, which includes words spoken to the people of God as they struggled in exile. Given as a promise of redemption in the future, these words serve as a source of hope in the present: God promises a new age in which the brokenness of the current age is overcome on every level. As we look at the marks of this new age, we get a beautiful picture of the full redemption that God longs for and promises to deliver in the age to come.

> "See, I will create
>   new heavens and a new earth.
> The former things will not be remembered,
>   nor will they come to mind.
> But be glad and rejoice forever
>   in what I will create,
> for I will create Jerusalem to be a delight
>   and its people a joy.
> I will rejoice over Jerusalem
>   and take delight in my people;
> the sound of weeping and of crying
>   will be heard in it no more.
>
> Never again will there be in it
>   an infant who lives but a few days,
>   or an old man who does not live out his years;
> the one who dies at a hundred
>   will be thought a mere child;
> the one who fails to reach a hundred
>   will be considered accursed.
> They will build houses and dwell in them;
>   they will plant vineyards and eat their fruit.

No longer will they build houses and others live in them,
> or plant and others eat.
For as the days of a tree,
> so will be the days of my people;
my chosen ones will long enjoy
> the work of their hands.
They will not labor in vain,
> nor will they bear children doomed to misfortune;
for they will be a people blessed by the LORD,
> they and their descendants with them.
Before they call I will answer;
> while they are still speaking I will hear.
The wolf and the lamb will feed together,
> and the lion will eat straw like the ox,
> and dust will be the serpent's food.
They will neither harm nor destroy
> on all my holy mountain,"
says the LORD. (Isa. 65:17–25)

This signpost suggests that God will delight in his people, dwelling so closely that he will know their desire for him before they even call. No longer will people feel like they cry out and God does not hear them. No longer will people be enslaved as the fruit of their labor goes to someone else; they will be able to enjoy the work of their hands. The animals that formerly preyed on each other will live together in peace, and God will eliminate all sources of weeping and crying, including the death of babies and the elderly alike.

These marks of the new age correspond closely with God's vision of shalom and reverse the implications of the fall that need to be overcome. God's closeness with his people is restored as they delight in one another and share intimate fellowship. God's call to his people to steward creation is fully restored through joyful work rather than drudgery. Nothing that causes harm to any living creature will be allowed in God's future kingdom.

Another hopeful signpost is found in Revelation. As in Isaiah, we're given a promise of "a new heaven and a new earth," anticipating a new age that God will bring about:

Then I saw "a new heaven and a new earth," for the first heaven and the first earth had passed away, and there was no longer any sea. I saw the Holy City, the new Jerusalem, coming down out of heaven from God, prepared as a bride beautifully dressed for her husband. And I heard a loud voice from the throne saying, "Look! God's dwelling place is now among the people, and he will dwell with them. They will be his people, and God himself will be with them and be their God. 'He will wipe every tear from their eyes. There will be no more death' or mourning or crying or pain, for the old order of things has passed away."

At each and every level, justice and righteousness will fill everything in every way because God himself will fill all things. Here, at last, all *will be fully set right.*

He who was seated on the throne said, "I am making everything new!" Then he said, "Write this down, for these words are trustworthy and true." (Rev. 21:1–5)

When I (Bethany) was fourteen years old my brother David and sister Ann gave me a Bible. I carried that Bible with me for years until the pages literally fell out—not even tape could keep them in. As I began reading that Bible one of the very first Scriptures that I clung to was the promise of God wiping every tear from our eyes. Even at the age of fourteen I had gaping aches in my soul that couldn't be comforted except by this truth that God will one day heal it all. The promise in Revelation is that God's consistent desire for justice will be finally and fully realized—no more death, mourning, crying, or pain. God's faithful and steadfast love will be on full display as he completely fills his covenant promise to dwell intimately among his people.

In another signpost passage in Revelation we see that the new age will include the fulfillment of God's desire for a people who not only dwell with God but also rule (in perfect unity with one another) on God's behalf, *on this earth*. Through God's fulfillment of his redemptive promises, the original call to God's people to live in union with God and one another while they have dominion over God's created world is finally and fully realized. As we read in Revelation, God's people, who are drawn from "every tribe and language and people and nation . . . will reign on the earth" (Rev. 5:9–10).

At each and every level, justice and righteousness will fill everything in every way because God himself will fill all things. Here, at last, *all* will be fully set right.

This Earth Renewed

The books of Isaiah and Revelation both use the language of "new heaven and new earth" to describe the age to come, but scholars disagree on what exactly is meant by *new*. In its most general sense it refers to a new age ushered in by God. But more specifically, does it mean that this earth will be renewed? Or does it mean that this earth will be entirely replaced by something new?

> *Eternal life with God does not mean an escape from this earth but rather new life on this earth. Our bodies and all of creation matter to God, even now.*

In his exploration of the book of Revelation, biblical scholar Ben Witherington III suggests that the biblical witness could support either interpretation. He notes that other parts of Scripture, along with Jewish understandings of resurrection at the time of the writing of Revelation, could go either way on the question of whether this earth will be renewed or entirely replaced. What cannot be denied is that this vision of fulfillment involves God's kingdom coming *to this earth*. When God promises to make all things new, he is not promising an escape from this earth but the redemption of this very world:

> It is important to remember that John's vision is not merely about salvation from the world and its injustices. It is also about salvation *of* the world, including the redemption of the earth and the material cosmos itself. John, like other early Christians such as Paul, was not interested in propagating an otherworldly or world-negating religion. To the contrary, John believes this is still God's world, and God intends to remedy the human dilemma, ultimately within space and time.[8]

God's vision of the renewal that will take place when Christ returns is, as Witherington concludes, "the invasion of earth by heaven, thereby finally entirely sanctifying the earthly realm."[9] It is the holiness of God drawing near, making this earth and all of its inhabitants holy as God is holy. And we know from the witness of the entire biblical narrative that God's holiness makes itself known as justice and righteousness.

Eternal life with God does not mean an escape from this earth but rather new life on this earth. Scripture makes it clear that the afterlife with God includes both spiritual and physical dimensions; while this earth and our human bodies will most certainly be transformed, our bodies and the earth will still exist. Our bodies and all of creation matter to God, even now.

In Paul's first Letter to the Corinthians he offers a vigorous defense of the belief that our bodies will be resurrected as Christ's body was resurrected. He writes, "The body that is sown is perishable, it is raised imperishable; it is sown in dishonor, it is raised in glory; it is sown in weakness, it is raised in power; it is sown a natural body, it is raised a spiritual body" (1 Cor. 15:42–44). That our resurrection bodies will be in continuity with our earthly bodies while being deeply transformed, as witnessed in the resurrection body of Christ and attested to in Paul's first Letter to the Corinthians, is a microcosm of what will be true of the creation as a whole.

According to Paul, when the physical body is changed into its imperishable form we will know that death finally has been overcome. He continues:

> Listen, I tell you a mystery: We will not all sleep, but we will all be changed—in a flash, in the twinkling of an eye, at the last trumpet. For the trumpet will sound, the dead will be raised imperishable, and we will be changed. For the perishable must clothe itself with the imperishable, and the mortal with immortality. When the perishable has been clothed with the imperishable, and the mortal with immortality, then the saying that is written will come true: "Death has been swallowed up in victory."
>
> > "Where, O death, is your victory?
> > Where, O death, is your sting?"
>
> The sting of death is sin, and the power of sin is the law. But thanks be to God! He gives us the victory through our Lord Jesus Christ. (1 Cor. 15:51–57)

Romans 8 anticipates that nothing will be able to keep creation from being all that God intended it to be in the age to come. We will no longer need to lament the sin that keeps things from being the way they should be. Our hope in the age to come is that the reconciliation that we experience now in Christ will be extended to and visible throughout the entire world, as God in Christ finally and fully reconciles all things.

The New Creation Matters for Justice

The belief that Christ is going to return and renew this creation has profound implications for the way we live into God's justice calling today. If we accept the gnostic premise discussed in chapter 6, that salvation involves only our souls and not our bodies, we will understand Christian life and ministry primarily in terms of saving souls, not caring for bodies. If the life to come is located in a heavenly realm apart from this created world, we will think in terms of rescue from this world rather than how to help people live faithfully and justly right where we are now.

Within the past two centuries, a pervasive belief has developed that understands evangelism as a call for sinners to jump from a sinking ship into the lifeboat of Christ.[10] This analogy teaches that this sinful world is going down, but if we jump into the lifeboat by believing in Christ, our souls will be saved for all eternity as we flee to heaven. With its focus on souls, not bodies, on the spiritual, not the physical, this picture of salvation presents a false dichotomy that is not faithful to the biblical narrative. It does not honor the degree to which God loves this world. God's love for his creation can be seen throughout Scripture—from the act of creation itself to God taking on flesh in the person of Jesus Christ to the promise of full redemption for our bodies and this created world.

Jesus did not ask us to follow him away from this world. He taught us to pray,

> your kingdom come,
> your will be done,
>   on earth as it is in heaven. (Matt. 6:10)

Creation groans toward redemption, and one day our redemption will be complete (Rom. 8:18–24). The new age will be full of resurrected bodies who will join with "*every* creature in heaven and on earth and under the earth and on the sea, and all that is in them" to sing blessing and honor and glory and might to the Lamb on the throne (Rev. 5:13, emphasis added).

Understanding Christ's ultimate redemption of all things helps us to live into our calling here and now—to love God and others with justice and righteousness, addressing needs that are inextricably spiritual and physical. From the beginning of the story to the end, we see God caring about the flourishing of humanity and creation on every level. We too are called to care about this flourishing on every level. The signposts we receive from Scripture that give us glimpses into the age to come must impact our commitment in the age in which we are living now. As Brad Harper and Paul Louis Metzger write, "God's eschatological promise of justice and peace means the church should work to establish these realities on earth now. Paul's vision of the future healing of the earth and humanity in ways that go beyond spiritual regeneration (Rom. 8:15) means that the church should work for the healing of earth and humanity now."[11]

The signposts we receive from Scripture that give us glimpses into the age to come should impact our commitment to the age in which we are living now.

In place of the image of the world as a sinking ship, Scripture and the teachings of Eugene Peterson have inspired us to hold the image of a rose garden.[12] God created this world to be a beautiful garden, and though it was overrun by weeds and thorns that cause real pain, God did not abandon it. In Christ God came to this garden, redeemed and transformed it, and remains active in it through the Spirit. With the presence and power of God in our lives and in this place, we can and ought to work together to pull the weeds and overcome the thorns even as we await the day when the Master Gardener will come to decisively pull all the weeds and remove the thorns that keep it from being the beautiful, flourishing, thorn-free rose garden he intended.

Our Labor Is Not in Vain

"Christ has died. Christ has risen. Christ will come again." Still used in churches today, this ancient liturgical refrain reminds us that the most important work has been done and will be done by Jesus Christ. Nowhere in Scripture do we read that Christ will come again as a result of our human activity. Nowhere do we read that we need to—or that we can—usher in God's kingdom ourselves.

And yet, strangely enough, the conviction that Christ is not relying on us for his return, that he will usher in his kingdom in his timing, is meant to motivate us to persevere in our kingdom work here and now. After Paul declares Jesus's victory over death, highlights the change we will experience in our resurrection bodies, and notes that this change will happen when Christ decides the time is ripe, "in a moment, in the twinkling of an eye" (1 Cor. 15:52 ESV), Paul concludes, "*Therefore*, my dear brothers and sisters, stand firm. Let nothing move you. Always give yourselves fully to the work of the Lord, because you know that your labor in the Lord is not in vain" (1 Cor. 15:58, emphasis added).

Believing that Christ will usher in his kingdom in his own way and time does not make our efforts irrelevant. Rather, our work is animated by our certainty that Christ's justice will prevail over the deepest injustices we encounter. Our response to God's call to justice is inspired by the wholeness and reconciliation we anticipate and know God longs to see in this world. Just as the apostles' certainty of Christ's kingship and victory empowered their ministries, sustained them in times of darkness, and provided hope in times of suffering, hope in the promise of Christ's return should shape our action here and now. Consider the apostle

> *The conviction that Christ is not relying on us for his return, that he will come again to usher in his kingdom in his timing, is meant to motivate us to persevere in our kingdom work here and now.*

Peter, who declared the end of all things near and then encouraged Christians to—above all—pray, love one another deeply, offer hospitality, use their gifts to serve others as faithful stewards of God's grace, speak the words of God to one another, and serve others with the strength God provides (1 Pet. 4:7–11).

Invitation for Today: Persevere in Hope

As we live in hope of Christ's return to fully and finally set all things right, how do we become a people who witness to persevering hope in the face of the real injustices of our world? How do we hold fast to hope for victims of injustice who wait to be rescued? And what about those who perpetrate injustice? What is our hope for Mala's trafficker and for all who commit horrors of abuse in our world?

Apart from God, our first response to this trafficker would likely be more focused on the need for (severe) punishment than the hope of redemption. At least, that is my (Bethany's) own raw response. But justice begins in the heart of God, and justice doesn't end when a perpetrator is finally put in jail. All of creation is aching and groaning for redemption, for justice that not only protects victims from violence and holds criminals responsible for their crimes but also for justice that stretches all the way to the final fulfillment of shalom—to the redemption and reconciliation of even the most vile evil (and human perpetrators of evil) known to our world. No sin, no brokenness, no injustice falls outside the reach of God's love; no suffering and no brutality is beyond the power of the ultimate restoration and culmination of God's glory in the age to come.

Loving violent criminals with the love of Jesus is certainly not beyond the scope of how God can use us in this world. Love for all people is at the heart of what Jesus teaches, at the core of what it means to be holy and set apart. What could be more counter-cultural than loving our enemies? And in what way could we be more obedient to Jesus's direct call?

No sin, no brokenness, no injustice falls outside the reach of God's love.

My husband, children, and I (Bethany) recently had the privilege of joining our neighbors, Hope and Jeremy, for their Passover Seder. This particular year the first night of Passover fell on Good Friday, bringing a stunning connection for us. Our Jewish neighbors were celebrating the blood of the lamb, which saved Israel from the plague of death brought upon Egypt as a result of their enslavement of God's people, the final plague that opened the way for the Israelites' exodus out of slavery. We too were celebrating the blood of the lamb—Jesus Christ, crucified on the cross and risen on the third day, the blood that saves us from death and frees us from all slavery to sin and death.

Moving through the Haggadah (the order of prayers and Scriptures that guide the Passover meal), I was particularly struck by the liturgy's instructions as to how to regard Pharoah's army and their deadly destruction in the waters of the Red Sea:

It is said: "When Israel saw the great deed the Eternal had done against the Egyptians, the people stood in awe of God. . . ."

AT THAT TIME, the ministering angels began to sing a song of praise before the Holy One, but God rebuked them, saying, "My children are drowning, and you sing praises!"

And then all join together to pray:

O God, teach us to rejoice in freedom,
but not in its cost for us and our enemies.

> let there come a day when violence is no more,
> and we shall be free to rejoice without sadness,
> to sing without tears.[13]

As we prayed these words aloud together, sitting around my neighbors' table, I couldn't help but think of all of us who are working and yearning for justice today. Even as we long for and plead with God to rescue the oppressed and to restrain the oppressor, our celebration when the oppressed are freed is not to come at the expense of those who have perpetrated injustice. When traffickers are finally put in jail, we don't rejoice at their demise but rather pray and ache for the fullness of justice and the redemption of flourishing new life to reach them as well.

Personally, I long for the day when we might hear the story of how, under the restraint of the law, Mala's trafficker and many others like him encountered the limitless grace of God in Christ, repented of the horrific violence brought on scores of young girls, and shared a wealth of underground intelligence to bring down trafficking rings all over India and the rest of the world. We need to remind and teach one another to hope and long for the day when we might stand side by side with even those we are tempted to write-off as most evil and beyond hope in this world, receiving new life and wholeness and freedom together in Jesus Christ.

This hope is not too great for our God, who created and sent his Son to redeem Mala's trafficker just as he created and sent his Son to redeem you and me. God longs for a restored relationship with Mala's trafficker just as he longs for deeper relationships with you and me. God can change the heart and life of this trafficker as he changed the heart and life of John Newton. To be recipients of God's grace and mercy is to be reminded that we live in utter dependence on God's forgiveness and that we need to do all we can to extend God's offer of forgiveness to others. We serve a God who, while dying on the cross, prayed that those who unjustly killed him would be forgiven (Luke 23:34). The extravagance of God's reconciling and redeeming love knows no limit.

In Revelation 7 we read of "a great multitude that no one could count, from every nation, from all tribes and peoples and languages, standing before the throne and before the Lamb, robed in white, with palm branches in their hands," united in praising God (7:9–10 NRSV). Jesus Christ came in fulfillment of God's covenant promise to Abraham, in which God said that all peoples would be blessed through his descendants. In this final act of the story we see all peoples united through Christ in worship of God. This vision can invigorate us here and now as we bear witness to God's saving and reconciling grace before all people—grace that can break down every barrier and overcome all hostility (Eph. 2:14–15).

But our lives and our churches do *not yet* fully reflect this new reality. Most churches continue to reflect the world's divisions more than the kingdom's unity. Most churches continue to reflect culturally constricted responses to evil and injustice more than God's commitment to redeem and reconcile all things. How do we become a people whose lives reflect God's hopeful vision of reconciliation? How do we become a people who live with active love and persevering hope for the victims and the perpetrators of injustice?

Worship

One of the central ways that God forms us into a people of persevering hope is through worship. In worship, we come together to honor and glorify God in grateful acknowledgment of the grace of God in Christ enables us to live as God's holy people. At the same time, worship nourishes us and forms us through the work of the Holy Spirit. By the grace of God, it helps us to see more clearly who God is and what the kingdom of God entails so that we can become more fully who we are called to be as God's covenant people, seeking the justice and righteousness of God's kingdom. As Justo González writes, "Worship is also an act of rehearsal. It is an anticipation of things to come. . . . It is practice for the Kingdom. It is a foretaste of the Reign of God."[14]

> *To be recipients of God's grace and mercy is to be reminded that we live in utter dependence on God's forgiveness and that we need to do all we can to extend God's offer of forgiveness to others.*

It is common today to emphasize that *every* part of our lives should be offered to God as worship, and this rationale is sometimes used as an excuse not to gather together with other believers for communal worship. But our desires and practices are shaped in every moment of our lives by influences all around us that are far more powerful than we realize. We have to be intentional about gathering together in worship to allow God to shape us through this foretaste of the kingdom. To become people who live with hope in a hopeless world, who live for God's justice in a world marked by injustice, we need to be regularly and consistently formed into kingdom people.

Through worship we can be shaped into people who share God's kingdom vision for others and this world. Mark Labberton vividly describes worship as "the dangerous act of waking up to God and to the purposes of God in the world, and then living lives that actually show it."[15] In Labberton's book *The Dangerous Act of Worship* he probes the ways in which worship ought to open our eyes to God's vision for the world and propel us to live in light of that vision. The worship that God calls us to is centered on the "glory and honor due God—Father, Son, and Spirit" and includes "the enactment of God's love and justice, mercy and kindness in the world."[16] These aspects of worship are mutually related: as we enter into

> *The things we undertake in the rest of our lives need to be "tethered to and nourished by the practices of Christian worship."*

worship of God, we come to learn more about who God is and what he cares about, which in turn forms us into people who deeply love God and deeply care about the things God cares about.

As we engage again and again in practices of worship, they "get hold of our heart and 'aim' our love toward the kingdom of God"; they form us into people who *desire* the kingdom, as James K. A. Smith puts it.[17] Worship isn't just a nice thing we do that helps us to become kingdom-desiring people in the rest of our lives. According to Smith, the things we undertake in the rest of our lives actually need to be "tethered to and nourished by the practices of Christian worship."[18] Without regular worship with the body of Christ and the formative power of Christian liturgies of worship that shape us as we move "beyond Sunday" into the rest of our lives, what we undertake in the rest of our lives will be shaped instead by cultural distortions of the kingdom.

Eucharist

The Eucharist (also called the Lord's Supper, Mass, or communion) is perhaps the component of worship that most deeply forms us into people who live with persevering hope. Despite many different traditions, interpretations, and practices that have arisen since the time of Christ, the church has been united in understanding Jesus's Last Supper as an invitation to regularly remember the life, witness, and death of Jesus. In the communion liturgy of the church that I (Kristen) worship in, we describe the Lord's Supper as a feast of remembrance, communion, and hope.[19] Through this meal, God helps us to *remember* what Christ has done by offering himself in our place as the Passover Lamb so that we might be freed from our slavery to sin and become God's holy people, living the way of justice and righteousness. God enables us to *commune* with God and one another, receiving the reconciliation that Jesus Christ made possible so that we can live as beloved children of God, united with God and one another.

And God shapes us into people of *hope* as we receive a glimpse of the abundant feasts that all will enjoy and of the fully reconciled relationships that all will experience in the new age, when all will be set right. As Smith writes, we can view "the Eucharistic feast as a tiny normative picture of the justice that characterizes the coming kingdom of God." Just as "the bread and wine are freely and equally distributed" in communion, so in the age to come there will be no hunger or thirst. Just as the communion table is "a table where God sits down with those who were once his enemies" (Rom. 5:10; Col. 1:21), so in the age to come all enmity and discord will be overcome.[20] As we receive the eucharistic feast, we are being shaped into people who freely receive from God so that we can freely share with others, who can receive reconciliation from God so that we can seek reconciliation with others.

Receiving the Eucharist is intended to be a practice that the Holy Spirit uses to shape us more and more into the holy people of God seeking God's kingdom of justice and righteousness in this world. Orthodox theologian Alexander Schmemann goes so far as to suggest that the church cannot fulfill its calling to bear witness to the kingdom, cannot enter the world in mission, without first receiving the Eucharist.[21] Receiving the Eucharist leads us to the table in the kingdom, and from that kingdom table we can see creation become "what it always was to be and yet failed to be."[22] The Eucharist forms us into eucharistic people who gratefully offer our lives to God in service of God and his kingdom vision. As we are sent back into the world after receiving the Eucharist together, we do so with Spirit-shaped kingdom vision for who we are to be and what creation as a whole is to be. God uses this vision to strengthen us to move into this world and its messy and broken places; to be formed into the people of God by the Spirit is to be formed into a justice-seeking people.

Year after year, IJM closes its Global Prayer Gathering with a time of Eucharist. Followers of Jesus from across the globe and across the theological spectrum join together at this table. Even those who are uncertain about taking the elements of the body and blood of Christ outside of their own church come forward; with arms crossed, they receive a prayer of blessing as clergy and laypeople join in the unity of being the body of Christ together—broken, spilled out, sent into the world. It's our very last act together as we close two days of intensive prayer and worship and prepare to move forward into life with God and pursuit of his justice in the year ahead.

This past year, pastor and seminary president Steve Hayner offered a sermon during our time of Eucharist. Steve was a dear friend and mentor to me (Bethany), as well as a significant adviser for IJM and many global organizations. We didn't know it at the time, but Steve would not live to join us for another Global Prayer Gathering. His sermon for our Eucharist was one of his last public engagements: two weeks later he learned that he was dying of pancreatic cancer.

Even as we didn't know what lay ahead for Steve, I remember the profound power his words imparted to us as we prepared to leave the gathering and enter the work of justice to which God was calling us. Now that Steve's life has been swallowed up by Life eternal (2 Cor. 5:4), his words bear the power, truth, and beauty of Jesus Christ all the more. As we close this biblical story, we invite you to receive the words that Steve offered and be formed in persevering hope as you consider how God is calling you to join his work of justice in the days and years before the fullness of Life ushers in a world where all things have been made new.

> We can view "the Eucharistic feast as a tiny normative picture of the justice that characterizes the coming kingdom of God."

For the past two days we have listened to stories of violence and oppression, of suffering and agony, and of courage and deliverance. Through all of the darkness, which we would rather not have to encounter, we have prayed and we have sat in silence.

I can't help but wonder what the watching world might think of what we are doing here. No doubt some would applaud us for at least paying attention to what is happening to people throughout the world. But I'm afraid that others would just say that we are hopelessly naïve to think that praying accomplishes anything, or that a few successes really don't mean much in light of the evil which is in our world and in our human hearts. . . .

So are we just naïve after all? Is all of this finally a waste of time?

Jesus knew that this is what his disciples would soon be asking as they watched him tortured, beaten, and finally die on the cross. All their hopes that he was really the one who could save Israel would be shattered. And for them there were likely sleepless nights and anxiety filled days as they huddled together in the upper room taunted by their own inner voices that yelled, "You were just so naïve to think that he was actually the Messiah who would bring healing, freedom and wholeness."

Jesus knew the pain and the helplessness which his disciples would feel then and now. He knew that there would be plenty of people who would say that we are not sensible—that we are just naïve. And so he told the disciples on the night before he died that along the journey they should frequently take the bread and the cup as he had done—and when they did, they should remember that hope is not found in looking at the "facts on the ground," but rather in looking to the One who was himself Hope—who walked out of a tomb and became the first fruits of a future guaranteed by the Sovereign God of the universe.

Every time we come to this Table, we declare that we are not merely wishful believers, but we are faithful disciples with our eyes fixed on the risen Lord.[23]

Amen. Come, Lord Jesus. Fill us with persevering hope.

Conclusion: Abide in Jesus

Justice and Perseverance

The night before his crucifixion, Jesus described himself as "the true vine" (John 15:1). Those who follow Jesus are branches of this true vine. He teaches that if we remain rooted in him we will bear much fruit but warns that apart from him we can do nothing (John 15:5).

If ever there was a moment in history for Christians to remain firmly affixed to the vine that is Jesus Christ, it is now. We are able to be aware of the needs of every neighbor on the planet in a way that has never been possible before. Opportunities to live our faith in a world full of suffering and injustice abound. If we root ourselves in any other vine than the vine of Jesus Christ—if we lean on our own ability to save rather than the saving love of Christ, our own strength rather than the enduring strength of the Holy Spirit, our own

> *If we lean on our own ability to save rather than the saving love of Christ, our own strength rather than the enduring strength of the Holy Spirit, our own visions of the "good life" rather than God's vision of flourishing—we will wither on that vine.*

visions of the "good life" rather than God's vision of flourishing—we will wither on that vine. Unless we abide in Christ, our very best efforts and successes are ultimately fruitless.

I (Bethany) vividly remember the day I was introduced to the phrase "prayer-less striving." It was June 1, 2004—my very first day as an employee of International Justice Mission (IJM)—and all IJM staff in the United States were gathered for a day of prayer.[1] Our president, Gary Haugen, was teaching about what it means to do the work of justice first and foremost as a fruit of being formed in Jesus Christ. "Prayerless striving," he explained, is a daily temptation for anyone who desires to work against injustice. Prayer, he continued, needs to be understood simply and essentially as "talking to God about what it is that we are doing together."

Working against injustice and all that is broken in our world begins with seeking God, who loves justice and who longs for the world to flourish. Our work begins with Jesus Christ, whose very life and death embodied the fullness of the call to justice that we are seeking to obey and who continues to be alive and active in this world as King and Lord. Our work begins with the Holy Spirit—who fills us, strengthens us, intercedes for us, and draws us into life with Christ and the ongoing mission of God in this world.

But the work of justice is hard and long. And while seeing justice accomplished brings one of the most exhilarating joys a follower of Jesus Christ could ever know, the journey to victory is fraught with difficulties. More often than not, perseverance is the deciding factor.

> *The work of justice is hard and long. . . . More often than not, perseverance is the deciding factor.*

Moving forward together, one step at a time as the body of Christ, we need to engage our justice calling with passion *and* perseverance. Perseverance comes as we recognize more fully that justice begins in the heart of God, not in our faltering ideas and intentions, our anger at injustice, our desire to make a difference, our frustration, our ambition, our sadness in the face of pain, or our desire to please others or do what others are doing. Justice that perseveres is justice that is intimately connected to our life in Christ. Life that is rooted in Jesus Christ by the Holy Spirit, who draws us into the story of Scripture and connects us to the ongoing life of the church, sees the present and future mission of God's kingdom as integrally connected with this Jesus-rooted justice.

Jesus commands us to love and to seek justice—not as frantic and reactive producers of justice but rather as bearers of the fruit *he* is producing. Jesus invites us to abide in him as branches of a vine; in so doing, we allow his fruit to be born *through* us, not *because* of us. Jesus is the one who will produce fruit through us, enabling us to bear the fruit in due season. But given the enormity of the need around us, we are easily lured to attach instead to vines that are not Christ. We run after justice as a pursuit of our own rather than knowing justice as fruit born out of deep abiding in Jesus.

Jesus's call to abide in him is the cornerstone of understanding his call to seek justice for those who suffer oppression and violent abuse. The act of abiding is not passive. It does not mean inactivity or disregard for the needs around us. It simply means that we respond to every need and every moment from a place of deep trust in Jesus Christ and an understanding that our identity lies in him, not in our ability to seek and bear justice.

> *We run after justice as a pursuit of our own rather than knowing justice as fruit born out of deep abiding.*

The work of justice is guaranteed to bring about discouragement, sleeplessness, intense questioning, physical danger, roadblocks, and spiritual attack. While our unprecedented access to stories of injustice and violence in our world today can spark passion, indignation, and a desire to act, it is nearly impossible to sustain an impulsive and emotionally driven response over the long haul. Reactive, emotion-driven action suffers from a lack of healthy roots from which to draw nourishment. To use another biblical image, our passion can sprout up quickly and then wither just as quickly, like seeds that fall on rocky, shallow soil (Matt. 13).

In contrast to seed planted in rocky, shallow soil, the Gospels offer the vision of seed that falls on good soil, takes root, and bears fruit. This imagery of seeds, roots, living water, and the fruit that results is found throughout the biblical story. My (Bethany) husband and I were inspired by the imagery found in Psalm 1 and Jeremiah 17 to name our son Beckham, which means "one who lives by a stream."

> Blessed is the one
> who does not walk in step with the wicked
> or stand in the way that sinners take
> or sit in the company of mockers,
> but whose delight is in the law of the LORD,
> and who meditates on his law day and night.

> That person is like a tree planted by streams of water,
>   which yields its fruit in season
>   and whose leaf does not wither—
>   whatever they do prospers. (Ps. 1:1–3)

> Blessed is the one who trusts in the LORD,
>   whose confidence is in him.
> They will be like a tree planted by the water
>   that sends out its roots by the stream.
> It does not fear when heat comes;
>   its leaves are always green.
> It has no worries in a year of drought
>   and never fails to bear fruit. (Jer. 17:7–8)

A tree planted by a stream—with roots that reach into the very water itself and leaves that stay green even through trial—is a powerful image for what our justice calling can be when rooted in the living water of Jesus.

With this in mind, we believe that justice is most faithfully understood as a fruit of our formation in Jesus Christ.[2] As we sink our roots into the faithful, merciful loving-kindness of Jesus Christ by the grace of God, we are able to bear fruit beyond anything we could engineer out of our own strength or imagination. When we, the people of God, have deep roots in Christ, strengthened even more as our roots intertwine with one another, we will find the nourishment and strength and life we need to persevere in the justice calling.

It is nearly impossible to sustain an impulsive and emotionally driven response over the long haul.

The spiritual practices we have offered through the "Invitation for Today" sections at the end of each chapter are intended to foster Spirit-led cultivation of deep roots that stretch into living water. The Holy Spirit uses spiritual practices to help us more faithfully live into our identity as God's holy people who seek first the kingdom of God and his justice and righteousness. Through understanding the whole story of Scripture and intentionally engaging in practices of spiritual formation with others, the Spirit can form us into people who are holy and set apart, bearing witness to abundant life in Christ through justice, righteousness, and shalom.

As we know and immerse ourselves in the whole story of Scripture, we can better see that God has always cared about justice and has always called his people to care about justice. In knowing God's original vision for creation, we are invited to keep the Sabbath as a way to remember God's commitment to the flourishing of the world. If we understand how sin and injustice entered and marred God's good creation through the fall, we can take intentional steps toward suffering and darkness in this world. Through our exploration of the history of Israel and the covenant promises and law God gave to his holy people to help them live the way of justice and righteousness, we can lament the injustices that we encounter in the darkness and reconnect with the life God intends for us in following his ways rather than our own. By understanding the centrality of Jesus for delivering justice to this world as priest, prophet, and king, we can be formed by the Holy Spirit into people who live as saints (not heroes) as we seek justice. By studying the rocky and beautiful history and mission of the church, we can remember to rely on the Spirit to do his continual work of sanctifying and sending as we respond to God's kingdom mission. And finally, by anticipating the day when Jesus Christ will make all things new, we can together be formed into people who persevere in hope through worship and the Eucharist. In all of this, by the grace of God, Jesus invites us to abide in him. In all of this, the Spirit will sink our roots more deeply into the living water of Jesus and allow us to persevere in his work of justice.

> *Justice is most faithfully understood as a fruit of our formation in Jesus Christ.*

> *If we do not abide in Christ, if our work is not the abundant fruit of being deeply formed in Christ through the Spirit, our work is dross. We will wither.*

Our life of faith is not fully formed if we have no passion for justice. At the same time, our passion for justice is weak and can ultimately be destructive to our faith if not grounded in Christ. When the Spirit draws us near to the heart of God as we seek the justice of God embodied in Jesus Christ and demonstrated in the whole story of God's Word, the action that flows forth in our lives can be action that lasts. In Christ, we can continue the fight for justice for the long haul. Empowered by the Holy Spirit, we can live lives marked by a passionate, persevering pursuit of righteousness and justice.

If we do not abide in Christ, if our work is not the abundant fruit of being deeply formed in Christ through the Spirit, our work is dross. We will wither. But in Jesus there is no reason to fear. In Jesus there is abundance of life beyond all we could ever ask or imagine. When we abide in Jesus, God himself will bear his fruit through us.

> I am the vine, you are the branches. Those who abide in me and I in them bear much fruit, because apart from me you can do nothing. (John 15:5 NRSV)

Notes

Introduction

1. Global Slavery Index 2014, www.ilo.org/wcmsp5/groups/public/---ed_norm/---declaration /documents/publication/wcms_243391.pdf.

2. International Labor Organization 2014. *Profits and Poverty: The Economics of Forced Labour*. www.ilo.org/wcmsp5/groups/public/---ed_norm/--declaration/documents/publication /wcms_243391.pdf.

3. Isa. 61:6; Eph. 3:21.

4. N. T. Wright and Samuel Wells have each offered renditions of Scripture as a five-act play in recent years. While influenced by their respective versions, our own engagement with Scripture has led us to use different language to capture the biblical story and to identify six key movements within the story. See N. T. Wright, *The New Testament and the People of God* (Minneapolis: Fortress, 1992), 140–43; and Samuel Wells, *Improvisation: The Drama of Christian Ethics* (Grand Rapids: Brazos, 2004), 53–57.

Chapter 1: Engage the Whole Story

1. All records for Boola's case are confidential and on file with International Justice Mission.

2. The definition/requirements for applying the term *human trafficking* and/or *slavery* to a crime have been carefully refined over the past fifteen years. Note that there is often an assumption that movement or international border crossing is required for a crime to be considered trafficking, but this is not the case; trafficking is defined primarily by use of force/coercion for exploitation, whether movement or borders are involved or not. This document from the 2014 US Department of State Trafficking in Persons (TIP) Report gives a helpful overview of the variety of standard definitions in use today: www.state.gov/documents/organization/233944 .pdf. As an alternative visual, the chart from the 2008 TIP Report is helpful for understanding the elements involved in legally defining whether a situation involves human trafficking and the distinctions between defining trafficking for minors versus adults. www.state.gov/j/tip/rls/tiprpt /2008/105487.htm.

3. The International Labor Organization (ILO) estimates human trafficking to be a $150.2 billion industry. Estimates for each company listed are derived from current figures available publicly.

4. See Kevin Bales (*Disposable People: New Slavery in the Global Economy*, 3rd ed. [Berkeley: University of California Press, 2012]) for a study of the twenty-first-century abolition movement.

5. This is the way Cornelius Plantinga Jr. captures the heart of sin in his book *Not the Way It's Supposed to Be: A Breviary of Sin* (Grand Rapids: Eerdmans, 1995).

6. N. T. Wright describes "God's project of justice" as "setting the existing creation to rights rather than scrapping it and doing something else instead," in *Evil and the Justice of God* (Downers Grove, IL: InterVarsity, 2006), 73. Writing about the Hebrew verb *sapat*, Christopher Wright says, "In the widest sense, it means 'to put things right'" (*Old Testament Ethics for the People of God* [Downers Grove, IL: InterVarsity, 2004], 256). Oliver O'Donovan notes that biblical justice is distinct from the classical and Aristotelian notion of justice, which entails receiving one's due and being in social equilibrium. Biblical justice is first and foremost a judicial activity to be carried out rather than a state of affairs. See O'Donovan, *The Desire of the Nations: Rediscovering the Biblical Roots of Political Theology* (Cambridge: Cambridge University Press, 1996), 39. Nicholas Wolterstorff, who is more comfortable than O'Donovan with the classic definition of justice as receiving one's due, nonetheless notes that "though Christian Scripture speaks often about justice, it neither gives a definition nor offers a theory of justice. . . . What it does do, over and over again, is enjoin its readers to act justly and to right injustice" (*Journey toward Justice: Personal Encounters in the Global South* [Grand Rapids: Baker Academic, 2013], 70).

7. See Wayne A. Meeks, *The Moral World of the First Christians* (Philadelphia: Westminster, 1986), 154–59. Meeks notes that Irenaeus had "a very influential way, as it turned out—of combining these diverse witnesses into one complex and doctrinal lesson, into a *story*" (154, emphasis in original). This was captured in Irenaeus's work *Proof of the Apostolic Preaching*.

8. Meeks, *Moral World*, 160.

9. Ruth Padilla DeBorst, "Liberate My People," interview by Andy Crouch, *Christianity Today*, August 8, 2007, www.christianitytoday.com/ct/2007/august/12.30.html.

10. DeBorst, "Liberate My People."

11. I (Bethany) gleaned this idea from some of my favorite thinkers and writers: Gary Haugen and Andy Crouch.

12. See Skye Jethani, "Tim Keller on Justification and Justice," *Parse*, April 28, 2010, www.christianitytoday.com/parse/2010/april/tim-keller-on-justification-and-justice.html.

13. For example, see Gen. 18:19; Ps. 103:5; Isa. 9:7; Jer. 9:24.

14. Moshe Weinfeld, "'Justice and Righteousness'—משפט וצדקה—The Expression and Its Meaning," in *Justice and Righteousness: Biblical Themes and Their Influence*, ed. Henning Graf Reventlow and Yair Hoffman (Sheffield, UK: JSOT Press, 1992), 137, 228.

15. See Bruce V. Malchow, *Social Justice in the Hebrew Bible* (Collegeville, MN: Liturgical Press, 1996), 16. The root of this word lies in the verb *shapat*, which is linked to the ideas of judging, governing, and bringing situations to appropriate resolution.

16. Elizabeth R. Achtemeier, "Righteousness in the Old Testament," in *The Interpreter's Dictionary of the Bible: An Illustrated Encyclopedia* (New York: Abingdon, 1962), 4:81.

17. Christopher J. H. Wright, *Old Testament Ethics for the People of God* (Downers Grove, IL: InterVarsity, 2004), 257.

18. Malchow, *Social Justice in the Hebrew Bible*, 16.

19. Amy Sherman, *Kingdom Calling: Vocational Stewardship for the Common Good* (Downers Grove, IL: InterVarsity, 2011), 46–58.

20. Achtemeier, "Righteousness in the Old Testament," 83.

21. See, e.g., Ps. 86:15; Neh. 9:17; Joel 2:13; and Jon. 4:2.

22. See Ellen Davis, sermon at Grace Cathedral, San Francisco, podcast audio, November 20, 2011, itunes.apple.com/us/podcast/sermons-from-grace-cathedral/id80855926?mt=2&i=10 6862645. With thanks to Travis West for bringing this sermon and translation to our attention.

23. John Webster, *Holiness* (Grand Rapids: Eerdmans, 2003), 43–46.

24. Karl Barth, *Church Dogmatics*, vol. 2, pt. 1, ed. G. W. Bromiley and T. F. Torrance (Edinburgh: T&T Clark, 1957), 386.

25. Barth, *Church Dogmatics*, II/1, 386.

26. Wolterstorff, *Journey toward Justice*, 76–77.

27. Todd Cioffi expresses this connection between divine justification and human justice well in his exploration of Barth's theology. See Todd V. Cioffi, "The Politics of Justification and the Case of Torture: The Political Theology of Karl Barth from 1938 to 1946" (unpublished dissertation, Princeton Theological Seminary, May 2007), 98.

28. Jennifer Ryden, "Reflection in Response to Karl Barth," February 18, 2014, Western Theological Seminary.

29. Abraham J. Heschel, *The Prophets: An Introduction* (New York: Harper Torchbooks, 1969), 1:204, 207 (emphasis added).

30. www.a21.org.

Chapter 2: Receive God's Vision of Flourishing

1. Bethany Hoang, *Deepening the Soul for Justice* (Downers Grove, IL: InterVarsity, 2012).

2. Douglas J. Harris, *Shalom: The Biblical Concept of Peace* (Grand Rapids: Baker, 1970), 14.

3. Nicholas Wolterstorff, *Until Justice and Peace Embrace* (Grand Rapids: Eerdmans, 1983).

4. One of the earliest and most significant articulations of the argument that Christians are responsible for the environmental problems of the day can be found in Lynn White Jr., "The Historical Roots of Our Ecological Crisis," *Science*, March 10, 1967, 1203–7.

5. Later in the chapter we read of God creating a woman to help the man with this work of stewardship (Gen. 2:18–25). It is important to understand what is meant by the biblical term *helper* since within the history of biblical interpretation this verse, and more specifically this word, have been used to sanction the domination of men over women. The Hebrew phrase, which is translated "helper suitable for him," contains two words. The first of these words, translated as "helper," suggests a person who assists and encourages, who "provides support for what is lacking in the one who needs help" (David Atkinson, *The Message of Genesis 1–11: The Dawn of Creation* [Leicester, UK: Inter-Varsity, 1990], 68). In the majority of times that this word is used in the Old Testament, it refers to help provided by God to his people and does not convey the idea of inferiority. The second of these words, *suitable*, is linked to the idea of a person who is fit to stand before the man—like him but also in contrast to him (ibid., 69). As biblical scholar John E. Hartley writes, the Hebrew word translated "'suitable' suggests a person who was significantly different from him so as to contribute distinctively to his life, yet one who was of the same essence and on the same level" (*Genesis*, New International Biblical Commentary [Peabody, MA: Hendrickson, 2000], 61). According to these interpretations, the man and woman are to live together in fellowship, help each other, and care for creation.

6. Israel understood sovereignty very differently than we do. Kings demonstrated a deliberative sort of sovereignty; they consulted with counselors, and the declarations they made were the result of this collective decision-making process. This is likely the context behind the divine counsel (the "us" in Gen. 1:26, "Let us make humankind in our image, according to our likeness" [NRSV]). While God's sovereignty manifested itself as a deliberative power, this does not minimize the power at his hand, for at the conclusion of this deliberation, God's word goes forth and the world is created. Culturally, this is the kingly model by which Israel understood God's role in creation.

7. See Andy Crouch, *Culture Making: Recovering Our Creative Calling* (Downers Grove, IL: InterVarsity, 2013), for his argument that God calls us to join him in creating and cultivating culture.

8. See Matt. 2; 3; 5; Luke 17:21.

9. Augustine, *Concerning the City of God against the Pagans*, trans. Henry Bettenson (Harmondsworth, UK: Penguin Books, 1972), 14.1.

10. Augustine's commitment to advocacy on behalf of slaves whom he considered to be victims of unjust practices as well as the ministry in which his church was engaged to rescue and receive these victims best come to light in his letters of correspondence. In particular, see

Augustine, Letters 10 and 153 in *Augustine: Political Writings*, ed. E. M. Atkins and R. J. Dodaro (Cambridge: Cambridge University Press, 2001), 43–47, 71–81. This is not to overlook Augustine's conviction that slavery was a result of sin and would always be a part of the fallen world.

11. Augustine, *City of God* 19.13.

12. Augustine, *City of God* 19.20. Augustine wrote in Latin, so the word translated here as "peace" is not *shalom* in his original text.

13. Augustine, *City of God* 19.17.

14. There are three references to "image of God" in the Old Testament, all of which are in the first half of Genesis (1:16–17; 5:1–2; 9:6). We see the language used a bit more in the New Testament, often in reference to Jesus as the true image of God (2 Cor. 4:4; Col. 1:15). This means that the image of God has to be carefully considered in light of Jesus Christ as the true and full human.

15. Wolterstorff, *Until Justice and Peace Embrace*, 69–70 (emphasis in original).

16. Wolterstorff, *Until Justice and Peace Embrace*, 69–71.

17. See Wolterstorff, *Until Justice and Peace Embrace*, 38–41.

18. Norman Wirzba, *Living the Sabbath: Discovering the Rhythms of Rest and Delight* (Grand Rapids: Brazos, 2006), 14–15.

19. Eugene Peterson, *Christ Plays in Ten Thousand Places* (Grand Rapids: Eerdmans, 2005), 110.

20. Wirzba, *Living the Sabbath*, 38.

21. See the chapter titled "Stop" in Hoang, *Deepening the Soul for Justice*.

22. Tim Keller writes on the importance of thoughtfully chosen recreation that refreshes on the Sabbath as well as enjoying God's works of creation through "outdoor things" and the arts. See Keller, "Wisdom and Sabbath Rest," Q, accessed April 14, 2015, qideas.org/articles /wisdom-and-sabbath-rest/.

23. Keller, "Wisdom and Sabbath Rest."

24. Peterson, *Christ Plays in Ten Thousand Places*, 111.

25. In his book *The Just Church* Jim Martin gives a detailed road map for churches wanting to engage justice issues at home and in cross-cultural contexts. See also ijm.org/get-involved /churches for more resources to aid your community in getting involved.

26. www.slaveryfootprint.org is a helpful starting point for grappling with slavery in the supply chain of our everyday products.

Chapter 3: Move toward Darkness

1. "Rosa" is a pseudonym used to protect this client's identity. All records for Rosa's case are confidential and on file with IJM.

2. The case involved an uncle who had sexually abused his two nieces. All records are confidential and on file with IJM.

3. Emmanuel Katongole and Chris Rice, *Reconciling All Things: A Christian Vision for Justice, Peace, and Healing* (Downers Grove, IL: InterVarsity, 2008), 13. Their language echoes that of Cornelius Plantinga.

4. Cornelius Plantinga Jr. *Not the Way It's Supposed to Be: A Breviary of Sin* (Grand Rapids: Eerdmans, 1995).

5. "God graciously gave the couple garments of skin. . . . With this gift God, acting as their sustainer, expressed his intention to continue to support and fellowship with humans" (John E. Hartley, *Genesis*, New International Biblical Commentary [Peabody, MA: Hendrickson, 2000], 72).

6. David Atkinson, *The Message of Genesis 1–11: The Dawn of Creation* (Leicester, UK: Inter-Varsity, 1990), 96.

7. Atkinson, *Message of Genesis*, 97.

8. The story of Noah and the flood relayed in Gen. 6–9 vividly and disturbingly reflects this fallen reality, while it also reflects God's continued commitment to love this world and humanity with justice and righteousness. By the time of Noah, the world had become so marked by corruption, violence, injustice, and chaos, in such clear contrast to the shalom vision of creation, that God decides to allow "the outworkings of the results of sin and wickedness to be their own judgment. For what God decreed was to be destroyed (6:13) had already in truth destroyed itself (6:11–12)" (Atkinson, *Message of Genesis*, 136). God calls the righteous man Noah (Gen. 6:9) and his family to be a new beginning in continuity with God's original desire for shalom, justice, and righteousness in this world. Indeed, we see clear parallels between the account of God's re-creation after the flood and the original account of creation. In making a covenant with Noah, God demonstrates his faithfulness to his world and commitment to see all of humanity and creation flourish and thrive.

9. Augustine, *The Trinity*, ed. John E. Rotelle, OSA, trans. Edmund Hill, OP (Brooklyn, NY: New City, 1991), 13.17.

10. See Andy Crouch, *Playing God: Redeeming the Gift of Power* (Downers Grove, IL: InterVarsity, 2013), for more on power used rightly and power abused.

11. Augustine, *The Trinity* 13.17.

12. Karl Barth, *Church Dogmatics*, vol. IV, pt. 1, ed. G. W. Bromiley and T. F. Torrance (Edinburgh: T&T Clark, 1956), 41–42.

13. Barth, *Church Dogmatics* IV/1, 41–42.

14. As R. R. Reno writes, the sin committed is "infected with the depth and breadth of Satan's prior rebellion," which makes it "universally consequential" (*Genesis*, Brazos Theological Commentary on the Bible [Grand Rapids: Brazos, 2010], 79).

15. Bethany has written about some specific prayer practices in her book *Deepening the Soul for Justice*. We hope these practices might be an encouragement as you step out.

16. A few examples of organizations (alphabetically ordered): A21 (Abolishing Injustice in the 21st Century, global), Free the Slaves (UK), International Justice Mission (global—visitors are invited to join 11 a.m. prayer time at headquarters outside Washington, DC), International Institute (St. Louis), The Justice Conference (global), Mosaic (Atlanta), Polaris Project (US), Rescue Freedom (Seattle), Restore NYC (NYC), Safe Horizons (NYC), Salvation Army (US), Saving Innocence (LA), Shared Hope (global), World Relief (global), World Vision (global).

17. For a good selection of documentary films, go to www.slaverynomore.org/get-informed /documentaries-and-films/.

18. For one of many gathering ideas, go to www.noondaycollection.com for ideas and stories for hosting a fashion-oriented fundraiser. Go to fundraising.ijm.org to create your own individual or community online-based fundraiser.

Chapter 4: Lament

1. Scripture passages detailing God's call for protection of widows and orphans and his rebuke for those who harm them are manifold. A sampling of Scriptures to begin study: Exod. 22:22; Deut. 10:17–18; 27:19 (among many laws specifying how to care for widows and orphans); Ps. 146:9; Isa. 1:10–20; James 1:27.

2. A United Nations brief on widowhood estimates that 44 percent of women over 60 years old and 16 percent of women aged 45–59 in sub-Saharan Africa are widows (United Nations, "Women 2000: Widowhood; Invisible women, secluded or excluded" [New York, 2001], 1–20). Over half the widows in one district of Uganda have experienced attempts to grab their land (Land and Equity Movement in Uganda, "Why Is the Legal System Failing to Protect People's Land Rights?" [National Refugee Council, 2009]). "No woman should lose her rights when she loses her husband, but an estimated 115 million widows live in poverty, and 81 million have suffered physical abuse" (UN Secretary-General Ban Ki-moon on International Widows Day, June 23, 2014).

3. Ghana Child Labor Survey 2003, Ghana Statistical Service Study.

4. "Trafficked children frequently [dive] to disentangle the fish nets from the numerous tree stumps that are scattered throughout the lake. . . . Diving is a dangerous job that can have dire consequences for the children, from catching water-based diseases such as bilharzia and guinea worm to death from drowning" (UNDOC, www.unodc.org/unodc/en/frontpage/child-trafficking -in-ghana.html). "Child workers usually work from 1 a.m. to 5 a.m. on cold, windy nights to reel in nets weighing as much as 1,000 pounds when they are full of fish. Skeletal tree limbs submerged in Lake Volta frequently entangle the fishing nets, and slave masters will throw weary, frightened children into the water to free the trapped lines, sometimes drowning them. I didn't meet one child who didn't know another who had drowned" (Lisa Kristine, photographer, *The Atlantic*, www.theatlantic.com/international/archive/2012/09/slavery-still-exists/262847/).

5. Richard Bauckham, *Bible and Mission: Christian Witness in a Postmodern World* (Grand Rapids: Baker Academic, 2003), 28.

6. For example, see Jer. 4:1–2. See also Bauckham, *Bible and Mission*, 30–31.

7. As theologian R. R. Reno writes, "God's plan is universal *in scope*—it sets about to redeem the entire cosmos" (*Genesis*, Brazos Theological Commentary on the Bible [Grand Rapids: Brazos, 2010], 138) (emphasis in original).

8. Note that when Jesus asks the disciples to eat bread and drink wine in remembrance of him, he is calling them to take action in light of his sacrifice. This active "remembrance" is built into our ongoing celebrations of the Lord's Supper in the church today.

9. Abraham J. Heschel, *The Prophets: An Introduction* (New York: Harper Torchbooks, 1969), 1:203.

10. See John Calvin, *Institutes of the Christian Religion*, ed. John T. McNeill, trans. Ford Lewis Battles (Louisville: Westminster John Knox, 1960), 2.7.6–9. For more on Calvin's understanding of the law, see I. John Hesselink, *Calvin's Concept of the Law* (Eugene, OR: Wipf and Stock, 1992); and Guenther H. Haas, *The Concept of Equity in Calvin's Ethics* (Waterloo, ON: Wilfred Laurier University Press, 1997).

11. See Calvin, *Institutes* 2.7.10.

12. Calvin, *Institutes* 2.7.12. For more on the second use of the law, see Calvin, *Institutes* 2.7.10–11.

13. Calvin, *Institutes* 2.7.12.

14. Calvin, *Institutes* 2.8.5.

15. Calvin, *Institutes* 2.8.7.

16. J. Todd Billings, *Union with Christ: Reframing Theology and Ministry for the Church* (Grand Rapids: Baker Academic, 2011), 111–12.

17. Billings, *Union with Christ*, 113.

18. Calvin, *Institutes* 2.8.55.

19. For example, see Exod. 22:21; 23:9; Deut. 10:19; Lev. 19:33–34; 24:22. See Bruce V. Malchow, *Social Justice in the Hebrew Bible* (Collegeville, MN: Liturgical Press, 1996), 22–24.

20. For example, see Exod. 22:26–27; 23:6; Lev. 25:35–37; Deut. 24:10–15, 17–18.

21. For example, see Deut. 24:19–22; Lev. 19:9–10; 23:22.

22. The Sabbath-year law, given in Exod. 23:10–11, takes a different form in Deut. 15:1–2; rather than the fields lying fallow every seven years, all debts are to be canceled every seven years as another way to help the poor. Between the time the law was given in Exodus and the time the law was articulated in Deuteronomy, social conditions had changed for the worse. See Malchow, *Social Justice in the Hebrew Bible*, 25.

23. Malchow, *Social Justice in the Hebrew Bible*, 25–26.

24. N. T. Wright, *Evil and the Justice of God* (Downers Grove, IL: InterVarsity, 2006), 53.

25. Heschel, *Prophets*, 1:202.

26. See Heschel, *Prophets*, 1:168.

27. "It is one of the essential paradoxes of prophetic thinking that, although the prophet speaks continually of the people's guilt and of dreadful punishment in store for them, once

the disaster comes he is stunned, puzzled, unable to justify completely the full measure of suffering" (Heschel, *Prophets*, 1:177).

28. See Heschel, *Prophets*, 1:181–86.

29. While this new covenant ushers in a new age for God's people, it is in continuity with the old covenant God made with Israel. The old covenant is chronologically prior to and lays the groundwork for the new covenant, while remaining significant.

30. For a thorough, groundbreaking treatment of violence against the poor and the effect of cultures of impunity on global poverty alleviation and development efforts, see Gary Haugen and Victor Boutrous, *The Locust Effect: Why the End of Poverty Requires the End of Violence* (New York: Oxford University Press, 2014).

31. Much of my (Bethany's) understanding of the context and interpretation of Habakkuk was derived from Tim Keller's work on this prophet in a five-part sermon series from 2009. See Redeemer Presbyterian Church, NYC online sermon archives for access, www.gospelinlife.com /living-by-faith-in-troubled-times.html.

32. Emmanuel Katongole and Chris Rice, *Reconciling All Things: A Christian Vision for Justice, Peace, and Healing* (Downers Grove, IL: InterVarsity, 2008), 78, emphasis added.

33. Katongole and Rice, *Reconciling All Things*, 77–87.

34. The significance of Job for understanding biblical justice has been beautifully explored by Tim Keller in his book *Generous Justice* (New York: Riverhead, 2010).

35. J. Todd Billings, *Rejoicing in Lament: Wrestling with Incurable Cancer and Life in Christ* (Grand Rapids: Brazos, 2015), 12.

36. According to UNICEF, human trafficking involves 1.2 million children each year (UNICEF, "The State of the World's Children 2006: Excluded and Invisible," www.unicef.org/sowc06 /pdfs/sowc06_fullreport.pdf).

37. For more on rape as a weapon of war and conflict in the Democratic Republic of the Congo learn from Lynne Hybels and World Relief by visiting www.tenforcongo.org.

38. Psalm 10:15.

39. A 2013 study of Kenyan police files found that in nearly two out of every three felony cases that went to full trial (64 percent) the police never gathered enough evidence to charge the accused person with a crime, much less convict them. See Independent Policing Oversight Authority, "Baseline Survey on Policing Standards and Gaps in Kenya" (Nairobi, 2013). www.ipoa .go.ke/images/downloads/IPOA%20Baseline%20Survey%20Report_06.09.2013_revised2.pdf. Another report states that every year about ten million people will enter pretrial detention where they can be held without any proceedings to determine their guilt or innocence (Open Society Foundations. *Pretrial Detention and Torture: Why Pretrial Detainees Face the Greatest Risk* [2011]. www.opensocietyfoundations.org/sites/default/files/pretrial-detention-and-torture-06222011.pdf).

Chapter 5: Live as Saints (Not Heroes)

1. Superman originally fought for truth and justice; only later was the "American way" added to his mantra. See Erik Lundegaard, "Truth, Justice and (Fill in the Blank)," *International Herald Tribune*, June 30, 2006, www.iht.com/articles/2006/06/30/opinion/ederik.php.

2. Uncle Ben tells this to Peter Parker in the 2002 *Spider-Man* movie, and it becomes a recurring source of motivation for Peter's work as Spider-Man.

3. The NIV uses the term *holy people*, while the NRSV, NKJV, NET, and ASV use "saints." See, e.g., Acts 9:13; 1 Cor. 1:2; Eph. 1:1; 3:18; Heb. 2:11; 1 Pet. 2:9.

4. Mark Labberton, *The Dangerous Act of Loving Your Neighbor: Seeing Others through the Eyes of Jesus* (Downers Grove, IL: InterVarsity, 2010), 23–25.

5. Julie Canlis, "Sonship, Identity, and Transformation," in *Sanctification: Explorations in Theology and Practice*, ed. Kelly M. Kapic (Downers Grove, IL: IVP Academic, 2014), 240.

6. J. Todd Billings, *Union with Christ: Reframing Theology and Ministry for the Church* (Grand Rapids: Baker Academic, 2011), 108 (emphasis in original).

7. See also John 16:33, which records the very final words of Jesus's farewell discourse. Andreas J. Köstenberger notes that Jesus's words in John 14:27 and 16:33 closely reflect the customary Jewish use of *shalom* as a word of farewell, while in John 20:19 the word is used as a welcome. See Köstenberger, *John*, Baker Exegetical Commentary on the New Testament (Grand Rapids: Baker Academic, 2004), 443. In John 20:19, the Hebrew phrase translated "peace be with you" is *shalom aleichem.*

8. William H. Van Doren, *Gospel of John: Expository and Homiletical Commentary* (Grand Rapids: Kregel, 1981), 1128 (emphasis in original). Commenting on John 20:19, he writes that peace "is the message of Him who has conquered death for us, and who, hereby, assures us of the victory. It is the preaching of the atonement (at-one-ment), announcing the peace which flows from pardoned sin and complete reconciliation with God. . . . Christ's disciples must receive His peace into their own hearts before they can become apostles of peace to mankind" (ibid., 1369).

9. Elizabeth R. Achtemeier, "Righteousness in the Old Testament," in *The Interpreter's Dictionary of the Bible: An Illustrated Encyclopedia* (New York: Abingdon, 1962), 4:81.

10. Darrell L. Bock, *Luke*, IVP New Testament Commentary Series (Downers Grove, IL: IVP Academic, 1994), 184–85. The work of C. Kavin Rowe in *Early Narrative Christology: The Lord in the Gospel of Luke* (Grand Rapids: Baker Academic, 2006) was extremely helpful in our reading of the Gospel of Luke.

11. For example, see Luke 6:20–26; 12:13–21; 14:12–14; 16:14–29.

12. See C. Kavin Rowe, *World Upside Down: Reading Acts in the Graeco-Roman Age* (Oxford: Oxford University Press, 2009), 100–102.

13. See Bock, *Luke*, 151–61.

14. See also John 12:31; 14:30; 16:11; Eph. 2:1–2.

15. For example, see Rom. 1:7; 2 Cor. 1:1; Phil. 1:1; Jude 3; Rev. 13:7.

16. René Padilla, *Mission between the Times: Essays on the Kingdom* (Grand Rapids: Eerdmans, 1985), 79.

17. The following section is inspired by Samuel Wells, *Improvisation: The Drama of Christian Ethics* (Grand Rapids: Brazos, 2004), 42–44, 56–57.

18. See Wells, *Improvisation*, 43.

19. Holly Burkhalter, *The Washington Post*, May 8, 2015, www.washingtonpost.com/opin ions/a-safer-home-for-cambodias-girls/2015/05/08/549e0d40-f4e4-11e4-84a6-6d7c67c50db0 _story.html.

20. The work in Cambodia is far from "finished." IJM has identified several key priorities for the work that lies ahead: (1) *Ensure the Cambodian public justice system builds off its success.* Cambodia's public justice system must continue strengthening its capacity, addressing policy gaps, weeding out corruption and patronage, and extending the effective response seen in the anti-trafficking police to other police units such as military, border and local commune police. (2) *Continue to advocate for police to be granted legal authority to conduct undercover investigations and for increased budget for agencies carrying out important anti-trafficking work.* In Cambodia, police are not legally authorized to conduct undercover investigations. This stunts the police's ability to locate and rescue children trafficked into the sex trade. We continue to advocate for Cambodia's legislation to be changed in order to allow for this much-needed authority, in addition to calling for sustainable operational funding for police and social work units. (3) *Endeavor to sustain the gains made in Cambodia.* We've seen tremendous progress in protecting children from sex trafficking in Cambodia. We're continuing to stand alongside government partners to make sure we don't lose significant ground. (4) *Prepare well for the next fight.* Cambodia needs to address other issues of violence in a more focused and significant way, including labor trafficking. The good news is that the Cambodian government leadership, their public justice system, and the nongovernment organizations community now have increased capacity, legal foundations and experience gained from the fight against sex trafficking that can be applied to

combat other issues of violence. IJM is presently exploring the possibility of starting a project focused on labor trafficking in Cambodia. For more details see IJM's Results Summary at www .ijm.org/sites/default/files/download/cambodia/Results-Summary.pdf.

Chapter 6: Be Sanctified and Sent

1. Jonathan Aiken, *John Newton: From Disgrace to Amazing Grace* (Wheaton: Crossway, 2007), 11.

2. Kathleen Norris recounts this version of the story about Newton in *Amazing Grace: A Vocabulary of Faith* (New York: Riverhead, 1998), 97.

3. Adam Hochschild, *Bury the Chains: Prophets and Rebels in the Fight to Free an Empire's Slaves* (New York: Mariner, 2006), 29 (see also 19, 20, 28, 75, 77, 131). Hochschild drew this quotation from Newton's personal writings as recounted in *Memoirs of the Rev. John Newton, Some Time a Slave in Africa; Afterwards Curate of Olney, Bucks; and Rector of St. Mary Woolnoth, London: in a Series of Letters Written by Himself, to the Rev. Dr. Haweis, Rector of Aldwinckle, Northamptonshire* (London: A. Maxwell, 1813).

4. Darrell L. Guder, *The Continuing Conversion of the Church* (Grand Rapid: Eerdmans, 2000).

5. Richard Bauckham, *Bible and Mission: Christian Witness in a Postmodern World* (Grand Rapids: Baker Academic, 2003), 84.

6. See Bauckham, *Bible and Mission*, 43, 46–49, 72–77.

7. C. Kavin Rowe, *World Upside Down: Reading Acts in the Graeco-Roman Age* (Oxford: Oxford University Press, 2009), 123.

8. Rowe, *World Upside Down*, 123.

9. Theologian Oliver O'Donovan writes, "As the world is given back to us again no longer as a broken world but as a world repaired, we are drawn in love toward God and into the world in one motion, for it is as the work of God's redemption that we receive the world's good" ("Sanctification and Ethics," in *Sanctification: Explorations in Theology and Practice*, ed. Kelly M. Kapic [Downers Grove, IL: IVP Academic, 2014], 158).

10. Helen Rhee, *Loving the Poor, Saving the Rich: Wealth, Poverty, and Early Christian Formation* (Grand Rapids: Baker Academic, 2012), 187–88; see also 112–31. The entire book is exceptionally well researched and informative.

11. René Padilla, *Mission between the Times: Essays on the Kingdom* (Grand Rapids: Eerdmans, 1985), 191.

12. Padilla, *Mission between the Times*, 197. For more on these themes, see Padilla's essay, "The Mission of the Church in Light of the Kingdom of God," 186–99.

13. John M. Perkins, *Beyond Charity: The Call to Christian Community Development* (Grand Rapids: Baker Books, 1993), 83.

14. Padilla, *Mission between the Times*, 198.

15. Padilla, *Mission between the Times*, 198.

16. Within the New Testament, we are encouraged to do certain things and given lists of behaviors to avoid, but in every instance the reason we are told to do so is connected to the new identity we have already been given in Christ as God's holy and beloved children. In Ephesians, we are told that *we are dearly loved* children of God and should *therefore* imitate God by loving others, offering ourselves to others as Christ did, and avoiding any suggestion of sexual immorality, impurity, or greed (Eph. 5:1–3). In Colossians we read that *we have been* raised with Christ and so we should *therefore* put to death whatever belongs to our earthly nature (Col. 3:1–6). This sequence of thought appears repeatedly throughout the New Testament: identity in Christ shapes how we live.

17. Julie Canlis, "Sonship, Identity, and Transformation," in *Sanctification: Explorations in Theology and Practice*, ed. Kelly M. Kapic (Downers Grove, IL: IVP Academic, 2014), 240.

18. Bauckham, *Bible and Mission*, 49.

19. Benjamin T. Conner, *Practicing Witness: A Missional Vision of Christian Practices* (Grand Rapids: Eerdmans, 2011), 99.

20. See Rowe, *World Upside Down*, 124.

21. Bauckham, *Bible and Mission*, 77.

22. For a helpful summary of recent scholarship on this point, see Conner, *Practicing Witness*, 99–102.

23. Bauckham writes, "The church's mission is inseparable from continual repentance and constant heeding of God's call to God-given holiness, faithfulness and discernment" (*Bible and Mission*, 112).

24. Gary Haugen, *Good News about Injustice: A Witness of Courage in a Hurting World* (Downers Grove, IL: InterVarsity, 2009). Both authors are foundationally indebted to the work of John R. W. Stott in forming our first understanding of gospel as both word and deed inextricable.

25. For more on evangelical involvement in the needs of society and the factors involved in this "Great Reversal," see Timothy L. Smith, *Revivalism and Social Reform: American Protestantism on the Eve of the Civil War* (Baltimore: Johns Hopkins University Press, 1980); George Marsden, *Fundamentalism and American Culture: The Shaping of Twentieth-Century Evangelicalism: 1870–1925* (New York: Oxford University Press, 1980); and Donald W. Dayton with Douglas M. Strong, *Rediscovering an Evangelical Heritage: A Tradition and Trajectory of Integrating Piety and Justice* (Grand Rapids: Baker Academic, 2014).

26. See Wayne A. Meeks, *The Moral World of the First Christians* (Philadelphia: Westminster John Knox, 1986), 155.

27. David Bosch, *Transforming Mission: Paradigm Shifts in Theology of Mission* (Maryknoll, NY: Orbis Books, 1997), 405.

28. Mark Labberton, *Called: The Crisis and Promise of Following Jesus Today* (Downers Grove, IL: InterVarsity, 2014).

29. See James Davison Hunter, *To Change the World: The Irony, Tragedy, and Possibility of Christianity in the Late Modern World* (Oxford: Oxford University Press, 2010), 256–57.

30. Amy Sherman, *Kingdom Calling: Vocational Stewardship for the Common Good* (Downers Grove, IL: InterVarsity, 2011).

31. Hunter, *To Change the World*, 247–48.

32. Andy Crouch, *Playing God: Redeeming the Gift of Power* (Downers Grove, IL: InterVarsity, 2013), 169.

33. You can read more about Don Coleman in "Local Celebrity, TV Celebrity Brothers Reflect on Challenged Upbringing," *Richmond Times–Dispatch*, January 5, 2015, www.rich mond.com/life/article_32849145-2e1d-5ada-9b2d-4aad7e8fd36c.html.

34. For more on the significance of Christian engagement with public education, see Nicole Baker Fulgham, *Educating All God's Children: What Christians Can—and Should—Do to Improve Public Education for Low-Income Kids* (Grand Rapids: Brazos, 2013).

35. To read more about this group of friends, particularly in relation to their decision to send their children to the local public school, see Amy Julia Becker, "The New School Choice Agenda," *Christianity Today*, April 9, 2012, www.christianitytoday.com/ct/2012/april/school-choice.html.

Chapter 7: Persevere in Hope

1. A pseudonym has been used for the protection of this IJM client. All records for Mala's case are confidential and on file with IJM.

2. All quotations from trafficking survivors and IJM staff were gleaned through staff-conducted interviews.

3. We're indebted and grateful to our friend Ruth Padilla DeBorst for the phrase "persevering hope." She used it in a chapel message at Hope College at roughly the same time that we were grappling to find the right language for this chapter.

4. Michael Horton, "'Let the Earth Bring Forth . . .': The Spirit and Human Agency in Sanctification," in *Sanctification: Explorations in Theology and Practice*, ed. Kelly M. Kapic (Downers Grove, IL: IVP Academic, 2014), 148.

5. This idea is expressed by theologians as early as Irenaeus of Lyons. See Irenaeus, *Against Heresies*.

6. N. T. Wright, *Surprised by Hope: Rethinking Heaven, the Resurrection, and the Mission of the Church* (New York: HarperOne, 2008), 132.

7. Wright, *Surprised by Hope*, 132.

8. Ben Witherington III, *Revelation*, New Cambridge Bible Commentary (Cambridge: Cambridge University Press, 2003), 266, emphasis in original.

9. Witherington, *Revelation*, 276.

10. The sinking ship was an image used by Dwight L. Moody, a leading American revivalist in the nineteenth century. See Paul Boyer, *When Time Shall Be No More: Prophecy Belief in Modern American Culture* (Cambridge, MA: Belknap, 1992), 95.

11. Brad Harper and Paul Louis Metzger, *Exploring Ecclesiology: An Evangelical and Ecumenical Introduction* (Grand Rapids: Brazos, 2009), 66.

12. Drawn from Eugene Peterson, who is playing with the imagery of T. S. Eliot. See Peterson, "Teach Us to Care, and Not to Care," in *Subversive Spirituality*, ed. Jim Lyster, John Sharon, and Peter Santucci (Grand Rapids: Eerdmans, 1997), 155–69.

13. Chaim Stern, *Gates of Freedom: A Passover Haggadah* (West Orange, NJ: Berhman House, 1982), 35, 36.

14. Justo González, *For the Healing of the Nations: The Book of Revelation in an Age of Cultural Conflict* (Maryknoll, NY: Orbis, 1999), 109.

15. Mark Labberton, *The Dangerous Act of Worship: Living God's Call to Justice* (Downers Grove, IL: InterVarsity, 2007), 13.

16. Labberton, *Dangerous Act of Worship*, 13.

17. James K. A. Smith, *Desiring the Kingdom: Worship, Worldview, and Cultural Formation* (Grand Rapids: Baker Academic, 2009), 33.

18. Smith, *Desiring the Kingdom*, 214.

19. The "Order of Worship for the Lord's Day," which includes the Lord's Supper for the Reformed Church in America, can be found at www.rca.org/liturgy.

20. Smith, *Desiring the Kingdom*, 201.

21. See Alexander Schmemann, *For the Life of the World* (Crestwood, NY: St. Vladimir's Seminary Press, 2004), 25, 46.

22. Schmemann, *For the Life of the World*, 38; see also 39.

23. Bethany Hoang, "A Tribute to IJM Board Chairman Steve Hayner," February 3, 2015. news.ijm.org/a-tribute-to-steve-hayner. To experience the way Steve and his wife encountered God throughout their cancer journey in the months following this sermon, see Steve and Sharol Hayner, *Joy in the Journey: Finding Abundance in the Shadow of Death* (Downers Grove, IL: InterVarsity, 2015).

Conclusion: Abide in Jesus

1. "All IJM staff in the United States" at that point totaled 37 people. More than 200 serve in the United States today and about 700 worldwide. Ninety-five percent of IJM staff are nationals of the countries where each of our offices is located.

2. It would be difficult to exaggerate just how much I (Bethany) have learned from Gary Haugen, the founder of IJM, about God's passion for justice, our biblical call to join God in this calling to justice, and most important, how to persevere over the long haul. His leadership and teaching permeate the whole of this book, and the conviction that justice is a fruit of our formation in Christ stems directly from what Gary has been teaching the IJM team for years.

Subject Index

Scripture Index